MISSISSAUGA

City of Excellence

Sponsored by the Mississauga Board of Trade

| *Photo by Michael Scholz*

MISSISSAUGA

City of Excellence

By Ric McDonald
Featuring the photography
of Jeff Chevrier

Corporate profiles by
Stuart Foxman
and
Bruce O'Neill

CREDITS

Mississauga: City of Excellence

Sponsored by the
Mississauga Board of Trade
(905) 273-6151

By Ric McDonald
Photography by Jeff Chevrier and Michael Scholz
Corporate profiles by Stuart Foxman and Bruce O'Neill

Community Communications, Inc.
Publishers: **Ronald P. Beers and James E. Turner**

Staff for **Mississauga: City of Excellence**

Publisher's Sales Associates	Sheli Ferrand, Elizabeth Kibodeaux and David G. McKinney
Executive Editor	James E. Turner
Managing Editor	Linda Moeller Pegram
Design Director	Camille Leonard
Designer	Scott Phillips
Photo Editors	Scott Phillips and Linda M. Pegram
Production Manager	Cindy Lovett
Editorial Assistants	Katrina Williams and Kari Collin
Sales Assistant	Annette R. Lozier
Proofreader	Wynona B. Hall
Accounting Services	Sara Ann Turner
Printing Production	Frank Rosenberg/GSAmerica

Community Communications, Inc.
Montgomery, Alabama

James E. Turner, Chairman of the Board
Ronald P. Beers, President
Daniel S. Chambliss, Vice President

© 1997 Community Communications
All Rights Reserved
Published 1997
Printed in Canada
First Edition
Library of Congress Catalog Number: 97-21428
ISBN: 1-885352-64-6

Every effort has been made to ensure the accuracy of the information herein.
However, the authors and Community Communications are not responsible
for any errors or omissions which might have occurred.

Photo by Jeff Chevrier

| *Photo by Jeff Chevrier*

*O*n behalf of members of Council of the City of Mississauga, I
am delighted to introduce **Mississauga: City of Excellence**, *a book
devoted to our dynamic city.*

*Within the Greater Toronto Area, Mississauga offers a unique envi-
ronment for success in an urban setting. With the international airport
located right in Mississauga, seven major highways traversing the city,
low taxes, outstanding amenities and attractive business and office
parks, Mississauga stands above all other business locations.*

*These benefits, plus the fact that Mississauga, alone among
Canadian cities of its size, is debt-free, have rightfully earned us the
reputation as the "City of Excellence." Small wonder that it has been
one of the fastest growing cities in the country for the past decade.*

*It is wonderful to have a book that reflects this growth and the
future potential of our exciting city. As you read through the pages,
you will discover Mississauga's vibrancy, its multiculturalism and its
diversity. You will realize that Mississauga really is the place to be!*

Mayor Hazel McCallion

FOREWORD

On behalf of the Board of Directors of the Mississauga Board of Trade, I am pleased to present to you **Mississauga: City of Excellence.** What better title could capture the spirit and the economic vitality of Mississauga, Ontario. The book describes the advantages the city holds for business by virtue of its location within the Greater Toronto Area and the strength of its commitment to providing an environment in which business can compete and prosper. In our estimation, this beautiful book is a celebration and exploration of the unique qualities of life created by the blending of Mississauga's rich cultural backdrop with its diverse industries, and the people who help make this city great through their values, strong work ethic and friendly nature. I am proud to be a part of this unique and dynamic community.

Since its incorporation in 1974, the city of Mississauga has continually set the pace for other cities, and has emerged as a key player in the region and in Canada. Its favourable business climate, solid economic base and well-educated workforce attract business and industry to the area from all over the world. The city's many amenities, diverse cultural, entertainment and educational opportunities, and community hospitality attract workers and families.

This book provides an overview of the history, thriving economy, quality education, business climate, state-of-the-art health care, technology and cultural richness of Mississauga, as well as a look at the arts, sports and attractions. It also profiles some of the companies who find that the city of Mississauga is an ideal place to do business.

Sincere thanks to author Ric McDonald, business profile writers Bruce O'Neill and Stuart Foxman and photographers Jeff Chevrier and Michael Scholz for making this book possible. Their contributions will be appreciated for generations to come.

The Mississauga Board of Trade is pleased to publish this book and hopes that it will provide a glimpse at what makes Mississauga special for those who have never visited this community. At the same time, we hope that lifelong and newer residents will gain a new perspective by seeing our city through someone else's eyes.

Nance MacDonald
1997 President
Mississauga Board of Trade

Photo by Jeff Chevrier

PREFACE

*O*ne of my first thoughts when asked to write this book was, "This city's only been incorporated since 1974. How much can there be to tell?" Having only lived in Mississauga for a couple of years when the project started, I decided not to jump to conclusions and accepted that there would simply be a considerable amount of research required if I was going to find much to say. True, the exploratory car rides we conducted while house hunting had uncovered several pleasant discoveries. So maybe we had barely exposed the tip of the iceberg.

Well, I was right. But, oh, my—what an iceberg! I recall thinking after just a few days of research, "How am I going to tell it all? There's so much to say!" I was—and continue to be—astounded by the richness of the history, the diversity of culture and the depth of community pride which are the cornerstones of this vibrant young city.

There is also a sense of remarkable potential, a feeling of leading the way into the 21st century. And everywhere, in neighbourhoods and in business, there is a genuine enthusiasm that says, "We love it here. This is the place to be."

I couldn't agree more. From the moment when, within 20 minutes of our moving van's arrival, new neighbours were shaking my hand, this began to feel like home. Since then, it has become just that in every sense of the word, and much more quickly than I would have imagined possible. And that, perhaps, is the real story that Mississauga has to tell.

In assembling the background for this book, I've spoken to many people who make up the fabric of this community—movers and shakers, old timers, the famous and not-so-famous. And no matter what insights or yarns they had to offer, their views of the city as a great place to live and prosper were unanimously positive. So to the dozens of people who contributed to this book, through interviews, research and encouragement, I thank you. This is your story, too.

The funny thing is that I still feel that I've only scratched the surface on getting to know the city. So much is happening so quickly that it's hard to keep up. One thing I can tell you, however, is that this iceberg appears to be moving inexorably toward greatness, and I for one am extremely happy to be on board. I think you will be too.

Ric McDonald

M

Photo by Jeff Chevrier

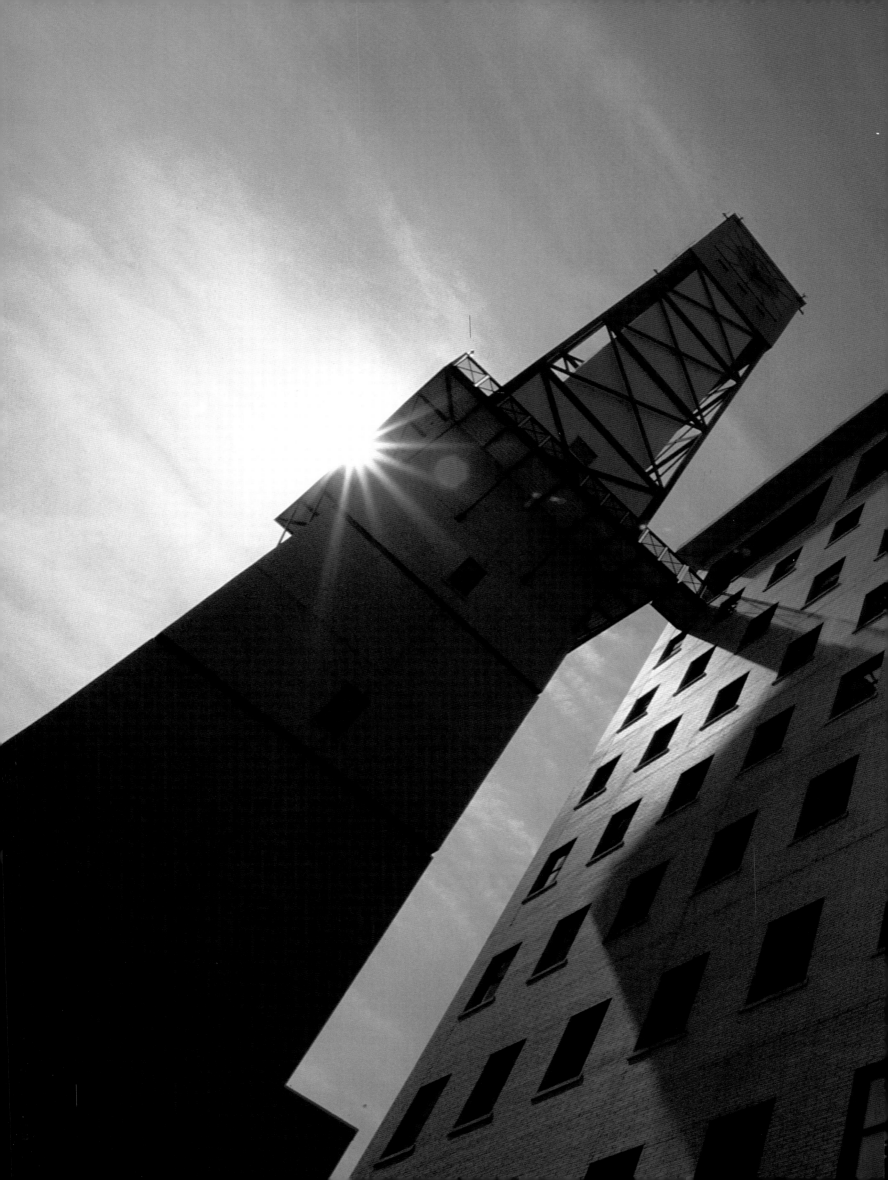

Part I

CHAPTER I

Pioneers

Ⓜ

For such a young city, Mississauga's history is astonishingly rich, rooted in tales of fur traders, pioneer settlers and the Mississauga Indians for whom the city was named. Today, over 200 years of heritage thrives in places like Streetsville, Port Credit and Clarkson—the "villages within the city."

Photo by Jeff Chevrier

This 1911 barn-raising was a familiar sight as settlers pulled together to literally build their communities from the ground up. *Photo courtesy Region of Peel Archives.*

Opposite page: **Earl Madill, the city's last full-time dairy farmer, ponders the incredible development that has surrounded his homestead at Eglinton Avenue and McLaughlin Road. The clock tower of City Hall stands in striking contrast to the once rural landscape of the entire region.** *Photo by Jeff Chevrier.*

It must have been a curious sight: John Graves Simcoe, the first lieutenant-governor of Upper Canada, and his wife traversing the Credit River in a canoe with two Mississauga Indians as tour guides. Like so many who would follow, Simcoe was looking for a new home—not for himself in this case, but for his planned Government Inn. It was June 1796. Seeking refuge from a stormy Lake Ontario, Simcoe's boat anchored at the mouth of the Credit. He decided he wanted to see some of this vaunted river for himself, with its abundant salmon and majestic forested shorelines. The Mississaugas obliged.

The Government Inn was to complement the Government House in Burlington in a chain of stopovers, intended to facilitate travel from Newark (Niagara-on-the-Lake) to York (Toronto). When it was erected according to Simcoe's wishes in 1798 on the east bank of the Credit River, it became the first building constructed by European settlers in the Region of Peel. This marked the start of English settlement in the area and, by many accounts, the birth of Mississauga. But the area's earliest recorded history of development and commerce and, indeed, the origins of the city's name are actually far older.

For at least 10,000 years, native Indians had flourished throughout southern Ontario. In the late 1690s, the Anishinabeg (part of the Algonquian linguistic family) pushed south, displacing the Iroquois through a decade of bloody warfare to occupy the area bounded by Lakes Ontario, Erie and Huron. Though most were called Ojibwas (or Chippewas) by Europeans, the French and later the English referred to those who lived along the north shore of Lake Ontario as *Mississaugas*.

The precise origin of the name is unclear, which would perhaps account for the spelling variations that have appeared, such as Mississaugua, Mississaga and Mississague. But a couple of possible explanations are known. Jesuit fathers first recorded the term *oumisagai* in 1640 in reference to an Algonquin band near the Mississagi River, the "river of the north of many mouths," on the remote northwest shore of Lake Huron. Perplexed as to why Europeans applied this name to Lake Ontario bands as well, the natives developed their own theory: many of the western Mississaugas belonged to the Eagle clan or totem, which in their dialect was pronounced *Masesaugee*. Hearing this reference was evidently enough for Europeans to assume the connection, and the name stuck.

Some Iroquois names have survived, such as Lake Ontario, the "beautiful great lake." Toronto, which the Mississaugas took to mean "looming of trees," was adopted by the French in 1720 as the name of their fort near the mouth of the Humber River. But the Mississaugas soon attached their own names to places. On a clear day at *Menecing*, "on the (Toronto) islands," mist could be seen rising like a cloud from *Kahkejewung*, "the water falls" of Niagara. *Adoopekog* was the "place of the black alders"—the Etobicoke Creek which today forms the eastern boundary of Mississauga. *Missinnihe*—roughly translated as the "trusting creek"—was the site of annual trading with Europeans, who often allowed the natives to trade on credit. It became known to all as the Credit River.

Eventually, the name Mississauga was coined not only for its native residents, but also for the region. In 1781, during the American Revolution, thousands of United Empire Loyalists began immigrating from the U.S. But since Britain's Royal Proclamation of 1763 officially recognized the Great Lakes Indians' title to their lands, the purchase of Indian lands by private individuals had been prohibited. To satisfy land settlement pressures, the Crown signed a series of agreements with the Mississaugas between about 1781 and 1788 to acquire lands stretching from Kingston to the Etobicoke Creek, and from the Niagara River to Burlington Bay. The remaining areas to the

north of Lake Ontario became known as the Mississauga Tract.

Ironically, Simcoe had preferred to preserve the Tract, both for Indian use and as a source of the tall pines and oaks required for the Royal Navy's ship masts. But his selection of the town of York as the new capital of Upper Canada in 1793 made the Mississauga Tract indispensable in linking "the population of the Colony with the seat of the King's Government... ." Three years later, his visit up the Credit on that summer day would ensure that the area's heritage as a transportation corridor and centre for trade would thrive on an unimaginable scale.

On August 2, 1805, eight Mississauga chiefs signed a treaty with British representatives at Government Inn. The First Purchase, as it is now known, transferred land rights to the Mississauga Tract from the lakeshore inland to a depth of eight or nine kilometres, or about as far north as the present Eglinton Avenue. The Mississaugas retained a strip of land extending 1.5 kilometres either side of the Credit River, their camps along the Etobicoke, 12- and 16-Mile Creeks, as well as sole fishing rights for all four waterways.

For the next few decades, growth would be explosive. Members of the illustrious Queen's

Workers take a break in Port Credit's harbour, the epicentre of the area's history. From its early days of commerce and stonehooking, the harbour has evolved into a modern hive of recreational waterfront activities. *Photo courtesy Region of Peel Archives.*

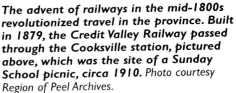

Rangers had carved a military trail through the forest, naming it after British Home Secretary Henry Dundas. The purchased land was surveyed and divided into the three townships of Nelson, Trafalgar and Toronto. (Mississauga now encompasses all of the original Toronto Township, plus some surrounding areas.) At the time, a district was the primary unit of land administration in Upper Canada. Perhaps as an omen for the future, all three townships became part of the "Home District."

By 1818, with virtually all of the "Old Survey's" 200-acre lots claimed along popular Dundas Street, officials and chiefs found themselves back at the Government Inn to negotiate the Second Purchase. This extended Toronto Township north to present-day Steeles Avenue.

Two years later, the Mississaugas relinquished their control of the watershed areas reserved under the First Purchase, except for 200 acres on the west bank of the Credit

The advent of railways in the mid-1800s revolutionized travel in the province. Built in 1879, the Credit Valley Railway passed through the Cooksville station, pictured above, which was the site of a Sunday School picnic, circa 1910. Photo courtesy Region of Peel Archives.

about two kilometres from the lake. From 1826 to 1847, this was the site of the Credit Reserve of the Mississaugas. For settlers, this removal of barriers to the major waterways meant access to power and transportation, and the development surge was on!

The Original Pioneers

By 1806, they had already begun to arrive: British settlers, Loyalists from the U.S. and resident Canadians. They came from places like Pennsylvania, New Jersey, New York, Massachusetts, Niagara, New Brunswick and directly from England. And they came by the thousands.

Though the War of 1812 slowed immigration, it actually spurred economic development in Toronto Township. With the English, French and natives fighting side by side, the invasion attempts of the "Long Knives" (Americans) were repelled and peace was restored in 1815. The timing was perfect, as thousands emigrated from the British Isles in the wake of the Napoleonic Wars to settle in Upper Canada.

With settlement came the emergence of villages and hamlets—lots of them. At that time, each of these small centres was by necessity quite self-sufficient, with sources for employment, supplies and mail service all established locally to varying degrees. The day-to-day world was, after all, a pretty small place. Most sprouted up around a new industry, a large

roadway (such as Dundas) or a post office at a significant crossroads. By 1877, 16 such settlements dotted the township, each with its own founders and heroes.

Though many hamlets have vanished, several flourished and survive today. To understand their roots is to better appreciate the fabric that is Mississauga.

Port Credit was home to the Government Inn and the area's first white resident—Thomas Ingersoll, father of War of 1812 heroine Laura Secord, who became the Inn's operator in 1805. But the area's growth was delayed by the Mississaugas' land reserves bordering the Credit River. Port Credit didn't become a village until 1834, the same year that harbour facilities were substantially upgraded. Following the 1847 departure of the natives, the village enjoyed a period of exceptional growth. Unfortunately, this was abruptly halted in the mid-1850s by a fire which destroyed the harbour's west side, and the advent of railways which diminished the harbour's shipping traffic. The key to Port Credit's revival proved to be its attraction as a summer resort area for fishing, hunting and cottagers. It further prospered with the opening of the St. Lawrence Starch Company in 1889 and by 1900 had become the most populated village in Toronto Township. In 1961, it became the town of Port Credit.

The little village of Dixie was home to the township's first recorded settler—Philip Cody—who purchased land at the southeast corner of Dundas Street and Cawthra Road in 1807. Soon after building the area's first private inn and tavern, he was host to Joseph and Jane Silverthorne, who later built their own house on the lot across from Cody's. Called Cherry Hill House, it stands today as the oldest surviving house in Mississauga. Cody and Silverthorne helped spearhead the construction of the original, multidenominational Dixie Union Chapel in 1816. With a tavern and church established, Dixie became a favourite social gathering place. Though it never gained major prominence in the shadow of neighbouring Cooksville, Dixie landmarks survive today.

Immediately west of Dixie, Cooksville sprouted up around the tavern and stagecoach operations of Jacob Cook. The village was initially called Harrisville for Daniel Harris, the area's first settler, who arrived in 1808. In 1819, Cook purchased part of Harris's land. The following year, he was awarded a contract to deliver mail between York and Niagara, which, over the next decade, he successfully parleyed into a network of stagecoach routes throughout Upper Canada. In his honour, the thriving village was renamed Cooksville in 1836. It continued to prosper until 1852, when a fire destroyed most of its stores and homes. Plagued thereafter by economic misfortune, the area dabbled for a time in winemaking and oil refining. Ultimately, it was Cooksville's 1873 selection as the site of the Toronto Township Hall that restored its momentum. With the key arteries of Dundas Street and Centre Road (Hurontario Street) intersecting at its core, Cooksville soon became the centre of the township and, eventually, the site of Mississauga's first city hall.

Also circa 1808, the village of Clarkson got its start with the arrival of Loyalist Warren Clarkson from New Brunswick. His family and others—like that of Captain Lewis Bradley— settled in an area which they named Merrigold's Point, after fellow settler Thomas Merrigold. By 1819, Clarkson had built a frame house which still stands on Clarkson

The oldest surviving house in Mississauga, Cherry Hill House was named for the English-bred trees which builder Joseph Silverthorne planted along the driveway. The house was moved to Silvercreek Boulevard from its original site near Dundas and Cawthra in 1973 to allow the widening of Cawthra Road. In 1973, it opened as a restaurant. Photo by Jeff Chevrier.

The Bradley Museum in Clarkson was once the 1830s home of the family of Captain Lewis Bradley. The farmhouse has been restored and is now a living re-creation of the lifestyle of early settlers.
Photo by Jeff Chevrier.

The Atlantic Hotel in Dixie, circa 1905.
Photo courtesy Region of Peel Archives.

Road. He went on to operate a general store and post office, prompting locals to call the area "Clarkson's Corners." In later years, Clarkson's agriculture flourished. During the early 1900s, it was known as the "Strawberry Capital of Canada"—a testament to its agricultural prowess.

Streetsville burst onto the scene as a direct result of two events: the Second Purchase of 1818 and the Mississaugas' subsequent sale of most of their remaining lands bordering the Credit River. The first vestiges of settlement occurred when James Glendinning erected the area's first log shanty in 1818. Immediately following the Purchase, Niagara settler Timothy Street was contracted to conduct the "New Survey" of the acquired lands. As payment, he received 1,000 acres within this new section of the township; his hired surveyor, Robert Bristol, was granted 600 acres. Street took advantage of the freed up access to the power and transportation afforded by the Credit River, and Streetsville was born. Street set about building a sawmill, a grist mill and a tannery. The Barber brothers followed, constructing a woollen mill and stately homes in a southern section of the village that would be nicknamed "Barbertown." Local industry spurred rapid growth, making Streetsville one of the most prominent centres in Toronto Township for much of the 1800s. Its fortunes

faded somewhat late in the century, but rebounded during the population surge after the Second World War. Incorporated in 1858, it is the oldest official village in Mississauga and boasts more heritage buildings than any other part of the city. It gained town status in 1962 and amalgamated with the newly formed city of Mississauga in 1974. Streetsville's mayor at the time was Hazel McCallion—the future mayor of Mississauga.

Farther up the Credit, Meadowvale Village was founded around 1820 by Irish settlers from New York, apparently led by John Beatty. A clear example of the importance of local industry and stores to fledgling hamlets, Meadowvale struggled for years without these conveniences. It wasn't until 1831, when Beatty sold his land to John Crawford, that signs of promise emerged. Crawford, and later John Simpson, established saw and wool carding mills that started things rolling. Francis Silverthorne moved to Meadowvale in 1844; he expanded operations and added a grist mill. By the end of the decade, two hotels, a blacksmith shop and a school served the burgeoning population. Meadowvale Village's 19th-century atmosphere has survived to this day—so much so that in 1980, it became Ontario's first designated heritage conservation district. The first hotel, built by blacksmith George Ball, still stands on Derry Road.

Opposite page: Many of the historical homes of Meadowvale Village are still lovingly maintained as proud reminders of days gone by. Photo by Jeff Chevrier.

Dundas Street, circa 1900. It began as a muddy corduroy road dubbed the "Governor's Road" for Lieutenant-Governor Simcoe, who ordered its construction by military troops near the turn of the 19th century. For over a century, the "Dundas Highway" was the main east-west artery through Mississauga and a breeding ground for development and commerce. *Photo courtesy Region of Peel Archives.*

Around the same time as Beatty's arrival, the quiet village of Malton was taking hold, named for the Yorkshire, England, birthplace of early settler Richard Halliday. Its success as a distribution centre for agricultural products bound for the markets of York was greatly accelerated with the 1854 introduction of the Grand Trunk Railway. For more than a decade, Malton prospered until agriculture began to wane as the base of the economy. It became the county seat briefly in 1859 and in 1914 was incorporated as a "police village," gaining slightly less autonomy than a full village. But Malton was destined to retain its heritage. In 1937, land adjacent to the village was chosen as the site of the new international airport. Following the Second World War, Malton gained a reputation as an international leader in aeronautics. It remains a major transportation hub and the home of Pearson International Airport.

To the south of Streetsville and west of Cooksville, the village of Erindale traces its

origins to 1822 when Thomas Racey built—yes, another sawmill—on the east bank of the Credit. Within a few years, a village thrived around the mill and the other typical staples of a post office and hotel/tavern, as well as a brewery and chair factory. About 1825, St. Peter's Anglican Church—the first Anglican church west of York—was built with the support of General Peter Adamson and others. Reverend James Magrath became the minister and a prominent force in the community's development. Though unofficially dubbed Toronto, the village eventually became known as Springfield, a favourite stop for travellers of the "Dundas Highway." Magrath's contributions were recognized in 1890, when the village was renamed Erindale—the name which he had given to his house in remembrance of his Irish homeland. By 1904, the Magrath estate was the site of Price Dairy, the first Canadian producer of pasteurized milk.

These are the villages of Mississauga. Their enduring individuality has provided a rich and diverse history for the city, and living links to its small-town roots. Even today, many long-time residents cherish the idea of being villagers first, within the greater framework of the city—their families having called the area home for a very long time. Certainly, Mississauga would be much the poorer without these enclaves of community spirit.

The Modern Era

By the latter part of the 19th century, with the villages having taken hold, a myriad of industries began to form the basis of the township's economy. Some were unique, like the turn-of-the-century stonehooking schooners of Port Credit—crafts designed to carry tonnes of the grey-blue Dundas shale, retrieved from the lake bottom with long-handled rakes, which was coveted by Toronto builders. Railroads—the Grand Trunk, CPR and the Credit Valley Railway—played an increasingly important role in linking the area with other centres as they began catering to passengers rather than freight alone. These, and the Lake Ontario steamboats, helped spots like the 75-acre Lorne Park to emerge as favourite day trip destinations of Torontonians.

Though the massive fires which struck many of the villages during the mid-1800s were a thing of the past, disasters continued to have an impact. October 15, 1954, was the date of one of the most ferocious natural occurrences ever to strike this area. Though Hurricane Hazel pummelled much of southern Ontario, Mississauga was left relatively unscathed. But the fates balanced the score somewhat in 1979. Just before midnight on November 10, a CPR train containing extremely volatile chemicals was derailed at a level crossing in the south central part of the city. An explosion released poisonous chlorine gas into the night sky, forcing the evacuation of most of the city's population during the early morning hours of November 11. Conducted in remarkably orderly fashion, it would go down in history as the largest peacetime evacuation ever.

From the turn of the century until the city was created, the area was transformed beyond anything that Cody, Cook, Street, or any of the other founders would recognize. Development pressures from a sprawling Toronto snowballed as wheat fields became an airport and orchards turned into subdivisions.

Still, it took a new breed of pioneers to propel the march toward urban maturity. One the earliest of the modern era, perhaps none is more fondly remembered than "Old Man Ontario." Thomas Laird Kennedy, a resident of Dixie, was first elected to the provincial legislature in 1919. In the ensuing 39 years, he only lost one election and served the province as an MPP until his 80th birthday in 1958. Minister of Agriculture for a total of 15 years and Premier of Ontario in 1948, the names of T. L. Kennedy Secondary School and Tomken Road still bear his indelible stamp.

Many others followed. Visionaries like Gordon Shipp Sr. and his son Harold were thought by many to have lost their minds for building roadways and subdivisions in the hinterland to the west of the provincial capital. Likewise for Bruce McLaughlin, who spearheaded the development of a shopping centre criticized for being "in the middle of nowhere." But their visions were borne out, inspiring others. The early subdivisions became Applewood; the shopping centre is now Square One, the second largest in Canada.

The final defining strides toward the city's formation were evidently set in motion by former Township reeve Robert Speck. Fearful that the area would eventually be swallowed up by Metropolitan Toronto, he aggressively worked to establish a single, large municipality capable of forging its own identity. In 1968, the Town of Mississauga was incorporated, encompassing all of Toronto Township except for Streetsville and Port Credit. On January 1, 1974, the three towns were amalgamated, and the city of Mississauga was born.

The Mississauga of today still thrives on the pioneer spirit. Pulsing with the new frontier zest. Tempered by the lessons of an arduous history. On a summer day, the laneways of the original villages whisper of courageous settlers and bold entrepreneurs. In over two centuries of incredible change, it seems some things are constant. As a new millennium dawns, Mississauga continues to be the home of pioneers. **Ⓜ**

Workers proudly unveil the first Lancaster bomber built by the Victory Aircraft Co. on August 6, 1943. Victory laid the foundation of Mississauga's aircraft industry, employing 9,700 at its peak before eventually being sold to A.V. Roe—makers of the famous Avro Arrow. Photo courtesy Region of Peel Archives.

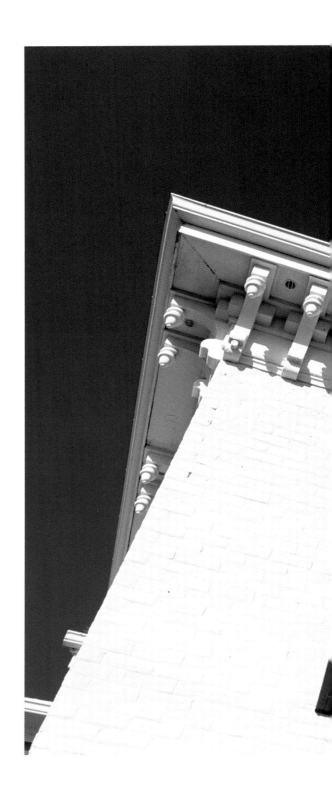

Opposite page and above: **Streetsville, incorporated in 1858, is the oldest official village in Mississauga.** *Photos by Jeff Chevrier.*

Photo by Jeff Chevrier

CHAPTER 2

A Modern Wonder

Ⓜ

In today's world of spiralling government deficits, Mississauga boasts a remarkable record of astute management and debt-free operation. This no-nonsense approach has attracted a diverse, thriving industrial base and fostered phenomenal development, making it one of the fastest growing cities in Canada over the past decade.

Photo by Michael Scholz

From an area population of 75,000 in 1961, Mississauga doubled in size each decade through the 1960s and 1970s. The torrid growth continued through the 1980s, with the largest absolute population increase in Canada between 1986 and 1991. With a current population of over 600,000, projections suggest that the city will be home to nearly three quarters of a million residents by the year 2030. There's little doubt that Mississauga will remain one of the fastest growing centres in the entire country well into the next millennium.

So how does one account for this incredible growth in such a short time? At least a partial explanation can be found in the city's management style.

City Government

Imagine for a moment a return to the good old days of balanced government budgets. Imagine the word "deficit" not being part of the common vocabulary of civic economics. Now try to envision major municipal developments and capital expenditures being undertaken without any need of bonds, debentures or other financing. And for a real stretch, picture a place where municipal property taxes hold steady, with no increase for years on end.

Amusing? Implausible? Well, here's one more for you: How about seeing your municipal tax

dollars go directly to providing new community facilities and services rather than to interest payments, because the city is debt-free!

The idyllic locale you've been pondering is alive and well in Mississauga.

While other cities have been reeling under the burden imposed by provincial funding cuts in recent years, Mississauga has managed to simultaneously hold the line on property taxes, push ahead with the construction of major new facilities and still balance the books. As a result, the city's industrial and commercial property taxes are among the lowest in Ontario, while business taxes consistently rank with the cheapest in the Greater Toronto Area (GTA). Other operating efficiencies have also had a positive impact. The city's electrical utility rates, for example, are the lowest in the GTA.

The origins of this no-nonsense approach to city government can be traced almost entirely to one individual—Hazel McCallion, the longest-serving mayor in Mississauga's history. Since taking office in 1978, her philosophy has been straightforward: 1) Run the city like a business; and 2) If you don't have the money in the bank to pay for it, you can't afford it.

Simple words that seem so difficult to adhere to. But it has been the ability of Mayor McCallion and city councils to consistently put this common sense credo into practice that has led to an amazing record of fiscal stability and controlled expansion.

A precedent-setting case in point was the construction of City Hall. Opened in 1987, the building's entire $59.5 million cost was paid for through a unique "savings plan." Beginning in 1979, monies were allocated annually to a fund which ultimately paid for the land and building, leaving the facility debt-free. This pay-as-you-go approach has since been applied to all new projects. Little wonder that the city has a AAA credit rating.

These keystones of solid planning and predictability have allowed the city to provide residents with the latest in recreational facilities and essential community services. They have also fostered phenomenal growth in both the industrial and residential sectors.

Growth in Mississauga's retail sector is both strong and diverse, ranging from Square One—the second largest mall in Canada—and huge "Power Centres," to the quaint European feel of the Sherwood Forrest Shopping Village. Photo by Jeff Chevrier.

A security guard pauses to take in the view from the Civic Centre clock tower. Below, 100,000 square feet of public activity areas feature a civic garden, amphitheatre, colonnades and a reflecting pool that transforms into a skating rink in winter. Photo by Jeff Chevrier.

The hand-painted ceiling of the Civic Centre's Council Chamber depicts the Mississauga Indian legend of the Great Bear (Big Dipper) and the seven hunters. Fibre-optic stars light the "night sky" 75 feet above the floor. Photo by Michael Scholz.

Xerox, whose already immense research facility was expanded by 34,000 square feet in 1995, is one of the anchors in the Sheridan Park Research Community. Photo by Jeff Chevrier.

Development

There's a chicken-and-egg conundrum at play in the growth of a new city. Development or infrastructure; which comes first? Without proper infrastructure, development is severely constrained and therefore difficult to attract. But without the tax base of new development, where does the money come from for an expanding municipal infrastructure?

Perhaps there's been a bit of "build it and they will come" optimism here at times that few will admit to. But the assurance of an aggressive yet systematic approach to growth by the city, pursued in tandem with developers and industry, has been a winning formula for attracting new players. In 1994 alone, the total value of construction in Mississauga was almost a billion dollars—the highest of any city in Canada and nearly double that of the city of Toronto. Not a bad year. Except that this was about equal to the annual average achieved for the previous decade. And though 1995 was generally regarded as a slow year for construction in Ontario, Mississauga still managed to maintain construction values in excess of $900 million for the year. Did someone say recession?

The magnitude of this activity prompted the city to implement MAX—the largest computerized development and building approvals system of its kind in Canada. Unveiled in 1996, the Mississauga Approval Xpress system is designed to eliminate bottlenecks in the building permit approvals process and gives city staff online access to 1,000 maps, with related data on zoning histories, active building applications and real estate transactions in general.

Economy

Some of the most compelling evidence of the effectiveness of the city's growth strategies lies in the strength and diversity of its industrial base. Mississauga is the fifth largest head office centre in Canada. There are mainstay industries, such as food distribution giant National Grocers, Cadbury Beverages, Dun & Bradstreet, Nissan, Rubbermaid, Revlon, Ralston-Purina and St. Lawrence Cement—the largest cement manufacturer in Eastern Canada—to name a few. In all, over 15,000 companies employ more than 300,000 people.

It's not surprising that in this city of the future, many of the prominent corporate citizens are within the key high-tech sectors which are expected to lead us into the 21st century: computer and information technologies, biomedical technologies, pharmaceuticals and aerospace. Names like General Electric, AT&T, Microsoft, Hewlett-Packard, DuPont, Glaxo Wellcome, Spar Aerospace and many others are sprinkled prominently throughout downtown office towers and more than 50 business parks.

But leading-edge industries are nothing new here. High-tech sectors have been firmly established in Mississauga since His Royal Highness Prince Philip officially opened the Sheridan Park Research Community in 1965. With original occupants like the Ontario Research Foundation and Atomic Energy of Canada, Sheridan Park immediately became a highly concentrated centre of public and private research facilities—one of the first of its kind in Canada. The centre still thrives with the addition of newcomers such as IMAX Corporation and Xerox, whose already immense research facility was expanded by 34,000 square feet in 1995.

And unlike the experience of many older cities, Mississauga's industry isn't crammed into one particular area, such as the waterfront. Sectoral clusters such as Sheridan Park can be found throughout the city. There's the

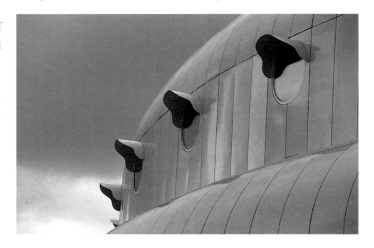

pharmaceutical industry concentration in Meadowvale; computer and software companies across the northern rim; petrochemicals in the southwest and into Port Credit. Given the way in which these blend with surrounding commercial and residential areas, it's hard to imagine that the city will ever suffer from the eyesores of decaying industrial tracts which often mar major urban centres.

For many, of course, Mississauga has become synonymous with the hive of activity which surrounds Pearson International Airport. The early aviation industry roots of Malton have spawned one of Canada's busiest industrial/commercial areas. Aeronautics and aerospace giants like McDonnell-Douglas, Pratt & Whitney and Spar have been joined by a tremendously diverse array of companies—from national associations to ad agencies.

To service all the airport comings and goings, there's one of the country's most intense concentrations of the hospitality industry. Virtually every major hotel chain is represented, accounting for an estimated 1,200 rooms and accompanying conference space. The International Centre alone houses some

900,000 square feet of prime space and hosts upwards of 100 trade and consumer shows annually. This cluster of facilities continues seamlessly across the boundary of neighboring Etobicoke, where roughly another 3,800 hotel rooms are readily accessible.

As another sign of things to come, the film industry is rapidly establishing its presence in Mississauga as well. The variety of settings and architecture, the lack of serious traffic congestion and availability of skilled technical crews make city locales an increasingly popular choice for television and movie producers. On one occasion a couple of years ago, a Mississauga Board of Trade official thought he may have had a brush with interdimensional travel when he entered city hall to find himself standing in a cavernous ancient Chinese temple. He regained confidence in his faculties when reassured that the miraculous transformation of the central Great Hall was courtesy of a film crew for use in the TV series *Kung Fu—The Legend Continues*.

As an ever-present undercurrent to all this growth and commerce, there is a tangible continuity of purpose here between the municipal government and business. The entrepreneurial

Mayor Hazel McCallion conducts her regular cable TV phone-in show, where she talks one-on-one to callers about municipal issues. She has been described as a dynamo, whose down-to-earth accessibility and common sense approach have helped make her one of Canada's longest-serving mayors. Photo by Jeff Chevrier.

Spar Aerospace is a major player in the thriving aerospace industry which has sprung from Mississauga's aviation heritage. Tremendous growth in several other high-tech sectors, such as computer and information technologies, biomedical technologies and pharmaceuticals, is expected to drive the city's economy into the 21st century. Photo by Jeff Chevrier.

Spar's "Canadarm" has greatly expanded the versatility of NASA's space shuttle program. Now a familiar sight, it allows satellites to be retrieved and equipment deployed through its sophisticated robotic manoeuvres. Photo courtesy NASA.

drive of the business community is reflected in the membership and initiatives of the Mississauga Board of Trade. Arguably the most vibrant chamber of commerce body in the country, the MBOT is a proactive force in the business community, fostering partnerships among businesses, governments and public institutions in matters of trade, municipal development and the environment. Echoing this is the city's Economic Development Office. In striving to be one of the country's most successful municipal marketing agencies, the EDO is careful not to concentrate solely on a traditional role of attracting new business to the city. Growth of local businesses is also encouraged through the efforts of the Business Services Initiative and the Small Business Self-Help Office.

With underpinnings like these, it's a safe bet that for this modern wonder of municipal efficiency and balance, growth and prosperity are not about to end soon. **ⓜ**

The Mississauga Board of Trade is considered one of the most vibrant and proactive chambers of commerce in the country. *Photo by Michael Scholz.*

The city core hums with construction. Throughout the mid-1990s, the value of new construction permits in the city has far surpassed that of neighbouring Toronto and virtually anywhere else in Canada. *Photo by Jeff Chevrier.*

With a capacity that is rapidly approaching 1 million square feet, the sprawling International Centre typically hosts more than 100 trade and consumer shows annually. Photo by Jeff Chevrier.

Workers take a break behind 77 City Centre Drive in the downtown core.
Photo by Jeff Chevrier.

Mississauga's Civic Centre (this view from the companion Central Library) was built as both a focal point for the burgeoning civic identity and a model of fiscally responsible, debt-free development. For some, it conjures up images of the area's farming past, with the office tower representing a farmhouse, the Council Chamber a silo, the facade building a barn and the clock tower a windmill. Photo by Jeff Chevrier.

Ready for action! **With its debt-free operating base, the city has been able to provide residents with the most modern municipal services and facilities to be found anywhere.** *Photo by Jeff Chevrier.*

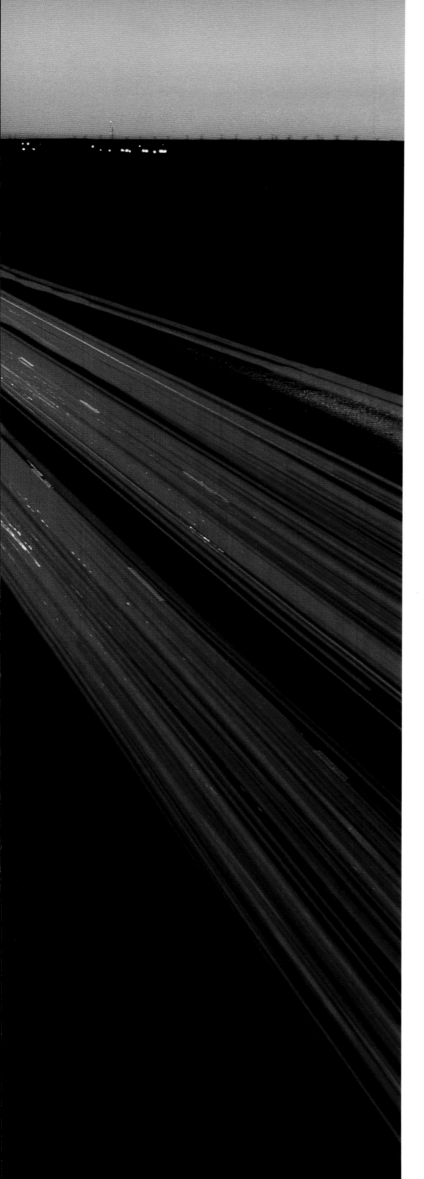

CHAPTER 3

At the Hub of the Golden Horseshoe

Ⓜ

The originator of the old axiom "location is everything" must have lived in Mississauga. Situated on the northwestern shores of Lake Ontario, Mississauga is at the epicentre of Canada's industrial heartland.

Photo by Jeff Chevrier

*T*here's yet another reason for Mississauga's astounding growth: It's strategically situated in perhaps the best all-around location in all of southern Ontario. Of course the dot on the map is just the beginning. Much of what makes a location "prime" has to do with convenient access—for people and products—and proximity to other important locales. In all these respects, Mississauga has been blessed.

First, a quick geography refresher. Since at least as far back as the early 1960s, the strip of land which borders the western perimeter of Lake Ontario has been dubbed the "Golden Horseshoe" because of its prominence as a key "engine" for the entire country. Stretching from the tip of the Niagara Peninsula to the city of Oshawa, the area is home to the highest concentration of industry and commerce in Canada, with a population of over 6 million—more than half that of the province. Yet it features some of the most fertile and productive farm land in the nation, including the vineyards of Ontario's burgeoning wine industry. Throw in a collection of the largest freshwater bodies in the world and you have a truly golden area which is undeniably the industrial and financial heartland of Canada.

In the midst of the region lies the economic powerhouse of the Greater Toronto Area (GTA), which encompasses Metropolitan Toronto and four other regional municipalities that surround it. Mississauga occupies the entire southern portion of the Region of Peel. With a combined population approaching 5 million, the GTA ranks fourth in size among major market areas within Canada and the U.S., virtually neck and neck with Detroit and behind only Los Angeles, New York and Chicago.

Situated at roughly the centre of the Golden Horseshoe and immediately west of Metro, Mississauga has become the gateway to the GTA. More multi-lane superhighways converge here than in any other city on the continent, and it's home to one of North America's busiest airports—Pearson International. It sounds like a hectic place, but with the most immense area of any major city in Ontario—111 square miles—Mississauga enjoys the advantages of being on the doorstep of the Toronto core without having to endure the congestion of most big cities. And that's precisely why so many prominent corporations now call Mississauga home.

By Air

Pearson International Airport is Canada's largest and most used, accounting for one-third of the country's total air traffic and a whopping 40 per cent of its air cargo. Pearson stands fourth in North America and is among the top airports in the world in terms of passenger volume. By the new millennium, officials expect to be processing more than 30 million passengers annually.

By any yardstick, it's a world-class facility that provides a crucial link to the world for business travellers and vacationers alike. With the addition of the newest of three terminals, the $300-million Trillium Terminal, Pearson services everything from private charter and corporate aircraft to the Concorde. An hour-and-a-half flight takes you to major centres like Chicago, New York and Boston. But if you'd prefer to avoid the bustle associated with large aircraft, walk across the tarmac, hand your luggage to the co-pilot and hop aboard one of the many general aviation charters or domestic commuter flights. Montreal and Ottawa are barely an hour away.

Modern, low-cost public transit covers all areas of the city, operating from a central terminal in the city core. *Photo by Jeff Chevrier.*

Photo by Jeff Chevrier

By Land

The significance of Mississauga's location is even more obvious from the standpoint of road access. As a society that's still very much enamored with the automobile and the lure of the open road, it helps to really put this epicentre thing into perspective when you consider that an estimated 125 million people live within a day's drive of the city. This is due in no small measure to the area's exemplary array of highways.

Historic highways 2, 5 and 10, each now a main thoroughfare, provided early access which has since blended into the city's network of high-volume roadways. But it was the opening of The Queen Elizabeth Way, Canada's first freeway, in 1939 that furnished a crucial artery stretching from downtown Toronto through Mississauga and around the lake to Niagara. With the 1956 completion of the final section linking Fort Erie to the U.S. border, the QEW immediately became the preferred roadway into and out of the Golden Horseshoe.

Highway 401—the MacDonald-Cartier Freeway—followed, slicing across the city's north to form the asphalt ribbon which spans southern Ontario from east to west. By far the most widely travelled highway in Canada, the 401 swells to an awesome 18 lanes in northeastern Mississauga. Today, a remarkable web which includes highways 403, 409, 410, 427 and the brand new 407 connects the QEW and the 401, allowing rapid movement through and around the city.

With a road infrastructure of this magnitude, it's not surprising that Mississauga is home to about 200 truck transportation businesses, complete with major truck terminals, bonded warehouses and freight transfer facilities.

The purple "People Movers" of the City Centre Shuttle Bus service transport people to and from offices, restaurants and shops throughout the downtown core. Thanks to an innovative joint venture between the city and major land developers, passengers ride free of charge. Photo by Jeff Chevrier.

By Rail

The main lines of Canada's two principal railways criss-cross through Mississauga to provide freight and passenger service. Intermodal freight terminals are located just north and east of city limits. Long-distance passenger service is available a short drive away at Toronto's Union Station.

By Sea

Yes, by sea. The St. Lawrence Seaway and the Great Lakes have for more than 160 years been a lifeline connecting the interior prairie regions to the Atlantic coast and everything in between. Ocean freight can be landed via one of two Lake Ontario

shoreline neighbours—the Port of Toronto just 18 km (11 miles) to the east or the busier Port of Hamilton, 33 km (21 miles) to the southwest. Two of the largest on the Great Lakes, these are full-service international ports of entry which offer truck and rail access, and a total of more than a million square feet of warehousing.

Getting Around Town

If you've read the previous chapter sections on the city's operation, you probably won't be surprised to hear that the same level of attention has been applied to the meticulous network of Mississauga's city streets. But it's true. Main arteries have clearly been designed with

A retired "laker"—like one of hundreds that continually ply the Great Lakes from Montreal to the Lakehead—now serves as a breakwater and silent testament to Lake Ontario's rich shipping heritage. Photo by Jeff Chevrier.

the eventual mature population of the city in mind. Lane expansions frequently occur well in advance of new development and the accompanying onslaught of higher traffic volumes (not in the after-the-fact manner that seems to plague some cities). Serious traffic snarls are the exception rather than the norm. Mind you, it's not all four-lane raceways here; there are hundreds of quiet, meandering neighbourhood streets that seem, quite simply, to be properly scaled to their intended use. It all comes back to the city's common sense approach to management.

But no city with a conscience can entertain aspirations of future growth without planning for the efficient movement of people, both logistically and from an energy conservation perspective, by means other than cars. Mass transit within the city comes in a variety of forms. There's conventional low-cost public transit with bus routes reaching all areas of the city, originating from a central terminal at Square One shopping centre in the downtown core.

Complementing regular transit is a unique City Centre Shuttle Bus service. Shuttle buses run continuously during the daytime, six days a week through a square mile of the downtown core. Thanks to an innovative joint venture between the city and major land developers, there is no cost to passengers for the service! This encourages those who work and shop in the downtown area to leave their cars at home

A web of high-quality expressways weaves in and around the city. More multi-lane superhighways converge here than in any other city on the continent.
Photo by Jeff Chevrier.

For those who prefer to leave the car at home, the GO Train speeds commuters throughout Mississauga and the surrounding Greater Toronto Area in comfort. Here, a rider gets ready to board at Port Credit Station, one of the city's nine commuter rail stations. Photo by Jeff Chevrier.

and still move easily and quickly between offices, restaurants and shops during the day.

Travel to and from Metro Toronto is a breeze via one of Mississauga's city buses that link up with the Metro subway system. Weekly or monthly GTA passes allow riders unlimited, seamless use of various transit systems across municipal boundaries. Or take the GO Train, which passes through Toronto's Union Station. More than 110,000 commuters from Mississauga, Metro and outlying areas rely on the GO Train to carry them across the GTA each day. This provincially operated passenger rail service serves nine rail stations throughout Mississauga, making it ideal for those who'd rather snooze or read a book than negotiate Metro's rush hour traffic.

For coming or going. Getting here, or just getting around. There isn't a more central or accessible city in Canada. **Ⓜ**

Above: **One of the dozens of luxury hotels in the airport area, the Sheraton is connected directly to Trillium Terminal 3 by a climate-controlled skywalk.** *Photo by Jeff Chevrier.*

Right: **Officials expect, that by the new millennium, Pearson International Airport will be providing service to more than 30 million passengers annually.** *Photo by Jeff Chevrier.*

CDN 5ZZ	LAGUARDIA
CDN 816	OTTAWA
AAL6553	OTTAWA
CDN1937	SARNIA
AAL6707	SARNIA
AALZ001	DALLAS FRESNO
CDN 888	MONTREAL
CDN6Z56	DALLAS
CDN19ZZ	KINGSTON
AAL6714	KINGSTON
CDN 5Z8	LAGUARDIA
AAL65Z8	LAGUARDIA
CDN6040	ROME
AZ 651	ROME
CDN 931	WINNIPEG
AAL6931	WINNIPEG
CDN6ZZ8	CHICAGO
AAL Z01	CH CAGO

A 45-foot-high, 1,000-foot-long skylit ceiling graces the departure concourse of the Grand Hall in Pearson's award-winning Trillium Terminal 3. Photo by Jeff Chevrier.

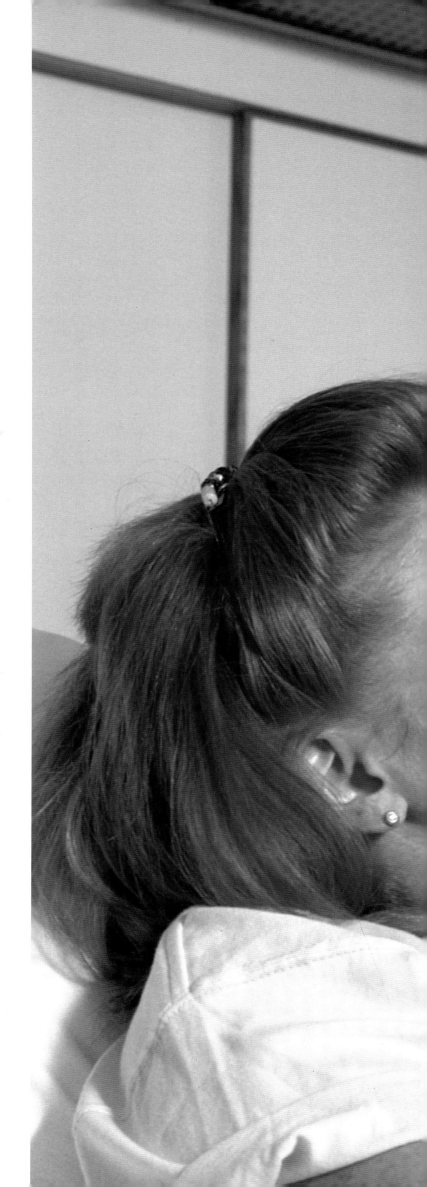

CHAPTER 4

Caring Hands

Ⓜ

There are a great many reasons why Mississauga's health care services are awe-inspiring: A universal health care system that is the envy of the world. Award-winning, state-of-the-art hospitals. Special care and retirement facilities of the highest calibre. But for those who live here, this is, above all else, a story of absolutely remarkable volunteers, compassionate people and the realization of dreams.

Photo by Jeff Chevrier

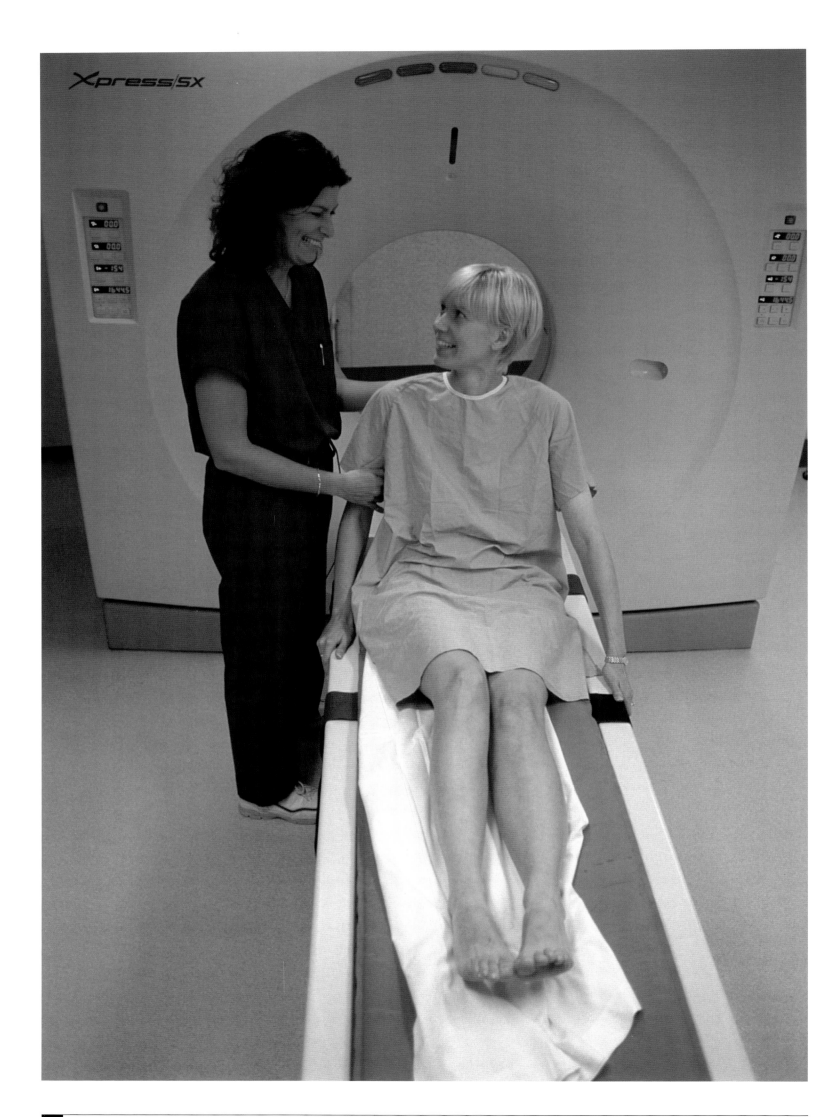

Some say that the true measure of a community's heart is revealed by its capacity to care for the sick, the infirm and the aged. If state-of-the-art facilities alone aren't enough evidence of Mississauga's heart, then one need only look at the incredible dedication of its health care workers and the support demonstrated by the public to be convinced.

Through its relatively short history, Mississauga has established a legacy of excellent and compassionate health care. It has been a cornerstone of the city's growth and well-being, and those associated with it have become integral threads in the fabric of the community.

As early as 1822, Dr. Joseph Adamson became the area's first licensed physician at a time when there were only 10 doctors in all of Upper Canada. In treating his patients—many of whom were Mississauga Indians—he would often accept payment through labour or other barter in order to ensure adequate health care for all. In his time, and for decades to come, he was not alone. When lean years hit a century later in the 1930s, Dr. Lionel "Ted" Brayley—himself a Mississauga institution—was known to often overlook a patient's finances if treatment was required. And health practitioner James Shaw, who also ran a blacksmith shop

and general store in Port Credit during the late 1800s, is said to have donated his medical earnings to the Methodist Church to help pay the minister's salary.

Today, Canada's version of "medicare" is the envy of the world. It ensures that medical care is accessible to everyone, regardless of race or ability to pay. Though beset in recent years by the same budgetary cutbacks that have been invoked by governments everywhere, the provincially administered universal health care system continues to meet the challenge: Provide world-class care with ever increasing efficiency.

Major Hospitals

In Mississauga, health care is principally delivered by two major hospitals—The Mississauga Hospital (TMH) and The Credit Valley Hospital (CVH). Both hospitals offer all the leading-edge equipment and technologies one might expect, like emergency heli-pads, CAT scanners and electronic diagnostic imaging systems. Yet each hospital has carved out its own identity and special place in the community.

Pure facts and figures say that TMH operates over 400 beds, reduced through efficiencies from a one-time high of 628. It is located on 23 acres in south central Mississauga. The CVH is a 440,000-square-foot acute care facility situated on 30 acres in a parkland setting in Erin Mills. Both are classified as community hospitals.

TMH specializes in cardiology and musculo-skeletal medicine, and is the regional centre for neurosurgery—quite a feat for a community hospital, considering this is territory usually reserved for teaching hospitals. And in the spring of 1997, the hospital installed the region's first Magnetic Resonance Imaging (MRI) unit. Each year, TMH oversees some 24,000 admissions and roughly 67,000 emergency visits. The CVH's areas of specialization include genetics and dialysis, and it is designated as the host site of the new $25-million Peel Community Cancer Centre. Each year, the hospital is host to nearly 4,000 births, over 10,000 surgical procedures, about 16,000 admissions and

In 1958, The Mississauga Hospital (TMH) was established as the area's first community hospital, built as a crucial alternative to the distant hospitals of Toronto. During the 1979 train derailment, all 462 of TMH's patients were efficiently evacuated to area hospitals using a fleet of 100 ambulances. Police had estimated this would take six to ten hours; it was accomplished in only three and one-half. *Photo courtesy of Consumers Gas.*

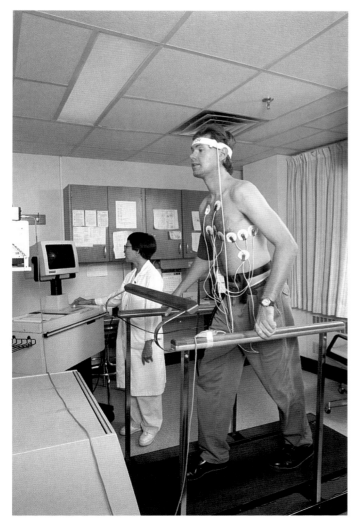

Opposite page: **A patient receives instruction and assurance during an MRI procedure at The Mississauga Hospital.** *Photo by Jeff Chevrier.*

Left: **The Mississauga Hospital cardiology specialists put a patient through the paces during a cardiac stress test.** *Photo by Michael Scholz.*

Though it looks more like an upscale hotel than a hospital in some respects, The Credit Valley Hospital (CVH) provides modern facilities and care second to none in the most computerized health care facility in Canada. Photo by Jeff Chevrier.

With its opening in 1986, The CVH ushered in a new era in health care. After just a year and a half of operation, it was awarded the highest honour bestowed by the Canadian Council on Health Services Accreditation for health care excellence. Photo by Jeff Chevrier.

62,000 emergency visits. Outpatient services number in the millions. But facts and figures, of course, tell only part of the story.

Established in 1958, The Mississauga Hospital has a rich legacy of its own which emphatically demonstrates the community's support for quality health care. The amazing saga which led to TMH's official opening began in the spring of 1952, when a Port Credit teenager involved in a traffic accident died before reaching the closest hospital—in Toronto. For local residents, this was the final straw in long-standing concerns over the lack of hospital facilities in the South Peel region. The Credit Valley Lions Club and the Port Credit Rotary Club initially took up the gauntlet that fall, planning a $500,000, 55-bed hospital in the face of stiff resistance from the Ministry of Health and Toronto Township's municipal council. As others joined the campaign, the story of perseverance which followed became even more remarkable.

In 1953, the public responded to a plebiscite on a new tax levy to pay for hospital debentures with a resounding 71 per cent approval. But this was a mere hint of the mammoth public support which would follow. The $2,500 down payment required to purchase the hospital site was raised through a peanut sale. Students donated proceeds from school dances and other events. Even a Brownie Pack contributed, raising $120 selling food and refreshments when 200 residents unexpectedly took refuge from

Hurricane Hazel at a Port Credit Secondary School dance. During the two years prior to the hospital's opening, women of the Hospital Auxiliary sewed 3,000 patient gowns and surgical smocks, and 450 pairs of baby booties from donated textiles and yarn. The examples go on and on.

Five years, a second levy, two major fundraising campaigns and thousands of door-to-door volunteer visits later, the hospital dream became a reality. Along the way, TMH had grown into a $1,625,000, 115-bed facility with nearly a third of the cost covered by public donations.

It's been a mutual love affair ever since. Subsequent expansions have been met with similar fund-raising success. And as it was during the infamous 1979 train derailment—when all 462 patients were evacuated—or in the wake of a disastrous 1980 fire in a large neighbouring nursing home, TMH is always there. The personal attachment was never more evident than during TMH's official opening, when more than 10,000 residents—about 13 per cent of the total population—toured the new facility in one weekend to examine their new hospital.

If TMH is the embodiment of the community's health care heritage, The Credit Valley Hospital is in many ways a microcosmic mirror of Mississauga today. Its official opening in 1986 marked the realization of yet another dream and the culmination of more than a decade of planning. In the short time since then, The CVH has enjoyed remarkable progress and garnered national acclaim as a leader in Canadian health care. And among staff there is that same pervasive excitement that seems to characterize the city.

Here's a snap quiz: Where might you find a coffee and espresso bar, a bagel specialty shop, a general store for healthy living and another for natural-source cosmetics, a hair salon, craft, jewelry and clothing kiosks, bank machines and someplace called the Skylight Restaurant? A major hotel? Another clue—how about a mini-zoo for kids, or art exhibits. A shopping mall? These are some of the shops and services of The Credit Valley Hospital. Its architecture at once conveys the aura of a new era in health care. But these are far more than skin-deep attributes.

The CVH has enjoyed numerous Canadian and North American firsts in utilizing technological advances, from the Philips Multidiagnostic III imaging system to a computerized optical scanning system for archiving patient records and hospital documents. There's a Sleep Laboratory and an Asthma Education Centre. The CVH even boasts satellite communications capabilities to enhance its fully catered conferencing services.

But again, it's the human side of The CVH that really tells the tale. In 1994, the hospital was named as one of the top 10 outstanding places to work in Canada. That's evident through events like the annual Teddy Bear Clinic—a favourite with staff, children and their families. Outreach programs focusing on issues such as alcohol abuse, parenting and nutrition extend care beyond the hospital's doors. And that affection has been echoed by thousands of community volunteers who, during the first 10 years of The CVH's existence, contributed in excess of an astounding 500,000 hours of their time to fund-raising and other hospital activities.

Together, these two hospitals continue to reward the public's unwavering support with unsurpassed, leading-edge medical service. Incredibly, not one, but both of Mississauga's hospitals are multiple award winners, judged as two of the best in Canada.

The Canadian Council on Health Services Accreditation (CCHSA) conducts voluntary peer reviews of the operation of more than 400 participating facilities across the country. After only a year and a half of operation, The CVH was awarded the prestigious three-year

Accreditation in 1987—at the time, the highest honour bestowed by the CCHSA. The feat was repeated with a second consecutive award in 1990. Then in 1993, The CVH became only the fourth hospital in the country to receive the new four-year Accreditation With Distinction, reserved for hospitals whose quality of care exceeds national standards in all respects. Not to be outdone, TMH was granted the same award in 1994, having previously won three-year accreditation awards since as early as 1961!

Special Care Facilities

The compassion and dedication to health care which the city has demonstrated stretches beyond traditional hospital services to numerous special care and family support organizations. For many, that has resulted not only in improved health, but also in a quality of life which otherwise might not have been possible.

A prime example is "Erinoak Serving Young People With Physical Disabilities." Nestled in a wooded Erin Mills enclave, Erinoak has quietly been making an immeasurable contribution to Mississauga and surrounding areas since 1978. Originally called the Credit Valley Treatment Centre for Children, Erinoak provides crucial medical, therapeutic and support services to over 1,600 young people and their families annually. As the organization's mission statement puts it, "Erinoak exists so that people with disabilities will maximize their individual potential."

The cap's on. Time to go enjoy the healing effect of The CVH's 30 acres of grounds, covered with 1,200 varieties of trees. Photo courtesy of The Credit Valley Hospital.

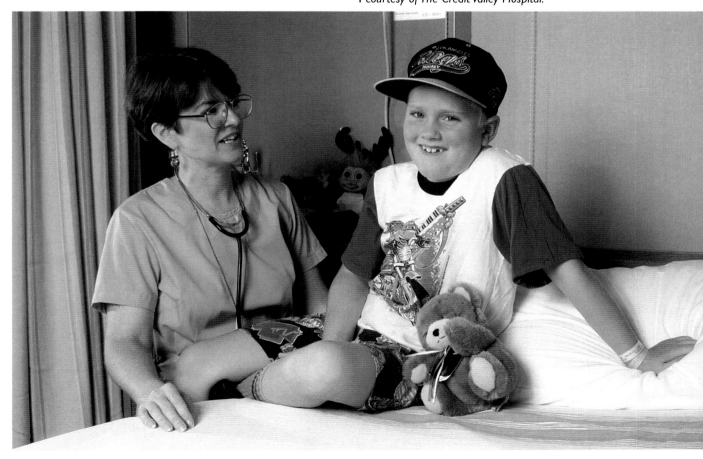

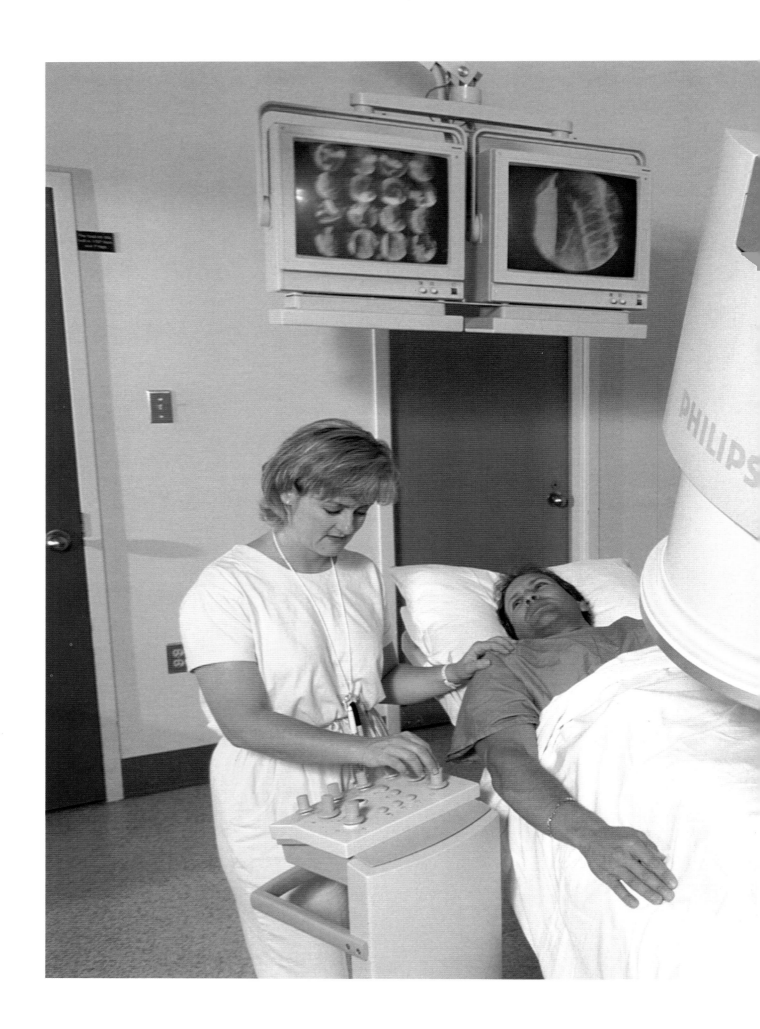

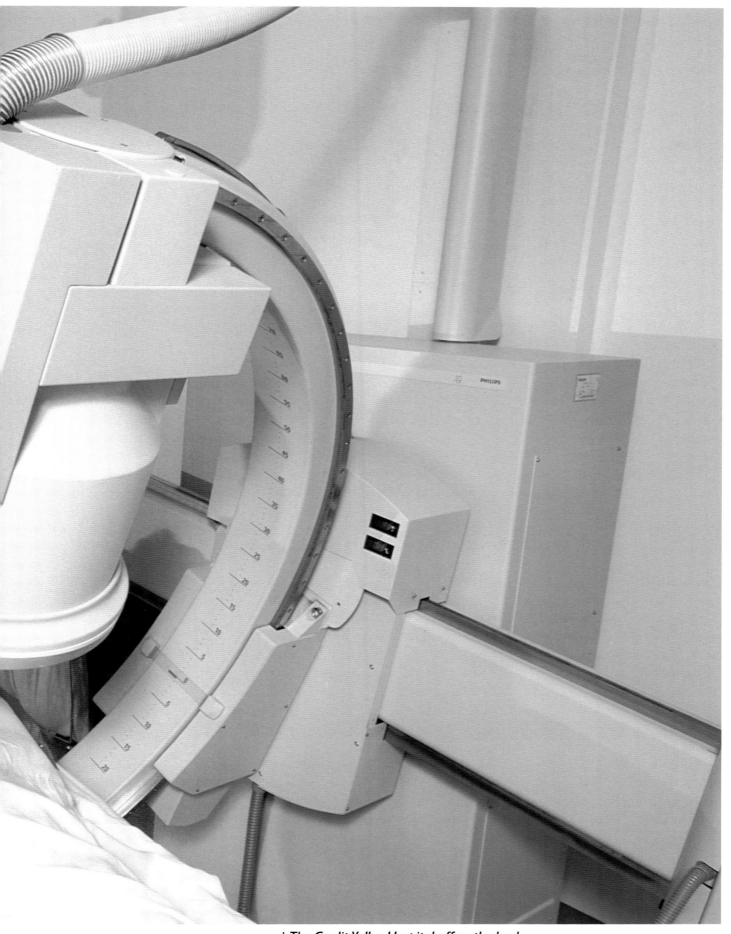

The Credit Valley Hospital offers the leading-edge equipment that health care consumers have come to expect, such as this multidiagnostic imaging system by Philips.
Photo by Jeff Chevrier.

Erinoak is an outstanding specialized health and support facility which helps young people with disabilities and their families to lead lives which are as normal, productive and self-sufficient as possible.
Photo by Jeff Chevrier.

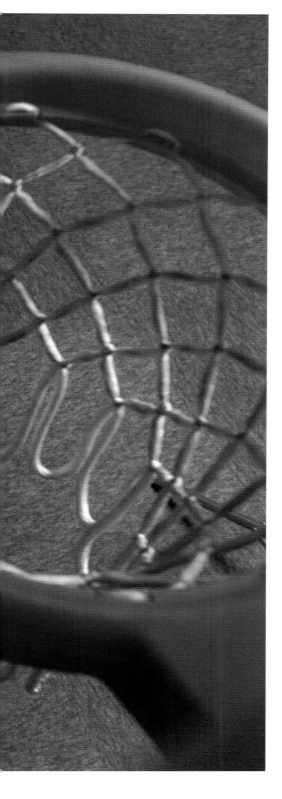

What does that mean? To the 136 staff and hundreds of volunteers, it means ensuring that youths with physical disabilities—from newborns to young adults—have access to the finest assessment, therapy, technical aids and devices, and moral support available. It means helping them to lead lives which are as normal, productive and self-sufficient as possible. And it means providing families with counselling in coping with the related challenges.

As with the hospitals, the public plays an important role as program supporters and financial benefactors. Volunteers assist with social, sports and creative activities, while donations and community fund-raising events account for a significant portion of operating funding.

What better evidence of Erinoak's value than these words from former client Annette Symanzik: "Over the past 10 years, I have utilized many (of Erinoak's) different services to aid in my mental and physical growth. Through a consistent, accepting and patient environment, I have learned important skills that are helping me to strive towards my potential." Annette is now an executive member of ABLE YORK, an on-campus student advocacy group for the needs of the physically challenged at nearby York University—the third largest university in Canada.

Retirement Facilities

Given the steadily aging North American population, care for the elderly is an increasingly crucial component of health care. For those who are fortunate enough to have little need of hospitals during their twilight years, a secure setting is provided by Mississauga's superb retirement facilities.

Chelsea Park Nursing Home in Streetsville has been just such a refuge since 1976. Well known for its cheerful warmth and homey atmosphere, Chelsea Park is home to 118 residents. Much of its appeal has been attributed to an excellent administration and staff (five of whom have worked there since the doors first opened), and—you guessed it—the wonderful efforts of local volunteers.

Industry Support

Mississauga's health care has benefited from one other advantage—a caring and generous local corporate sector. Donations in the tens of millions of dollars have poured in over the years. But the value of its teamwork with the health care community is inestimable.

The city has the good fortune to be home to one of the largest concentrations of pharmaceutical companies in the country. This sector is responsible for significant financial support during hospital fund-raising and for specific programs such as continuing medical education for physicians and community education nights. Through ongoing partnerships, companies like Astra Pharma help to ensure that the city's health care professionals always have cutting-edge information on drug and therapeutic developments.

Other industry collaboration has also reaped substantial benefits for health care in the city. A partnership with the Baxter Corporation resulted in The CVH's 1986 initiation of the Baxter Advanced Stockless Inventory System (BASIS), the most advanced cost-cutting hospital inventory management system in North America. At the opposite end of the spectrum, McDonald's Restaurants donated The CVH's Paediatric Playground and Playroom.

And so the saga continues—each year, a little more impressive, a little more advanced. Since the groundwork was laid by the area's pioneers of healing, the well-being of Mississauga's health care sector has never been in doubt. **Ⓜ**

A resident gets the sort of attention from a caregiver and friend that is typical at Chelsea Park Nursing Home, one of Mississauga's superb retirement facilities. Photo by Jeff Chevrier.

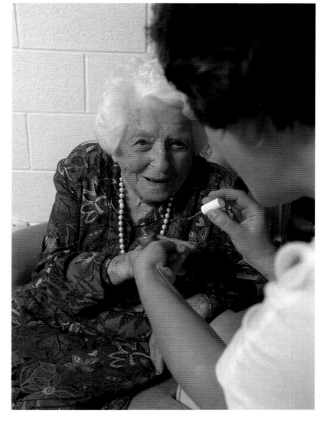

Events like The CVH's annual Teddy Bear Clinic encourage children and families to have some fun while becoming familiar with hospital procedures in a friendly setting.
Photos courtesy of The Credit Valley Hospital.

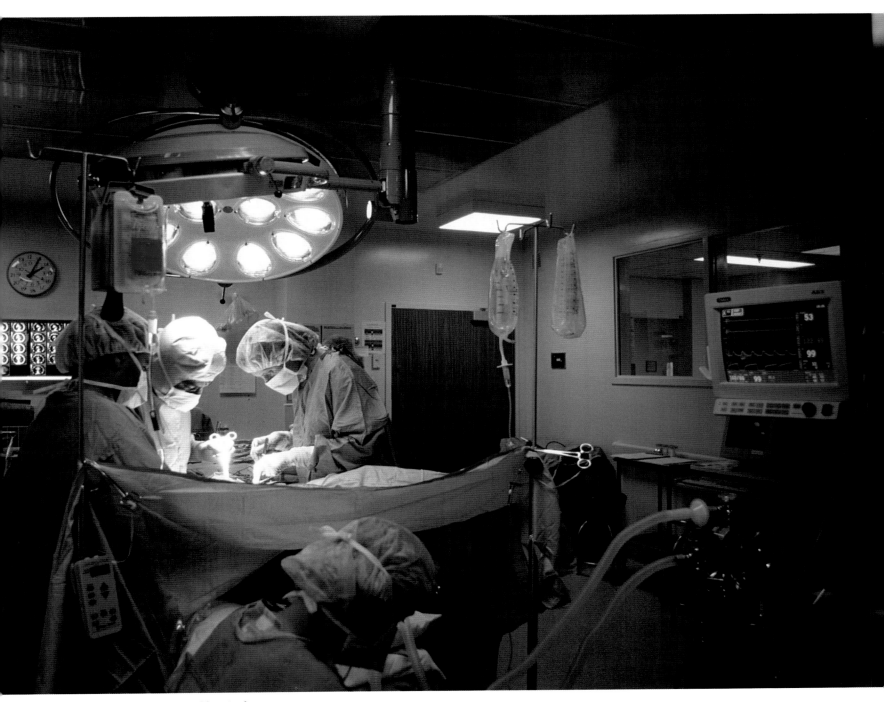

Like The CVH, The Mississauga Hospital has won multiple awards in recognition of its standing as one of the very best hospitals in Canada. *Photo by Michael Scholz.*

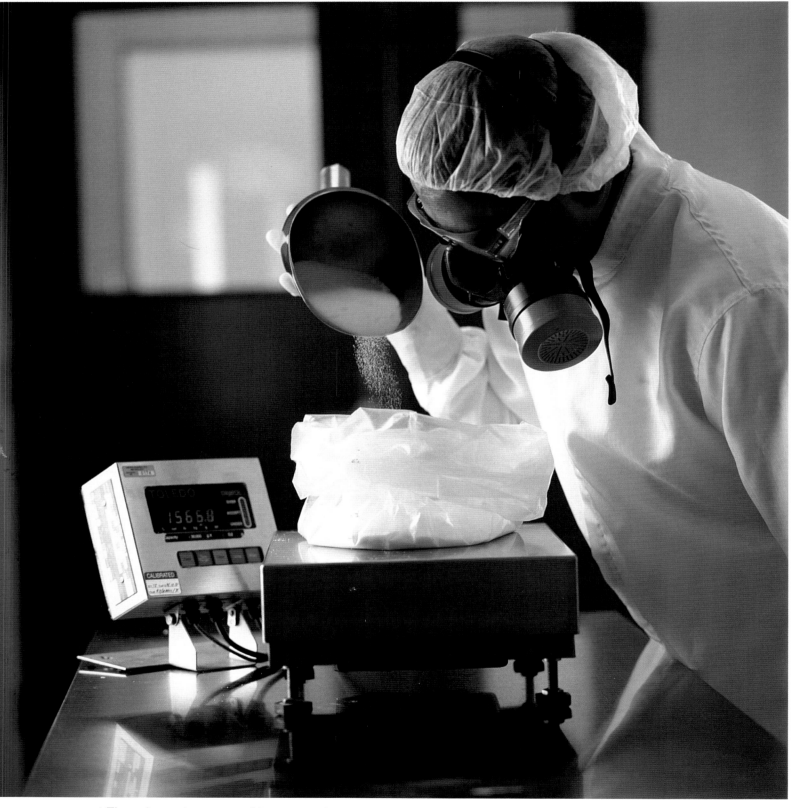

Through ongoing partnerships, companies like Astra Pharma help to ensure that the city's health care professionals always have cutting-edge information on drug and therapeutic developments. Photo courtesy of Astra Canada.

With a Canadian base of operations in Mississauga, Glaxo Wellcome Inc. employs more than 1,200 people in this country in pharmaceutical R&D, manufacturing, sales and marketing. *Photo courtesy of Glaxo Wellcome.*

CHAPTER 5

For the Love of Learning

Home of a highly educated workforce,
Mississauga enjoys exemplary education
systems. Two of the largest school boards in
Canada oversee the city's public and Catholic
elementary and secondary school systems.
The Erindale College campus of the renowned
University of Toronto is nestled in a parkland
setting in the heart of Mississauga, while 19
other major universities and community
colleges, and numerous other institutions
of learning, are within an hour's drive.

Photo by Jeff Chevrier

At Britannia Schoolhouse, children from local schools attend for a day to discover first-hand what life was like for students at the turn of the century. *Photos by Jeff Chevrier.*

Opposite page: **The Mississauga Central Library.** *Photo by Jeff Chevrier.*

Canadians take education seriously, which is why we as a nation have one of the highest literacy rates in the world. Virtually every recent forecast on Canada's economic future has suggested that our continued fostering of high-tech growth industries will be crucial to maintaining our prosperity in the new millennium, and that our highly educated workforce will be a key advantage in that regard. An educated workforce is dependent upon exemplary schooling, and nowhere is the exceptional quality of our education systems more evident than in Mississauga.

Education has been regarded as one of the cornerstones of society here since the early days of settlement. In most cases, once local businesses and churches became established, the construction of schoolhouses soon followed. Most of the city's villages included elementary schools by the early to mid-1800s. Streetsville had its own schoolhouse by 1824.

In 1851—a full seven years before the village was officially incorporated—it became host to the township's first Grammar School (the forerunner to high school), serving students from surrounding villages as well. That same year, Meadowvale Village opened its first elementary school. The Grammar School building still stands, as do the early 20th-century structures which housed the Dixie and Erindale Public Schools. Dixie Public School was founded as a log cabin in 1844; Erindale in 1872.

Most of the village schools experienced substantial growth in their attendance after the 1921 Adolescent School Attendance Act raised the compulsory schooling age from 14 to 16. Some, such as the Dixie and Erindale schools, were forced to construct larger brick structures to accommodate the influx of students. With the subsequent explosion of residential development throughout the city, the area's school attendance has experienced tremendous growth ever since.

Today, the city's outstanding education opportunities include something for everyone. Residents enjoy superb elementary and secondary schooling principally provided by two of the largest school boards in Canada. In addition to the conventional curricula provided by the public school system and the Roman Catholic "separate" school system, each offers continuing education for adults as

SCHOOL BUS

LAIDLAW

93531

ONTARIO
SD3·635

well as programs for those with special needs. Independent schools address private and alternative school requirements, and post-secondary education is widely available in virtually any discipline.

Elementary and Secondary Schools

The Peel Board of Education, which oversees public schooling in Mississauga and neighbouring areas, is the largest public school board in Canada. In Mississauga alone, the Board operates approximately 105 schools serving over 58,000 students with kindergarten through OAC (Ontario Academic Credits, formerly known as grade 13) programs. And as the country's largest provider of workplace training, the Board's Community Education Department offers a wide range of skills upgrading, computer courses, and career planning and counselling to adult and part-time students.

What's particularly impressive is the variety of programs which the Board offers to address changes in both the population and the workplace. These include English as a second language (ESL) training; specialized technical education; co-operative education; "special ed"

services for those with distinct learning needs; programs for gifted students; French immersion (intensive language training where all subjects are taught in French); arts programs and alternative secondary schools. Extra-curricular activities include everything from computer clubs to traditional sports programs.

The Dufferin-Peel Roman Catholic Separate School Board (RCSSB) operates approximately 71 schools in Mississauga serving about 49,000 students. Like the public system, the separate school system offers the full spectrum of Ontario education programs, including French language education throughout elementary and secondary school. The principal difference from the public system is the integration of religious education and faith development into all aspects of the curriculum, primarily through "the practice of prayer and worship, and the presence of gospel values...in the daily life of the schools." The Board is regarded as one of the leaders in Catholic education in Canada.

As a testament to the strong foundation of schooling in the city, the Dufferin-Peel RCSSB and the Peel Board have worked together on cost-saving initiatives to such an extent that a

Mississauga's outstanding educational opportunities include something for everyone. Residents enjoy superb elementary and secondary schooling provided by two of the largest school boards in Canada. Photo by Jeff Chevrier.

recent government commission highlighted
the Boards' efforts as new models of co-operative service delivery. Their joint efforts in areas
such as purchasing, transportation, special
education programs and curriculum have
saved thousands of tax dollars.

Complementing the two main school boards
are dozens of privately owned and operated
schools, including several Montessori-style
schools. In addition to the more personalized
teaching which these institutions attempt to
provide through smaller classes, some feature
specialty facilities of particular interest, such as
Mentor College's Marine Biology Centre or
Mississauga Private School's Computer
Technology and Robotics classes.

Training in the Arts

The city's education system as a whole continues to respond to the changes in skills and
knowledge which are required in our evolving
world of high-tech industries and global markets. But, as in all things, balance is essential.
There are numerous instances within
Mississauga of hands-on education which aug-
ments conventional classroom learning. As one
of the better examples of this, the city provides
some of the best opportunities in Ontario for
high-level training in various arts disciplines.

Within the school system, the prime example of this can be found at Cawthra Park
Secondary School. As one of two schools in
Peel's Regional Arts Program, Cawthra offers a
stunning array of training in music,
dance, drama and visual arts to
augment its conventional high
school curriculum. Admission is
based on demonstrated ability,
potential, enthusiasm and commitment, and is gained only through
individual auditions and portfolio
presentations. In return, students
receive top artistic instruction delivered in professional calibre facilities.
And to dispel any concerns that
academic results suffer from this
immersion in the arts, Cawthra produced OAC graduates in both 1995
and 1996 who achieved perfect 100
per cent averages.

A strong mandate for education
is evident in several of the city's
performing and visual arts organizations as well. The Springbank
Visual Arts Centre offers arts and
crafts classes for children, teens and
adults, including its popular

The U of T at Mississauga developed the first Forensic Science program in Ontario. Coordinated by internationally recognized anthropologist and skeletal biologist Dr. Jerry Melbye, above, the program is the realization of the work of 10 professors from different disciplines. Students in the Forensic Science program study anthropology, biology, psychology and chemistry. Photo courtesy of U of T at Mississauga.

Summer School of the Arts for ages 6-12. Classroom and studio settings are a key element in the Living Arts Centre's efforts to establish a working link with the artistic community. The Meadowvale Theatre participates in several educational initiatives, including cooperative theatre training programs for high school students, and as part of the community outreach of Ryerson Polytechnical University, a Toronto school renowned for its arts programs. Programs like these allow participants to gain valuable hands-on experience in set creation, lighting and other aspects of theatre production.

Post Secondary

It is estimated that about 70 per cent of Mississauga's workforce has some form of post-secondary education. A significant factor in attaining this status has been the presence of 20 universities and community colleges situated in and around the city, including 9 of the 42 English-speaking universities in the entire country.

Locally, the most prominent of these is the University of Toronto at Mississauga, Erindale College. Erindale is the largest faculty of Arts and Science at the University of Toronto—ranked as the number one medical/doctoral

university in Canada. Nestled on 90 hectares (224 acres) of picturesque park land bordering the Credit River, Erindale was opened in 1967. It has since grown to encompass a faculty of 250 and a student body of about 6,500. Acclaimed for its research in sciences, social sciences and the humanities, Erindale excels in the fields of molecular chemistry, theoretical computer science, environmental management and forensic physical anthropology.

In positioning itself for the 21st century, Erindale now offers degrees such as Bachelor of Commerce and is the home of the University of Toronto's Master of Management & Professional Accounting (MMPA) program. Community and corporate partnerships will also play a growing role at the university, as evidenced by the new Hitachi Survey Research Centre—the most advanced facility of its kind anywhere in the region.

From a student's perspective, a university is only as good as its teaching staff, and Erindale's is superb. Several faculty members have been nominated for international awards, including one for the Nobel Prize in Literature and another for a Pulitzer Prize. Faculty have earned the Governor General's Award and the prestigious Guggenheim Award for their excellence in

Located along the banks of the Credit River, the 224-acre University of Toronto Erindale Campus is larger in itself than five of Ontario's independent universities. Currently, 6,200 students attend full- and part-time classes, and the school is one of Mississauga's top 15 employers. Photos by Jeff Chevrier.

education, while seven professors have received province-wide awards in recognition of their outstanding achievements in the classroom.

Another impressive member of Mississauga's post-secondary education landscape is the Richard Ivey School of Business, part of the University of Western Ontario. Specializing in business schooling, Ivey's home base of operations is the J.J. Wettlaufer Executive Development Centre in Mississauga. Its principal programs include the renowned Premier FastTrak™ entrepreneurial training program, first offered through the University of Southern California, and Western's unique Executive MBA Program. The latter allows mature students to earn an MBA within two years without career interruption. And for those who can't attend the Mississauga centre, modern videoconferencing technology enables professors to simultaneously interact with classes in Vancouver, Edmonton, Calgary, London, Toronto, Ottawa and Montreal.

Sheridan College of Applied Arts and Technology, a community college with campuses in neighbouring Oakville and Brampton, also maintains a presence in Mississauga by offering continuing education programs in conjunction with local high schools. Sheridan is well known as one of the best arts, media and computer studies colleges in the province.

A number of other institutions offer various forms of training and skills upgrading for business and commerce, as well as technologies and skilled trades, such as the Toronto School of Business and DeVry.

Internationally acclaimed animation programs at Sheridan College in Oakville train students in both classical and computer animation. Graduates are highly sought after by major motion picture studios and related industries worldwide. Photo courtesy of Sheridan College.

Library System

Any university student can attest to the importance of readily available reference material. Few cities can boast a public library system that fulfills that need as effectively as Mississauga's. The Mississauga Central Library opened its doors in 1991 to become the hub for the city's network of 13 public library locations. Part of the Civic Centre complex, this 150,000-square-foot facility houses some 250,000 books, a full range of audio-visual media and CD-ROMs, access to global databases and the 244-seat Noel Ryan Auditorium, which occasionally hosts lectures and seminars. It has reportedly become the busiest library facility in Canada.

As in many cities, the libraries are linked by a computer cataloguing and search system which reflects the inventory of the entire network, the loan status of each title and its location by branch. But Mississauga's advanced system goes a step further, allowing users to check this in-branch database via modem from their own homes before venturing to the local branch. You can even phone in a renewal of your books with the use of an automated Touch-Tone™ system!

The Love of Learning

Mississauga is in a rather enviable position—one for which many individual educational institutions strive. Many universities face the challenge of how to grow large enough to be able to provide state-of-the-art facilities and attract top professors without losing the intimacy and personal touch offered in a smaller school. This city finds itself in something close to this middle ground as a starting point by virtue of its moderate size.

In turn, this has allowed Erindale College and the major school boards to offer some of the highest-calibre education available in the country while retaining close ties to the community. The evidence of this can be seen in the wealth of support programs, counselling and interaction with parents which is provided by the schools. As the Peel Board of Education's 1995 annual report put it, "To us…it means opening our doors and welcoming the community inside."

For Mississaugans, education is as much about providing rewarding, enriching experiences as it is the imparting of knowledge. For most of the city's educators, this has become not just a goal, but a living credo. It is also a reflection of the attitudes of the community as a whole toward teaching our children: Prepare them for the future, but handle with care, for no resource is more precious. **Ⓜ**

Like the public school system, the separate school system offers the full spectrum of Ontario education programs, including French language education throughout elementary and secondary school.
Photo by Jeff Chevrier.

Within Mississauga's education systems, academic excellence is complemented by the challenge of physical activities and sports. Here, the Erindale Secondary School football team prepares for a winning season. Photo by Jeff Chevrier.

Cawthra Park Secondary School offers a Regional Arts Program that attracts students from across the city of Mississauga. Students in the Regional Arts Program can specialize in visual arts, dance, drama or music. Pictured below is the school's Intermediate Jazz Ensemble. *Photo courtesy of Cawthra Park Secondary School.*

Not all learning takes place in the classroom! *Photo by Jeff Chevrier.*

CHAPTER 6

The Living Arts

Ⓜ

Mississauga's arts community is
vibrant, diverse and multicultural. Both the
Philharmonic and Symphony Orchestras are
well supported, as are dozens of choral,
dance and theatre troupes. These and existing
art galleries, concert and live theatre
venues find common ground through
the new Living Arts Centre.

Photo by Jeff Chevrier

*T*f health care is the embodiment of the city's heart, then certainly the arts are its soul. Creativity, artistic or otherwise, can be a difficult thing to sustain in isolation. But for the arts community in particular, it's as though a certain critical mass must be established for artistry to be at its best. It is not enough to simply erect performance venues, or hold public showings of artists' works. There is a "whole is greater than the sum of the parts" effect which collaboration within an artistic community invariably seems to produce. Musicians, actors, authors, composers, painters—whatever the discipline, artists seem to nourish one another. Ideas engender better ideas. Excitement builds. And when people get excited, marvellous things can happen.

Mississauga may be on the verge of attaining just the critical mass needed to propel it to new artistic heights. In recent years, the city has evolved rapidly into a wellspring of talent and innovation. Whether this is a result of the city's affluence, its cultural diversity or a high concentration of individual champions of the arts is hard to say. But there can be no denying the artistic explosion that is underway here.

Music, theatre and the visual arts have all been well represented in the area for many years. For example, historical accounts suggest that in the early 1900s, the Fortnightly Club met in Meadowvale to read poetry, perform musical works and engage in general discussions in matters of the arts. Eventually, as the level of activity grew, there was an increasing sense of the need for some means of bringing all facets of the arts together.

During the 1970s, an Arts Unit was established within the city's Community Services Department to see to the needs of community arts groups. But in 1981, as it became apparent that more guidance was needed from within the arts community, city council responded by forming the Mississauga Arts Council. Today, MAC's mandate is to "foster and promote artistic expression and appreciation of the arts…" within the city. With over 1,400 members, it has become the coordinating voice of Mississauga's arts community, providing training and development support, administering grants and forming liaisons with other councils, service groups and governments. Each year, MAC is responsible for operating the Mississauga Arts Awards and community outreach events, such as the Mississauga Arts Festival—conducted in conjunction with Square One Shopping Centre.

Still, there were those who dreamed of a greater synergy among the city's artistic disciplines and, in turn, with the community as a

whole. From such dreams, the Living Arts Centre was born.

The Living Arts Centre

There's little question that Mississauga's new Living Arts Centre (LAC) is presently the hub of a flurry of activity in the local arts community. When it opened its doors in late 1997, the LAC also opened a new chapter in interactive arts and entertainment—for Mississauga, and the world. This prototype facility features state-of-the-art performance venues, art studios, exhibition and fine dining areas. With its integrated fibre-optic, digital technologies—allowing worldwide digital broadcasting of voice, video and data—the LAC is unique. And it is designed to remain well ahead of any facility of its kind in the world for years to come.

The Atrium—where one might typically expect to find a lobby area—is accented by an 18.5 metre (60 foot) glass front wall, and houses a gift shop, fine dining restaurant and the box office. The connecting glass-roofed Galleria lets the public stroll amongst displays of the various creations produced by artists in the Centre, with views of all three levels of the Studio

The Stage West Hotel and Theatre Restaurant offers a marvelous blend of hotel accommodations, culinary delights and live theatre productions which, over the years, have featured a long list of international stars. *Photo courtesy of Stage West.*

Opposite page: **The Springbank Visual Arts Centre has built an enduring legacy of fostering art appreciation and learning in novices and accomplished artists alike.** *Photo by Jeff Chevrier.*

The Blackwood Gallery, located at the University of Toronto, Erindale College, features new exhibits every six to eight weeks and offers children's art classes each spring and summer. *Photo by Jeff Chevrier.*

The Mississauga Concert Band is a favourite, performing high-calibre renditions of everything from Gershwin to Glenn Miller. *Photo by Michael Scholz.*

Its massive stage is the same depth as that of the 3,000-seat Hummingbird Centre in Toronto's core; the stage left and right wings are even larger than Hummingbird's. And the acoustics are incredible. Not only are they classed as N1—the finest acoustic rating attainable for concert venues—but they're also adjustable. An array of moveable sound baffles allows the acoustics to be ideal for a chamber orchestra one evening and a rock concert the next. Complementing the Hammerson Theatre are two smaller theatres. For more modest productions, there's Theatre II, which features a retractable, tiered seating system with a capacity of 400, a sprung floor and full lighting grid. The 110-seat Theatre III is augmented by a projection room.

Perhaps most impressive is the versatility of the Centre. The Atrium's expansive central area is suitable for catered events and gatherings of up to 1,000 people. The Hammerson Theatre's immense "fly tower" (the overhead backstage area where backdrops are suspended until being lowered during a performance) comfortably conceals the sets for an evening's major touring production, while hosting a corporate product launch in the afternoon. Between them, the smaller theatres can be used for everything from banquets and film screenings to recitals and theatre-in-the-round. Then there's the teaching applications.

Thanks to its digital technologies and satellite link-up capabilities, worldwide simulcasts of performances are possible. Pretty incredible.

Wing. The latter offers studio space for several disciplines, ranging from the more traditional, such as pottery, sculpture and painting, to digital art and multimedia production. The Dance Studio on the third level is fully equipped, with sprung floor, mirrors and barres. Other features include an interactive Discovery Deck and a huge two-storey Staging Room.

The jewel of the Centre is its 1,300-seat Hammerson Theatre, complete with full proscenium stage and orchestra pit large enough to accommodate up to 80 musicians.

From their home base in the Huron Park Theatre, the Mississauga Players delight audiences with three plays each season, augmented by a summer cabaret. *Photo by Jeff Chevrier.*

But imagine a sculpting class being conducted in one of the art studios, with students asking questions of and receiving instruction from a master sculptor—directly from his home in Italy via an interactive satellite transmission! That's indicative of the kind of innovation which sets the LAC apart from regular performance venues. In addition, the Centre's sophisticated wiring allows camera equipment to be "plugged in" in any of its major areas to quickly be up and running for broadcast of, say, a fund-raising gala in the Atrium.

Technologically awesome. But the LAC is much more: It is a 210,000-square-foot celebration of the coming of age of the arts in Mississauga.

Music

One body which is busy settling into its new digs at the LAC is the Mississauga Symphonic Association. The city boasts not one, but three orchestras, for which the MSA is the umbrella organization.

In 1972, internationally renowned conductor Boyd Neel and a small group of volunteers founded the Mississauga Symphony Orchestra. From its original complement of 40, the MSO has become a thriving "community" orchestra comprised of more than 80 amateur, student and professional musicians.

Sinfonia Mississauga, the city's highly acclaimed professional chamber orchestra, was formed in 1986. It has performed throughout Ontario to rave reviews and has been featured on national broadcasts on CBC Stereo. The Mississauga Philharmonic Orchestra gave its first concert before a packed house in February 1996. The Philharmonic's repertoire ranges from Beethoven to an evening of the "Pops" (excerpts from movie sound tracks and other popular music) to children's entertainment.

The extent of the orchestras' outreach to the community is exceptional. This was certainly evident when, to mark its 25th anniversary, the Symphony invited the audience to bring

"noisemakers, flags and funny hats" to join in the celebration. Elgar's *Pomp and Circumstance* and Arne's *Rule, Britannia* may never be the same.

As prominent as these orchestras are, it's no exaggeration to say that they represent only the tip of the city's musical iceberg. Groups such as the Mississauga Chamber Players and the renowned Mississauga Youth Orchestra round out the classics; the versatile Mississauga Concert Band adeptly moves from Gershwin to Glen Miller, while the award-winning Emerald Knights Drum and Bugle Corps participates in parades and competitions throughout southern Ontario.

Evidently, this is also a city that loves to sing. The celebrated 70-voice Mississauga Choral Society is one the top choirs of its kind in Canada, having enjoyed nearly two decades as the city's premiere choral ensemble. And Opera Mississauga's efforts in continuing to bring high-calibre opera to the city received a major boost from their 1997 move to a new home in the Living Arts Centre.

Theatre

Theatre troupes in Mississauga are diverse and prolific, with styles ranging from the slightly avant-garde to traditional and comedy, at all performance levels. By co-operating, through vehicles like the Mississauga Theatre Alliance umbrella organization, this energetic theatre community has made tremendous strides in improving facilities, opportunities and the overall visibility of theatre in the city.

Certainly, the Living Arts Centre brings the promise of productions on a scale never before seen in Mississauga. But its predecessor as the city's foremost theatre showcase has for years been the Meadowvale Theatre. Opened in 1989, this 395-seat theatre hosts up to 225 public events per year, plus hundreds of corporate and fund-raising events. Some 90,000 people attend annually, usually to see troupes such as the Mississauga Players, the Mississauga Youth

The stirring sounds of the Mississauga Concert Band's brass section resonate in the rafters of the Meadowvale Theatre. Photo by Jeff Chevrier.

The stimulating effect of art finds its way into the shadows of Mississauga's downtown office towers. Photo by Jeff Chevrier.

The new Living Arts Centre exudes uniqueness and innovation, starting with its main Hammerson Theatre. In spite of its 1,300-seat size, the theatre's layout provides the shortest distance between the stage and rear seats of any comparable venue, giving it a truly intimate feel.
Photo courtesy of the Living Arts Centre.

The Living Arts Centre—the crown jewel of the arts in Mississauga—is so advanced that nothing in the world is expected to rival it for years. *Photo courtesy of the Living Arts Centre.*

Theatre, Music Theatre Mississauga, or one of many community-based troupes. And, as with the LAC, versatility is the watchword. Three "satellite" theatres which are managed by Meadowvale—Huron Park, Malton and Burnhamthorpe—each offer approximately 200-seat venues. Together, the four theatres masterfully accommodate everything from National Geographic lectures to cultural dance troupes and rock concerts.

Visual Arts

The city's flagship of visual arts is the Art Gallery of Mississauga. In operation since 1987, the AGM is a public (as opposed to commercial) gallery with 3,500 square feet of exhibit space and an outdoor sculpture garden. Its mission is "to bring art to the community and the community to art." In addition to its permanent collection of more than 50 works, the AGM promotes Canadian art, with a Mississauga emphasis. Apart from hosting, on average, 11 major exhibits per year, it offers an intimate setting for corporate launches and receptions. About 20,000 people—a large percentage being tourists—visit this highly acclaimed gallery each year.

Other artistic perspectives are presented by galleries like the Blackwood Gallery at Erindale College, the Springbank Visual Arts Gallery, the Harbour Gallery in Clarkson and the Gallery at Fairways.

Without question, all aspects of the arts are alive and well in Mississauga. The critical mass is taking shape, and the leap to a broader range of world-class performances and exhibits is at hand.

But what's particularly intriguing is the sheer number and diversity of community arts groups and associations which are sprinkled throughout the city—the grassroots evidence that the momentum is both real and sustainable. The spectrum of opportunities for people to get involved—to belt out a tune, deliver their lines, mould a masterpiece or just share their talents—truly is amazing.

Several vocal ensembles get together just for the fun of it, like the delightful mixed vocal group "Justus," who perform a variety of favourites at community events and annual variety shows. There are performing groups for seniors and youths of all ages. Traditional, native and multicultural singing and dance organizations abound, and modern dance, jazz and ballet are also well represented. Community associations and clubs are well established for numerous disciplines like photography, painting, sculpting— even rug hooking. And for the really adventurous, the National Circus School of Canada is here.

Overall, the arts play a vital part in helping to define us in a way which universally transcends the barriers of race and language. This becomes clear as Mississauga's social mosaic is wonderfully explored during Carrassauga—an annual city-wide festival of multicultural dance and music which promotes racial harmony through a better understanding of cultural diversities. And it is perhaps the missions of some of the arts groups themselves which best sum up the role of the arts in this city. The Association for Scottish Traditions and Arts promotes "anything Scottish that it thinks needs to be promoted"—a carefree credo that essentially says we don't need a special occasion or reason to celebrate our culture and our heritage. They are, after all, the truest expression of who we are. **Ⓜ**

The **Springbank Visual Arts Centre** offers adult classes in fine arts and crafts, as well as excellent art programs for children and teens, including its popular Summer School of the Arts for ages 6-12. *Photo by Jeff Chevrier.*

A **Springbank student sketches a live model.** *Photo by Jeff Chevrier.*

*A mainstay of the city's arts scene, the
395-seat Meadowvale Theatre hosts
90,000 patrons each year for plays, musical
productions and hundreds of corporate
and fund-raising events. Its combination of
intimate ambience, and massive rear and
backstage areas makes it a favourite venue
of performing troupes.* Photo by Jeff Chevrier.

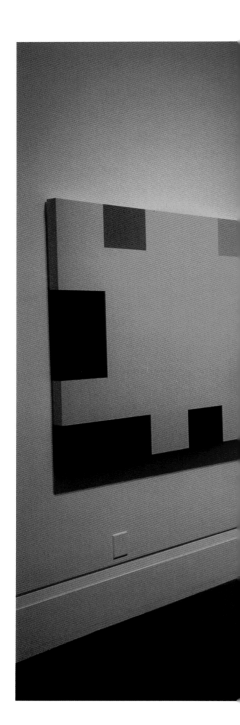

The highly acclaimed Art Gallery of
Mississauga promotes Canadian art with
a Mississauga emphasis. Its mission is "to
bring art to the community and the
community to art." *Photo by Jeff Chevrier.*

Public exhibits are not for famous artists alone! The talent of numerous budding artists is appropriately displayed on the site barriers surrounding the Living Arts Centre during its construction. Photo by Jeff Chevrier.

Photo by Jeff Chevrier

Photo by Michael Scholz

CHAPTER 7

People & Places

Ⓜ

This city is blessed with a cosmopolitan mosaic of cultures and neighbourhoods. From the stately homes lining Mississauga Road, to the quaint heritage buildings of Meadowvale Village and the clusters in Erin Mills, there's a pride that speaks volumes about the quality of life here.

Photo by Jeff Chevrier

*F*or all its other features and amenities, a city is most clearly defined by its people—how they live, work, play, interact and contribute to the community. Beneath the surface of Mississauga's bright lights and paparazzi lie the passion, the spirit and the warmth that distinguish it as not just a great city, but also as a great place to live.

Mississauga has certainly benefited from the efforts of countless founders and builders—people with the vision to imagine a great centre of commerce and society, and the courage to act. In recent times, the city has also enjoyed the advantages of being both very young and very old; tremendous opportunity and enthusiasm have been wisely tempered by a sense of community ownership that only time can provide. The result has been a blending of the new with just enough of the old to produce the ideal setting for relaxed suburban, almost country-style, living within a major city.

That continuity with the past helps to explain the undeniably strong sense of identity which permeates the neighbourhoods and businesses of this vibrant city. That in itself is a significant accomplishment, living next door to the largest metropolis in Canada. And it is a testament to the dedication and pride which its citizens have displayed in over two centuries of building their city.

Neighbourhoods

Much of the area's heritage is tangible today throughout the city's neighbourhoods and original villages. Port Credit has retained its seaside atmosphere, though yachts and sailboats now occupy the harbour which once served cargo ships and stonehookers. Tucked behind Streetsville's historic homes are the last vestiges of the grain mills that once propelled the village economy. And in both of these areas, an eclectic blend of quaint shops, restaurants and neighbourhood pubs gives the thriving main streets the unmistakable look and appeal of a small town. To the southwest,

Clarkson has also managed to preserve much of its small-town feel.

While Erindale and Malton have become bustling centres, Meadowvale Village remains a quiet little hamlet with a distinctly rural flavour. And perched next to the city's downtown core area, Cooksville and Dixie are still home to splendid taverns and landmarks like the Dixie Union Chapel. Jacob Cook and Philip Cody would be pleased.

Harkening to its early days as a favourite recreation spot, Lorne Park, with its winding streets, sprawling wooded lots and private enclaves, remains a haven of tranquility in the city's south. Winding north, along the banks of the Credit River, are the massive estates which line Mississauga Road—some of the most prestigious homes found anywhere in the region.

Suburban innovation has been at the forefront here since the postwar boom. Applewood, one of the city's first major subdivisions and among the first in Ontario to include "ranch style" bungalows, has matured into a cozy retreat for family living. Erin Mills began life on the city's west side as Ontario's first integrated, planned community. Its interconnecting system of paths and green spaces allows kids to play and move around their neighbourhood with a minimum of road crossing. In similar fashion, the

The interconnecting system of paths and green spaces in Erin Mills allows kids the freedom to play and move around their neighbourhood with a minimum of road crossing. *Photo by Jeff Chevrier.*

Opposite page: **The well-known landmark St. Peter's Anglican Church was the centre of social life in Erindale through much of the 1800s. The church recently celebrated the 170th anniversary of its founding.** *Photo by Jeff Chevrier.*

Left: **There's more than one way to beat the heat at Jack Darling Memorial Park.** *Photo by Jeff Chevrier.*

Mississauga officially twinned with Kariya, Japan, in 1974. The city celebrated the event's 10th anniversary by hosting Kariya dignitaries and dedicating this new Japanese-style park across from the City Centre in Kariya's name. Photo by Jeff Chevrier.

The quaint shops of Streetsville recall a bit of small-town Canada in the midst of Mississauga. *Photo by Jeff Chevrier.*

It seems that everywhere in Mississauga you will discover people who are here because they believe that there should be more to life in a big city than concrete and office towers. *Photo by Michael Scholz.*

"new" Meadowvale in the northwest features a charming mix of quiet suburban streets and secluded townhouse clusters dotted with ample parkland.

People

It seems that a long list of extraordinary people have been attracted to this area over the past 200 years. The historical chapter of this book scratched the surface by describing some of the founders, but many others have been celebrities in their day.

There was Dr. Beaumont Dixie, the Erindale doctor for whom Dixie was named and who donated a significant sum of money to the construction of the original Union Chapel. City landmarks and roadways bear the names of prominent founding families, like the Adamsons and the Cawthras. Of course, Dixie resident Thomas L. Kennedy was a long-standing member of the provincial legislature. And it was in Cooksville that one William Pierce Howland first settled in 1830. Thirty-seven years later, he would become known as one of Canada's Fathers of Confederation.

In the modern era, some of our better known citizens have included the likes of world-famous pianist Oscar Peterson, actor Don "Charlie Farquharson" Harron, and rock star and former Triumph member Rik Emmett. Some of Canada's premier Olympians have been Mississaugans, like Olympic medalists Silken and Danielle Laumann, Jeff Lay and Rob Marland (rowing); Lisa Alexander and Karen Clark (synchronized swimming); and sprinter Carlton Chambers—a member of Canada's 1996 Olympic gold medalist men's 4 X 100 relay team.

Several stars of the professional sports world have figured prominently here as well. Toronto Maple Leaf Tie Domi is particularly well known for his ongoing support of countless community and charity events. Numerous players and coaches of the Leafs, Blue Jays and Argonauts have called Mississauga home, including goaltending legend Johnny Bower and the man who scored the unforgettable winning goal in the

1972 Russia-Canada hockey showdown, Paul Henderson. There's sportscaster Don Chevrier—an institution in Canadian television—and, of course, the inimitable television personality and former coach of the Boston Bruins, Don Cherry.

Since the early 1800s, these people and others like them have distinguished themselves as leaders, achievers and role models and, in doing so, have helped immeasurably to define the character of this city. To all, Mississauga has been quite simply home.

But this is equally a city of the famous and the not-so-famous. Whether through summer street parties, community volunteer work or just a welcoming handshake to a new resident, it is the ordinary people of Mississauga who make this a special place to live.

So perhaps more than anything, Mississauga is about caring people and good old-fashioned home town spirit. More than the blend of old and new; more than the parklands and wide open spaces, marvellous wooded lots and quiet, well-kept streets—it's a mindset. And nothing sums it up better than the story of young Richard Wolniewicz and the waterfront preserve which still bears his name. Richard's Memorial Park was created not to commemorate an act of heroism, but as an expression of thanks from a grateful city for an ultimate act of human compassion. Following his death in 1971 at age 14, Richard's heart was donated for a transplant operation. That act saved the life of Robert Speck, Mississauga's first mayor. This is, indeed, a special place to live. Ⓜ

The quiet backyards of Meadowvale are a great place for breaking in your first set of wheels. *Photo by Jeff Chevrier.*

Soccer's the thing at Woodhurst Heights Park. *Photo by Jeff Chevrier.*

What better way to spend a summer day than taking advantage of the amazing facilities at the Rivergrove Community Centre in Streetsville. Photo by Jeff Chevrier.

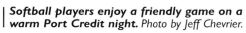

Softball players enjoy a friendly game on a warm Port Credit night. Photo by Jeff Chevrier.

CHAPTER 8

Bright Lights...

Ⓜ

Whether shopping, snacking or sightseeing, there's plenty to do in Mississauga. From live, world-class theatre productions, the symphony, art galleries or museums to fine dining and colourful pubs, the options seem to be growing exponentially each year. Ample shopping choices begin with the second largest mall in Canada. And if you've still got energy to burn, take the kids to Sega City or one of many regional family attractions.

Photo by Jeff Chevrier

$\mathcal{L}$et's face it. You can live in the greatest neighbourhood ever and still get bored if there's nothing to do but wave to your neighbours and watch the grass grow. It's a dilemma with which many suburban dwellers struggle: if you want to do anything interesting or shop for the latest fashions, you have to make the trek into some huge urban jungle, complete with "the big drive," traffic snarls and parking headaches. Not so in Mississauga! There's lots to do right here in the city.

Shopping

Any avid shopper can tell you that when it comes to retailing, Mississauga has definitely come of age. Square One is a mega-mall at the centre of the downtown core with over 350 stores and services. As the largest mall in the province, it is a mecca for shoppers from all over southern Ontario. Anchor stores include all three of Ontario's long-standing department store mainstays—Eaton's, Sears and the Hudson's Bay Co.—as well as what is reportedly the world's largest Wal-Mart.

Two other beautiful local malls are the Erin Mills Town Centre, with 235 stores, and the Sheridan Centre with over 165. Erin Mills even boasts an indoor nine-hole minigolf course, modelled after famous courses. Three other large enclosed malls, dozens of plazas and factory outlet-style retail "power centres" ensure tremendous shopping variety and convenience.

If you prefer, the downtown areas of some of the original villages offer a wonderful array of eclectic specialty shops, cafés and family operated stores. These "small-town Main Streets" are perfect for treasure hunting in any season when you'd like to mix a walk in the sunshine with your shopping. And when you're looking for the freshest ingredients for that special dinner, visit one of the city's seasonal farmers' markets.

Attractions

The Civic Centre is an attraction unto itself in a way that few city halls can claim. Its striking architecture inside and out makes it a favourite location for television and movie productions. The grandeur of the Great Hall and the indoor gardens of the Conservatory regularly attract wedding parties for photo sessions. At the top of the Great Stairs is the Mississauga Sports Hall of Fame, which pays tribute to the long list of outstanding athletes which this young city has already produced. Honoured are greats like track stars Debbie Van Kiekebelt and Angela Bailey, former NHL stars such as Paul Henderson, Fred Stanfield and Joe Primeau, CFL quarterback Chuck Ealey and jockey Sandy Hawley.

Shoppers pause to relax by one of the fountains in the mammoth Square One Shopping Centre, where a half million-square-foot addition is in the works. Dubbed the "Powerhouse," it will be themed to complement the surrounding entertainment district. Photo by Michael Scholz.

There are a number of historical sites in the city, beginning with the Bradley Museum in Clarkson. This 1830s farmhouse has been restored and staffed to recreate the lifestyle of early settlers. Sharing the museum grounds is the Anchorage, a restored 1830s cottage complete with gallery, gift shop and Sunday Tea Room.

The city's newest community museum is the Benares Historic House. Originally built in 1857, the house has been restored to its 1918 form to showcase the lives of the Harris family since their arrival in Clarkson over 160 years ago. But what makes this re-creation especially authentic is the presence of furnishings, photos and even children's toys preserved by living descendants of the Harris family.

Check out the Toronto Suburban Radial Line, a turn-of-the-century electric railway which connected Port Credit with Sunnyside in Toronto. Or tour the Gooderham Estate in Meadowvale Village, restored to its original opulence in 1996. Though currently in use as their area sales centre, residential developer Monarch Homes graciously allows the public to browse through this beautiful historical home. Several other such estates around Mississauga are owned and preserved by the city.

Heritage Mississauga has excellent material available to help people through self-guided historic walking tours of most of the city's original villages. Visit the 1837 stone building of the Dixie Union Chapel which replaced the original log structure built by Philip Cody, Joseph Silverthorne, et al., in 1816. Most of Dixie's earliest settlers are buried in its cemetery. Or

Opposite page: Ice skating is always best outdoors. When you can't find a pond, there's the public rink at the Civic Centre. It's also the site of the city's annual Christmas tree lighting ceremony. Photo by Jeff Chevrier.

The Benares Historic House and Visitor Centre is the city's newest museum. It is believed to have been the inspiration for Mazo de la Roche's famous Whiteoaks of Jalna series. Photo by Jeff Chevrier.

Benares was restored to reflect the daily lives of early settlers and contains family belongings preserved and furnished by descendants of the original 1857 builders—the Harris family. Photo by Jeff Chevrier.

explore central Streetsville to find more than 30 churches, buildings and homes from the 1800s, including the house of Timothy Street himself.

The young and the young at heart thrill to the sights and sounds of the $25-million Sega City at Playdium, the sports and games theme park situated north of Square One. Here, Sega has taken the world of their famous video arcade games to the next level of entertainment experience. Ride go-carts, shoot some hoops, go rock climbing; or venture into the high-tech simulations that let you race a Formula One

car at over 300 kilometres per hour; or lift off from the deck of an aircraft carrier.

For other live action, play laser "tag" in a converted warehouse, complete with mazes and darkened rooms, at Mississauga's Laser Quest.

Several other attractions are located within the immediately surrounding region, like Paramount Canada's Wonderland—the massive world-class theme park for the whole family. Make a day of it at African Lion Safari, a giant "zoo" through which you drive amongst lions, tigers, monkeys and other animals that roam

around the compound. Of course, all the amenities of Toronto's downtown core are only about a 20-minute drive away. Catch a game of one of Toronto's NHL, Major League Baseball, CFL or NBA teams—the Maple Leafs, Blue Jays, Argonauts or Raptors.

The Arts

Culture buffs can enjoy world-class live theatre and music, art galleries and exhibits, many of which have been featured in the Arts chapter of this book. In addition to mainstays such as the Living Arts Centre, the Meadowvale Theatre and the Art Gallery of Mississauga, there are numerous other venues throughout the city. One of the better known of these is the Stage West Dinner Theatre, renowned for its combination of high-calibre theatre and tasty buffets since 1986.

For film enthusiasts, Mississauga is home to dozens of movie theatres of all types and sizes. The most impressive and distinctive is the Famous Players Coliseum 10, the first circular stadium theatre in the world. The complex features 10 auditoriums with wall-to-wall screens, luxurious rocking chair seats and incredible digital sound. In-house food outlets include Pizza Hut, New York Fries, Baskin-Robbins and Starbuck's.

Night Spots

Experience elegant dining or paint the town at one of dozens of pubs and nightclubs.

If it's haute cuisine you're after, exceptional restaurants abound. Many are housed in the historical homes, some of which belonged to early settlers who are noted in this book's first chapter: The Barber House (William Barber) in south Streetsville; Cherry Hill House (Joseph Silverthorne) in old Dixie; the Elliott House and Barbizon to name just a few. With over 500 restaurants, the city's exquisite dining experiences satisfy virtually any taste—French, Italian, Mexican, Chinese, Japanese, Greek, Indian, Continental—the list goes on.

For those who prefer the ambience of the local "watering hole," the selection is equally diverse. There's down-home spots like "The Pump" in Clarkson or the Lone Star; British-style pubs like the downtown Fox and Fiddle or Streetsville's Winchester Arms; and contemporary family dining restaurants such as Kelsey's, the Keg, Montana's and Jack Astor's Bar & Grill.

Like to watch your favourite game on a big screen, play a game of pool or dance till you drop? Then you'll find that the city's many sports bars and dance clubs—like the Sports Café, Rendezvous Beach Bar & Grill,

Once a year, the base of the clock tower at Erin Mills Town Centre is magically transformed into a piece of the North Pole. *Photo by Jeff Chevrier.*

Erin Mills Town Centre entices shoppers with 235 stores. When it's time to take a break, you'll find a nine-hole miniature golf course in the centre of everything.
Photo by Jeff Chevrier.

C.C.'s Roadhouse and many more—are the places to go.

Events

In typical Mississauga style, there are a myriad of events held regularly across the city which celebrate old traditions and strive to establish some new ones. One of the oldest and largest events is Streetsville's Bread and Honey Festival. Early each June, the main streets are closed to traffic, and for three days the village takes on the atmosphere of a country fair. With help from the local Lions, Rotarians, Kinsmen and dozens of other volunteers, the festival features a parade, a carnival, beer garden, baking contest, craft competitions, a fishing derby, sports tournaments, a pancake breakfast, assorted other activities and, of course, free bread and honey for everyone.

This is but one of Streetsville's four seasonal events. On July 1, it's fireworks and flags. In September, the streets are awash with the aroma of hot buttered corncobs during the Harvest Hoedown. And at Christmas, it's Santa Claus, carollers, horse-drawn wagon rides, hot drinks and food, and maybe even an antique steam engine. In Clarkson, the annual Cornfest gala is held each August at the Bradley Museum. The gala features activities like line dancing, craft exhibits and corn-on-the-cob,

cooked the old-fashioned way in a huge cauldron over a bonfire.

The Civic Square in front of City Hall hosts several community and cultural events each year, such as the day of dancing, music and fireworks which marks July 1st Canada Day celebrations. In winter, the central fountain pool becomes a public ice skating rink. Each December, the city greets the season with the opening of the rink complemented by touches like free hot chocolate or a performance by the Mississauga Skating Club, and the official lighting of an immense Christmas tree.

To get everyone in the spirit ahead of time, the city hosts the annual Santa Claus Parade in November. Fifty thousand gather to watch the floats, bands and the jolly old elf himself wind their way through the downtown core.

But when the searing summer heat rolls around once again, it's Carassauga's turn to stir the city. This annual three-day festival provides a close-up look at the heritage of many different cultures, displayed in 12

The arenas have changed, but the love of the game hasn't. Perhaps these hockey stars of the future will one day join other Mississaugans like former NHL greats Paul Henderson, Fred Stanfield and Joe Primeau in the Mississauga Sports Hall of Fame. Pictured here, Mississauga's new Iceland Arena, which boasts two Olympic-sized rinks. Photo by Jeff Chevrier.

to 15 pavilions located throughout the city. Sample foods from around the world while dancers dressed in authentic costumes perform traditional cultural dances.

Getaways

Every so often, it's nice to get away and recharge your batteries—especially if it means not having to travel far. You can find a retreat to suit your tastes right in Mississauga.

For a serene woodland setting and cozy old stone fireplaces, escape to the charm of historic Glenerin Inn. For those who thrive on a quicker pace, there's the bustle of the many major hotels within the airport district. Relax in the spacious accommodations of downtown's Novotel Mississauga, or one of the city's hotels that specialize in oversized

apartment-style luxury suites such as Dodge Suites Hotel. Mix in some exercise by staying at the Delta Meadowvale Resort and Conference Centre, which features one of the most complete fitness and racquet facilities in the city.

When the day winds down and you've had your fill of shopping, sightseeing, dining and pub crawling, spend a night at one of Mississauga's superb hotels. Sometimes, a weekend refresher is the best entertainment of all. **Ⓜ**

While parents enjoy their shopping spree, youngsters have fun of their own on the rides at Kid's Place—the indoor mini-amusement park at Square One. Photo by Michael Scholz.

The arrival of the Bread and Honey Festival is a sure sign that summer's here! Streets are closed off and activities are everywhere for three days of fun in Streetsville's largest annual community event. Photo by Michael Scholz.

Outdoor concerts can be found around the city during numerous summer events. Photo by Michael Scholz.

What would Streetsville's famous Bread and Honey Festival be without the star attraction? Photo by Jeff Chevrier.

These festival-goers catch a bird's-eye view.
Photo by Jeff Chevrier.

Opened in the spring of 1997, Famous Players Coliseum 10 is billed as the first circular stadium theatre in the world, featuring 10 auditoriums with giant wall-to-wall screens, rocking chair seats and digital sound. Photo by Jeff Chevrier.

It's not just popcorn at this place! Coliseum 10's impressive menu includes premium food from Pizza Hut, New York Fries, Baskin-Robbins and Starbuck's. *Photo by Jeff Chevrier.*

Coliseum 10 sits in the northeast corner of a multifaceted entertainment district that is taking shape at an amazingly rapid rate. Already, Sega City, the Living Arts Centre, Civic Square, restaurants, huge specialty stores and Square One are within a few minutes' walk. *Photo by Jeff Chevrier.*

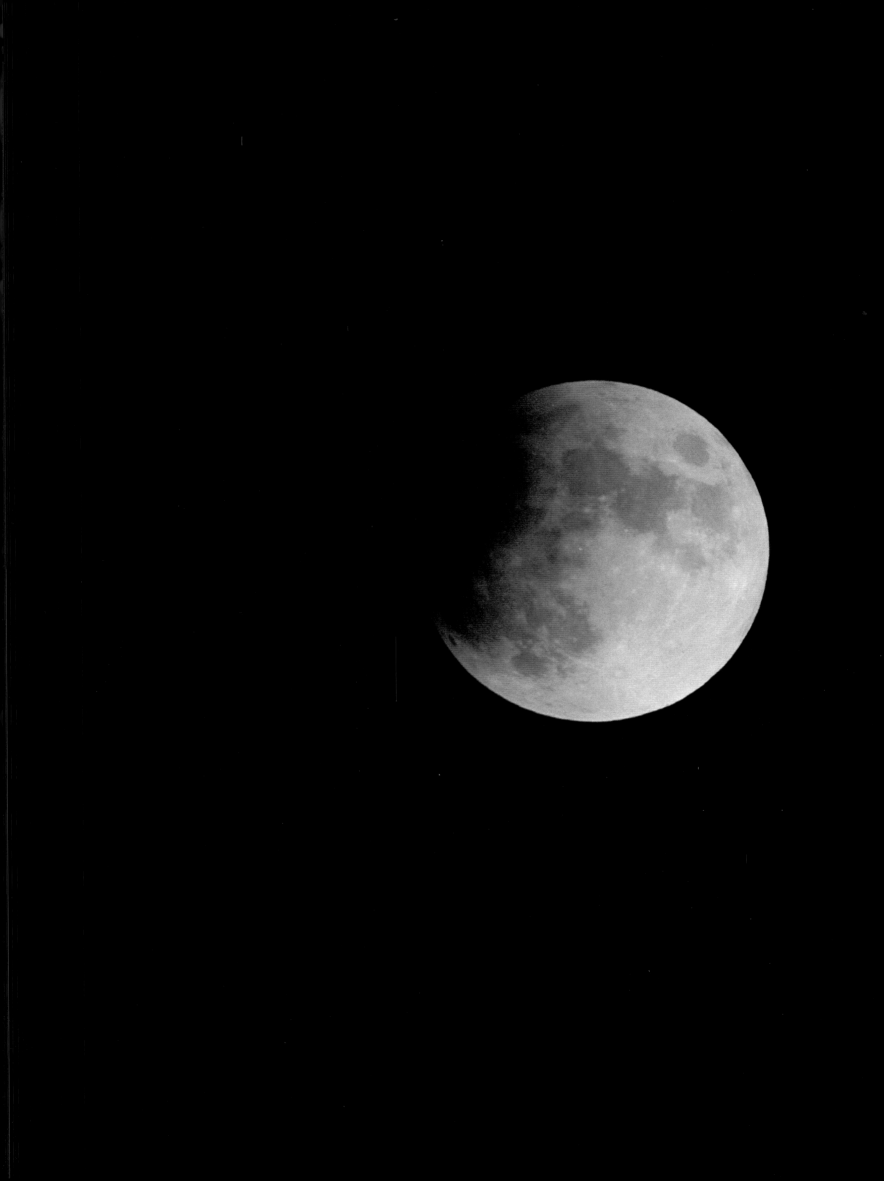

CHAPTER 9

...And Moonlit Nights

Ⓜ

With so many open spaces, it's no surprise that an incredible number of recreational opportunities await you in Mississauga. From moonlit canoe trips down the Credit River to birdwatching at Rattray Marsh, you're never far from the soothing tranquility of nature. And for the sports minded, there's an impressive array of recreational facilities ranging from neighbourhood baseball diamonds to world-class golf courses and major sports complexes.

Photo by Jeff Chevrier

Nothing lends more to the quality of life in an urban setting than the presence of nature. Without question, Mississauga's natural setting is the final ingredient in the mix that makes this city so eminently liveable.

Perhaps it's a harkening back to the city's rural origins, or just the common desire for a refuge from a hectic world. Whatever the reason, Mississaugans hold the city's natural amenities and recreational opportunities in high regard.

In spite of the rapid suburban growth which has occurred here over the past 20 years, the city's thoughtful approach to development has made the preservation of natural areas and green spaces a high priority. Some 3,200 acres of parkland have been set aside in the form of over 350 parks, ranging in size from neighbourhood parkettes to huge waterfront preserves. And many of the newer subdivisions are

Credit weaves its way from the Caledon Hills in the north, down through the neighbourhoods of the city to Lake Ontario. Along the way, the river and major tributaries like Sawmill Valley Creek undergo numerous changes in size and character, providing a marvellous spectrum of recreational and natural habitat areas.

Of course, it doesn't hurt to have the shoreline of one of the largest freshwater lakes in the world as the city's southern boundary. The immensity of Lake Ontario brings to Mississauga many of the recreational water activities normally associated with a seaside coastal town. Each summer, the harbour areas of Port Credit and Lakeview team with sailboats and yachts, while all manner of pleasure craft and windsurfers criss-cross the water, racing to and from the horizon in all directions.

Already one of the busiest recreational ports

*Opposite page: **The Credit River continues to play a major role in defining the character of Mississauga. Though narrower and shallower than it was during its fur-trading days, the Credit measures 22.5 metres (73 feet) at its deepest point in Erindale, and is a favourite spot for anglers and canoeists.** Photo by Jeff Chevrier.*

J.C. Saddington Park is one of several waterfront parks that line the shores of Lake Ontario along Mississauga's southern border. Photo by Jeff Chevrier.

adjacent to woodlots and dedicated greenbelts, mimicking the gorgeous tree-lined streets of the older areas in the south end.

That affinity for nature is well reflected in the number and variety of public parks, waterside trails and recreation facilities which the city continues to establish.

Waterways

It begins with the Credit River system. Still in many ways the lifeblood of the city, the

in the province, Port Credit is undergoing a major renaissance. Phase One of a $13-million six-phase redevelopment of the harbour area was concluded in 1996, adding a new docking facility for transient boats and improvements to pedestrian access, landscaping and parking.

Anglers from around the world are attracted to the Credit River system, which contains speckled, rainbow and brown trout, and smallmouth bass, as well as pickerel, carp and pike at the river's mouth. The waters off Port

Right: **Take a tour on the self-guided trail of Rattray Marsh, home to 428 species of plants, 227 bird species, 26 different mammals, 16 reptiles and amphibians, and 11 species of fish.** *Photo by Jeff Chevrier.*

Credit are renowned as one of the best salmon fisheries in the world, making the harbour the residence of one of Lake Ontario's largest fleets of charter boats. Trophy-size catches are common, with abundant coho, chinook and Atlantic salmon, and rainbow, lake and brown trout.

With all the attention garnered by the giant lake to the south, it's easy to forget about Mississauga's two other lakes—Lake Aquitaine and Lake Wabukayne, the little lakes of Meadowvale. They were created in the mid-1970s as storm management ponds designed to buffer excess run-off from area subdivisions as it entered the Credit. But time and considerable nurturing have turned the lakes into budding wetlands that are home to numerous bird species and naturally occurring fish. As an added bonus, the only access is via the surrounding paths which connect to Meadowvale's network of neighbourhood cycling and walking trails.

Parklands

Mississauga's parkland comes in many forms, from "passive" picnic areas and scenic spots to sports parks.

Miles of paths and bike trails border picturesque river valleys and the lake shore, and wind through wooded lots across the city. The Mississauga Waterfront Trail alone spans 15 km (nine miles) of parks, green spaces and scenic streets as part of a 325-km trail system which stretches from Hamilton to Trenton.

Expansion of the trail system is ongoing, with initiatives like the 1996 installation of a $200,000 pedestrian bridge across the Credit River in Pine Cliff Park. This is part of the Culham Trail, which will eventually stretch all the way from Erindale Park to the neighbouring city of Brampton in the north.

Some of Mississauga's largest parks are located along the Lake Ontario shoreline. Majestic trees, expansive picnic and play areas, and numerous beaches make these favourite weekend spots for families of all ages. Kids love to climb on the 60-foot ship-shaped apparatus, or run through the giant sprinkler at Lakefront Promenade Park. And to the delight of dog owners, some parks feature designated leash-free zones for dogs, which have proven to be even cleaner than parks where leash bylaws apply.

One of the city's most spectacular parks is Rhododendron Gardens, home to one of Canada's most extensive arrays of rhododendrons east of the Rocky Mountains. More than just pretty faces, these gardens feature beautiful hybrids of the popular flower which were created in Mississauga and can be found nowhere else in the world.

With a stunning natural beauty all its own, Rattray Marsh is the only lakefront marsh between Toronto and Burlington. The marsh is

Another prominent resident of Rattray Marsh. *Photo by Jeff Chevrier.*

an environmentally sensitive area which provides a unique habitat for 428 species of plants, 227 bird species, 26 different mammals, 16 reptiles and amphibians, and 11 fish species. A self-guided trail helps visitors identify plants, birds and animals.

Sports and Fitness

Mississauga also has more than its share of not-so-passive parks which are designed for sports uses. Many of these feature soccer pitches, football fields or tennis courts. And it seems like practically every community enjoys the ubiquitous neighbourhood ball diamonds.

The variety of city-operated sports and fitness facilities is absolutely amazing in terms of both numbers and calibre. Digest these figures for a moment: 12 arenas with over 20 indoor ice rink surfaces for public skating and hockey; 16 swimming pools, including nine indoor; 10 Community Centres housing 8 fitness centres, most with complete weight training and fitness equipment, gyms, racquet courts and a qualified training staff. In a city this young! And because of that, the facilities are new, and well maintained and equipped.

One of the newest facilities is Iceland Mississauga—the ice sports complex with an Olympic-size rink and three standard North American rinks, plus a restaurant, snack bar, pro shop, learning centre, skills arcade and lounge areas with floor-to-ceiling glassed viewing galleries.

Private sector facilities are equally impressive, beginning with one of the best-equipped YMCAs in the country. For avid baseball enthusiasts, there's year-round indoor action in one of Mississauga's domed facilities, such as Mini-Domes—the home of Baseball Academy, run by former Blue Jay great Ernie Whitt.

Perhaps the quality of sports facilities in the city is to be expected, given its sports heritage. From 1949 until 1996, the old Dixie Arena was the training grounds of top NHL stars like Paul Coffey, Mike Gartner, Brendan Shanahan, Mike Ricci and countless others. World-class gymnasts like Curtis Hibbert, Elfie Schlegel and Stella Umeh have excelled thanks to the special gymnastics training facility which the city and Gymnastics Mississauga have established. And consider that among Canada's 1996 Summer Olympians, Silken Laumann and relay sprinter Carlton Chambers were but two of a contingency of 14 Mississaugans accounting for a gold and four silver medals.

For golf enthusiasts, there are half a dozen golf courses within city limits, ranging from challenging recreational to world-class, as well as a number of driving ranges.

A rare sight—a red trillium—in the Credit woodlands. Photo by Michael Scholz.

Seen here in its more common white form, the trillium is Ontario's official flower and is protected by law against picking. Photo by Michael Scholz.

The six golf courses within Mississauga's limits, ranging from recreational to championship level, are perfectly suited to matching the growing popularity of this sport. Photo by Jeff Chevrier.

Aerial of the Lakeview course. *Photo by Michael Scholz.*

Other Activities

Twice each year, Mississauga Community Services publishes a catalogue of more than 100 pages of artistic, sports and fitness activities which are offered by Mississauga's Recreation and Parks department. From ballroom dancing to horseback riding, there truly is something for everyone.

And that's to say nothing of the activities offered by dozens of specialized dance and sports schools in Mississauga. In fact, there are so many other programs and activities available that each autumn, Square One Shopping Centre hosts a Registration Show for them to simplify winter program registrations for all interested parties.

To make sure that no one is left out, numerous city and community agencies also provide activities for seniors and those with special needs, including outstanding programs offered by Special Olympics Mississauga.

A quiet stroll on a hot summer night. A brisk tour of the glistening trails on cross-country skiis. Or watching the harvest moon bob and dance on the swirling surface of the Credit. It's not unusual to suddenly catch yourself thinking, "I'm in the centre of a big city?"

If it's hard to imagine a city of over 600,000 comfortably situated in a park-like setting, come to Mississauga. And don't forget to bring your hiking boots, fishing rod and—oh, yes—your camera. Ⓜ

Dusk settles on Lake Ontario. Photo by Jeff Chevrier.

The newly renovated Lakefront Promenade Park is a busy place in summer, with amenities like beach volleyball courts, a waterfront trail for walking, biking and in-line skating, picnic shelters, fishing facilities and a bustling marina. All of this is in the heart of the Port Credit village. *Photo by Jeff Chevrier.*

The lakefront area is home to thousands of ducks, geese, swans and other waterfowl. *Photo by Jeff Chevrier.*

The waters surrounding the Port Credit Lighthouse are a favourite spot for week-end anglers in search of salmon, trout and bass. *Photo by Jeff Chevrier.*

Kids of all ages catch a break from the blistering heat in the sprinklers at Jack Darling Park. Photo by Jeff Chevrier.

CHAPTER 10

On the Threshold of Greatness

Ⓜ

Having long drawn on its historical roots in developing a sense of itself, this city is currently working through the realization of its emergence as a major urban centre. It's a bit like a young adult who has received all the benefits of a strong upbringing, who is now coming of age and recognizing what possibilities lie ahead. For Mississauga, those possibilities seem limitless.

Photo by Michael Scholz

There's a sort of mission under way here. It's not about trying to become something more than a bedroom community, perched on the doorstep of a metropolitan area. Mississauga has long since distinguished itself as a leader, not a follower. Nor is it about searching for civic identity as some would suggest. You don't have to scratch far beneath the youthful, exuberant surface to discover what 200 years of history have done to give this city a character all its own.

No. In fact, this "mission" has its sights set on looking ahead, to becoming the new North American standard in "edge cities" (those which sit on the rim of a major metropolitan centre). It's a fitting goal for Mississauga—one that is eminently achievable and, in many ways, has already been accomplished.

The evidence is powerful and undeniable. The city's rapid contemporary growth has been nothing short of phenomenal. Yet one gets the sense that Mississauga is just beginning to hit its stride. Solid municipal planning and financial prudence have laid the foundation for tremendous future development. Now, with critical elements like available resources, infrastructure and land all well in hand, few if any apparent limits to the city's potential have appeared on the horizon.

Transportation infrastructure—one of Mississauga's long-time greatest strengths—is keeping pace with the area's growth. Upgrading of transportation systems in and around the city is already under way on a number of fronts. Extensions to Highway 407 will soon connect western and northern sections of Mississauga with points to the east of Metro, providing a bypass of the entire Metropolitan area.

The city is taking steps now to avoid any future congestion problems in the downtown core. Construction of a new, more efficient central terminal for city transit has been completed. Plans also call for the creation of a series of transit priority lanes which would improve links to the City Centre and access to Metro's subway system. Reserved bus lanes are to be constructed along the shoulders of Highway 403. For the longer term, planning includes the Transitway—a new express transit link between the city's core and the airport district.

Easily the most significant infrastructural change promises to be the massive 10-year redevelopment and expansion of Pearson International Airport. In December 1996, the Greater Toronto Airports Authority assumed control of Pearson from the federal government, as well as ownership of the buildings and runways. In of itself, this has Mississauga and the Greater Toronto Area (GTA) as a

whole excited: other North American cities have benefited measurably from creating local airport authorities, most notably Vancouver, where a similar move saw annual passenger traffic subsequently jump by 17 per cent.

Work is well under way. Flight capacity, already augmented by the new north-south runway which opened in 1997, will be further increased by two additional planned east-west runways. Most significantly, a $2-billion terminal building will replace Terminals 1 and 2. The already impressive Terminal Three will, in fact, be dwarfed by the new terminal, which will almost double overall passenger handling capacity.

But the sparkling new terminal and improved efficiencies aren't really what has everyone excited. Apart from the obvious financial benefits which the capital investment will have on the area, the magnitude of the potential ongoing economic spin-off is astounding. Even in its current form, Pearson has an enormous impact on the GTA's economy, generating nearly $10 billion in business revenue annually. According to a 1995 study, the airport is also

responsible for almost 100,000 direct and indirect jobs paying over $2.8 billion in wages and accounting for close to 2 per cent of employment in the entire province!

Now for the exciting part: if present projections for passenger traffic growth hold true, the resulting jobs and annual revenues generated by Pearson will increase by about 40 per cent by 2005. As the host city, Mississauga will be the clear beneficiary of much of this activity.

Opposite page: **Mississauga's solid municipal planning and financial prudence have laid the foundation for tremendous future development.** *Photo by Jeff Chevrier.*

Already an economic powerhouse, Pearson International Airport is slated for a huge expansion. It's estimated that the addition of a single weekly international 747 flight creates 90 jobs and some $9 million in annual economic benefits. *Photo by Jeff Chevrier.*

Mississauga is a budding metropolis, with lots of room still for growth. *Photo by Jeff Chevrier.*

All this coincides with aggressive GTA-wide initiatives to increase economic development and tourism. And a further indication of prospective growth was recently received as *Fortune* magazine named the Toronto region as the best international centre in which to live and work.

Other facets of infrastructure also continue to forge ahead. With roads, water, sewer and hydro services all remarkably well maintained, there is no looming financial crisis related to an aging municipal infrastructure. Plans for new facilities are forming, such as the new $25-million Peel Community Cancer Centre at The Credit Valley Hospital. And exceptional recreation and sports facilities are sprouting up at a tremendous pace, including the home arena of the city's new franchise in the Ontario

Mississauga appears to be poised for a substantial growth surge. In the meantime, other development has pushed on.

When a sagging national economy caused commercial development to stall throughout the GTA in the early 1990s, something unexpected happened in Mississauga. Rather than stagnate, energies were diverted to the creation of an entertainment district in the City Centre's northwest. Hammerson Canada, the owner of Square One and surrounding properties, came up with a scheme to blend power centre and traditional style retailing with entertainment in one dynamic area. The plan calls for a myriad of restaurants, night spots and other entertainment establishments to be added, building on the presence of "anchors" like the Living Arts Centre and Sega City. At the centre of the district is the 500,000-square-foot addition to Square One, the "Powerhouse," designed to complement the adjacent Living Arts Centre. An accompanying hotel complex and IMAX theatre may also be in the works.

At maturity, the district will provide a unique blend of experiences that run the entertainment gamut—playing, viewing, listening, shopping and dining. If the amazing draw which Square One already enjoys is any indication, these new attractions promise to make the City Centre a major tourist destination.

Other public and residential areas will see their share of activity as well. The six-phase redevelopment and refurbishment of the Port Credit Harbour area is expected to be a tremendous boost to the local community. The impressive new marina facilities and waterfront restaurant, constructed in 1996, are to be complemented by a boardwalk, picnic shelter, bandstand and children's play area. Completion is scheduled for 2002. And neighbouring vacated industrial land is expected to be converted to recreational and mixed residential/commercial use over the next few years.

In an effort to ensure sustainability, the torrid growth of subdivisions has been tempered by

Hockey League—the prolific "feeder system" of talent for the NHL.

With a solid infrastructure in place and ample land available, the city's capacity for growth in the industrial and commercial sectors is immense. Mississauga has by far the largest inventory of undeveloped "greenfield" industrial/commercial land in the GTA. This is quickly making it the preferred location for outer-Metro development. Within the City Centre area alone, the city's official plan allows for an eventual total of 22 million square feet of office space. To put that into perspective, the current inventory is about 3 million square feet.

Present vacancy rates for downtown office space are drastically lower here than in Toronto's core. With the Canadian economy rebounding, office space construction in

Upgrades to local expressways keep pace, with innovations like reserved bus lanes along the highway shoulders being planned. *Photo by Michael Scholz.*

A resident enjoys a quiet stroll through Erindale Park, where one of the amenities is an exceptionally well-maintained system of parks and recreation facilities.
Photo by Jeff Chevrier.

reason, through the preservation of greenbelts where possible and the occasional innovative twist. On the perimeter of the old Meadowvale Village, for example, housing developments are shaping up which revisit the village's historic architecture rather than supplant it.

The city's employment picture also holds the promise of great things ahead. Already a net importer of labour, Mississauga's position as a major employment centre continues to expand. And there is every reason to believe that the city's massive influx of knowledge-intensive industries—expected to fuel Canada's economy through the 21st century—will accelerate as Mississauga's numerous advantages continue to multiply.

Is there a simple explanation for the city's progress? Part of the answer may be found in these words from Mayor Hazel McCallion: "We have worked very hard together to build a city that...cherishes its past but looks to the future as well. We have had the opportunity to build this city from the ground up and to learn from the successes and mistakes of others."

But for all the apparent potential in the world, no city would have much of a future if it neglected the most important development of all—its people, and their quality of life. Again, Mississauga has excelled: parks and open spaces are exceptional; streets are safe, clean and inviting; and new schools and community sports facilities are busy turning out the next generation of scholars and elite athletes. People have responded by initiating a stream of new community groups, events and activities that shows no signs of letting up.

In the final analysis, this city will continue to thrive because people care about it. For although Mississauga is a place of commerce and entertainment, most of all, it is home.

The "people's mayor" may have summed it up best with her own personal reflection. "I love that I can look out on the Civic Square and see people of many cultures skating or sharing in community celebrations. I love that even though we've grown into a major centre of high-tech industry and commerce, I can still walk my dog along miles of wooded trails without having to leave the city. We've built a great community for which people feel a real sense of ownership and pride, and I see that getting even stronger as Mississauga matures."

As a philosopher friend once said, "Give good people the tools to create, and you will most assuredly be astonished by the results." For all the remarkable feats that have already been accomplished here, surely Mississaugans can look forward to being even more astonished in the years ahead. ⓜ

Part of the Civic Centre complex, the Mississauga Central Library houses some 250,000 books, a full range of audio-visual media and CD-Roms, access to global databases and the 244-seat Noel Ryan Auditorium. *Photo by Jeff Chevrier.*

Photo by Jeff Chevrier

Photo by Jeff Chevrier

The lake shoreline is a fitting backdrop
for the stately, historic Adamson Estate.
Photo by Michael Scholz.

Built by Agar Adamson, a son-in-law of
the prominent Cawthra family, the
Adamson Estate has been refurbished and
is now used by the Royal Conservatory of
Music. *Photo by Michael Scholz.*

**Swans drift majestically by the shores of
Lakeview.** *Photo by Jeff Chevrier.*

The historic Port Credit Lighthouse stands as a familiar symbol of the enduring harbour area. Photo by Jeff Chevrier.

You can pick your own apples right in the middle of the city at the Riviere Apple Farm. Photo by Jeff Chevrier.

Photos by Jeff Chevrier

The planned community of Meadowvale has matured beautifully, with lots of hiding places and watering holes for its feathered residents. Photo by Jeff Chevrier.

Another popular watering hole of a different kind—Streetsville's Sundance Saloon and Grill. Photo by Jeff Chevrier.

The city's rapid growth will continue to work because its well-planned development ensures that, no matter where you are in Mississauga, sights like these are never far away. Photos by Jeff Chevrier.

Part II

Photo by Michael Scholz

$\mathcal{R}$epresenting the "Voice of Business" in Mississauga, as it bills itself, the Mississauga Board of Trade (MBOT) has no trouble being heard. Not with more than 1,300 member companies and rising—that's over 10 per cent of the city's entire corporate population.

The MBOT's membership parallels the

Mississauga Board of Trade

makeup of Mississauga's commercial, industrial, retail, and professional communities. It's a far cry from the days of the Clarkson-Lorne Park Chamber of Commerce, one of the local business organizations that joined and evolved into the MBOT. Back in 1958, that group had just 12 members, and couldn't foresee the growth of both the city and what would become its Board of Trade.

Nowadays, the MBOT is one of Canada's largest Boards of Trade. It strives to create an environment in which Mississauga businesses can compete and prosper, not only creating a thriving business sector but also contributing

The 1997 MBOT Executives *left to right:* **Phil King, Martin Rosen, David Gordon, Craig Cowan, Nance MacDonald, Ron Mossman, Wayne Barrett, John Wouters, Dean Morrison, Steve Offer.**

to the quality of life for all citizens in the community.

As a non-profit, volunteer-driven organization, the MBOT is funded solely by membership fees—no government funding or corporate endowments. Managing Director and COO David Gordon says business people join the MBOT for three basic reasons: networking, lobbying and services. (Memberships are both individual and corporate, and all staff of corporate members can take advantage of MBOT's programs and services.)

He calls networking a "misused" word which actually entails any aspect of involvement in the organization. Educational seminars and workshops, for instance, expose members to business solutions and strategies that can give them a competitive edge. Social gatherings, meanwhile, facilitate more informal exchanges of ideas and promote goodwill in the business community.

By volunteering time for committee work, members help the MBOT develop and communicate policy on business issues, along with obtaining valuable business contacts, gaining

The Mississauga Board of Trade's humble beginnings—Clarke Hall, 1976

visibility for themselves and their company and enhancing their interpersonal skills.

More than a dozen committees offer monthly opportunities for participation, studying everything from the city's transportation infrastructure and education system, to environmental awareness and international trade.

Helping the business community extend its markets, locally and internationally, is a priority of the MBOT. Even before the North American Free Trade Agreement was ratified, the MBOT led a private sector trade delegation to Mexico to encourage alliances between Canadian, Mexican, and American companies. It did the same with the MERCOSUR countries, a trade bloc between Argentina, Brazil, Uruguay and Paraguay.

Today, the MBOT is proud to be part of the Canadian Business Networks Coalition, whose mandate is to promote worldwide and domestic strategic alliances. An example could be bringing together an architecture, a construction and an engineering firm to compete as a consortium on an international bid.

"Through our education, encouragement and opportunities for networking, we want to help companies look beyond the physical boundaries of Mississauga," says Gordon. "We want businesses to broaden their scope and horizon regionally, nationally and globally."

No matter what their intentions are on the local or world stage, all MBOT members benefit from the MBOT's lobbying efforts—Gordon's second reason to join the organization.

He says the MBOT offers strength in numbers, possessing the size and reputation to advocate effectively on behalf of its member companies. On issues from taxes to labour legislation, the MBOT knows how to convey the business community's views to decision-makers at all levels of government and to other interest groups.

As any business realizes, success depends largely on service. At the MBOT, members have access to an array of services which, in themselves, can make membership worthwhile.

Consider these value-added conveniences and money-savers—use of meeting rooms and private dining rooms, long-distance savings plans, special MasterCard and Visa merchant rates, discounted car and home insurance, notarizing of certificates of origin for export shipments, free professional advice, a group medical/dental insurance plan and much more.

"Because of our size, we drive revenues that allow us to do more for members," Gordon states. "For instance, we're one of the few places where a company of any size can obtain affordable group insurance, by using our national buying power."

He states that MBOT follows the philosophy it preaches, creating alliances with other industry associations and groups in Mississauga and elsewhere. "There's no sense replicating what other organizations are providing."

The MBOT's community networks, and positive relations with Regional Council and other Greater Toronto Area (GTA) Boards of Trade, create what he calls "mutual interest groups." The result is the MBOT's leadership in ongoing dialogue among GTA stakeholders on key collective issues, from waste management site selection to the airports authority.

While the MBOT is acknowledged as one of the most progressive Boards of Trade in Canada, Gordon deflects all the attention back to the member companies. In fact, to promote and recognize outstanding achievements, the MBOT confers numerous awards—not only

The Board's 1996 Business Award recipients *left to right:* **Doug Stewart, of Baxter Corporation, the Environment User award winner; Gerry Gentile, of InTELaTECH, the Small Business of the Year award winner; Ron Nolan, of Hatch Associates, the Large Business of the Year award winner; Joe Galati, of Motion Electric Motor Services; Duncan R. Hobbs, of Charton Hobbs, the Business Person of the Year; Michael Ruscigno, of InTELaTECH; Bill Auld, of Auld Butchers, the Small Business Community Involvement award winner; Hugh Middleton of Canadian School Book Exchange; George Clack, of Abbott Laboratories; and Dusanka Filopovic, of Halozone Technologies, the Environment Provider award winner.**

for top companies and business people, but also for supporting the arts, fostering sound environmental practices and community involvement.

"We're not just business, business, business," says Gordon. "We want to acknowledge contributions not only within the business world but for the entire community of Mississauga."

Gordon realizes that from a business standpoint, Mississauga is fortunate. The creation of the Region of Peel in 1974, coupled with the

amalgamation of several towns under the Mississauga banner, provided the opportunity to strategically plan the growth of the city.

It is a city, he notes, that is blessed with an international airport—a major engine driving the economy of Mississauga and the entire GTA—and one which offers the accessibility of more multi-lane highways criss-crossing through it than any city in North America.

These advantages, not to mention the MBOT's own guiding efforts, have unquestionably helped create a vibrant local business community, reflected in the Board of Trade's expanding membership. "We are fortunate," says Gordon.

Though the MBOT continues to grow, he says the organization doesn't measure success by the size of its membership or revenues from dues.

"The important thing isn't how successful we become, but how successful we make our members. When a company thrives because, in part, of the efforts we advocate and benefits we offer, that's what counts." Ⓜ

The Annual President's Dinner, 1997

Transportation, Energy & Communications

Ⓜ

Photo by Michael Scholz

*T*he people at Hydro Mississauga like to say their commodity is not just electricity.

"Energy value is the product we have to deliver," states Ron Starr, chair of the municipal utility.

Hydro Mississauga does just that, better than just about any utility in Ontario.

Hydro Mississauga

One of 306 independent electrical distribution utilities in the province, Hydro Mississauga boasts zero debt and an extremely low operating margin. That translates into better rates for the utility's 142,000 customers. At a margin of 8.4 per cent, Hydro Mississauga has positioned itself as a low-cost operator, relative to the Ontario municipal utility average of around 17 per cent.

Ron Starr points out that based on the utility's raw cost of power, this 8.6 per cent productivity difference equates to a savings

In 1997 Hydro Mississauga celebrates its 80th year in the business of providing energy in Mississauga. Hydro Mississauga was first established in 1917, when the Mississauga of today was known as Toronto Township. The company's business has changed immeasurably since then. Pole-climbing spurs and accounting journals have given way to aerial bucket devices and integrated computer systems. Highly skilled employees now make use of the very latest innovations in equipment and technology.

approaching $50 million annually. "This is a productivity dividend that we are able to deliver straight back into the hands of Mississauga customers in the form of lower energy rates," he said.

In fact, Hydro Mississauga offers lower standard rates than any major electrical utility serving the Greater Toronto Area, or neighbouring American states.

Hydro Mississauga is literally part of the city—it designs, operates and maintains thousands of kilometres of electrical lines that run through Mississauga, and provides all street lighting services.

As the second largest municipal electrical utility in Ontario, distributing five per cent of the province's total electric load, Hydro Mississauga is a leader in efficiency and reliability. Its energy services team is continually looking for pricing innovations and new service options, which help customers be competitive.

In business, time is money. This old cliché is especially relevant to utilities striving to find a competitive advantage for customers. With little ability to store electricity, the whole delivery system must have enough generation, transmission and distribution capacity to accommodate peak demands. Since there are times when electricity demand is high, and times when the available capacity is underused, this "time of use" factor is critical to pricing electricity.

The separate charge for peak usage is an important consideration for medium and large

Ron E. Starr, P. Eng.
Chair of the Mississauga Hydro Electric Commission

business. Introduction of sophisticated Time of Use (TOU) meters is providing a solution to managing this cost. Through TOU, customers are reducing their energy costs by shifting their electricity usage patterns to off-peak periods. More than recording energy use, these meters are connected electronically to Hydro Mississauga's computers, resulting in better demand planning and cost savings to the utility and its customers.

In this and other programs, as well as in the normal course of business, Hydro Mississauga is cataloguing the distinctive requirements of customers. The Customer Intelligence System lets the utility continually learn about the needs of those it serves, which is the first step towards satisfying those needs.

As for reliability, Hydro Mississauga engineers describe their electrical system as "robust." The emphasis is on preventative maintenance and quality material purchases, helping to ensure the integrity of the system.

Aging underground electrical systems and obsolete styles of street lighting are reconstructed or upgraded before problems occur. If power is interrupted, Hydro Mississauga investigates and repairs the cause quickly. With the automation and monitoring capabilities of a multimillion-dollar Supervisory Control and Data Acquisition System (SCADA), average minutes per year of customer interruptions have steadily declined to just 44 minutes in 1996, which is nearing world-class levels.

To improve the quality and speed of developing engineering designs, and boost the response to service calls, the utility makes use of an Automated Mapping and Facilities Management (AM/FM) system. Hydro Mississauga was the first electric utility in Canada to completely digitize its mapping using this system.

The AM/FM system includes 600,000 individual pieces of data—on transformers, poles, spans of wire and more—which can be delivered instantly to computer screens across the company.

Another tool helping Hydro Mississauga operators manage performance is the Supervisory Control and Data Acquisition (SCADA) system. It provides remote control and monitoring of switching devices at municipal substations and a growing number of sites along the lines.

SCADA can sense abnormal circuit conditions, alerting system operators to take action. It also saves the utility money through better system load management.

In its effort to provide customer value, Hydro Mississauga has been one of the chief boosters of reform in the electricity industry.

Some of the changes being discussed include separating control of the generation, transmission and distribution functions.

From Hydro Mississauga's standpoint, a key change anticipated is a separation of the "wires" side of the business from the electricity sales and energy services side.

"Simply put, this means the hard services, the poles and wires in a given geographical area, will be delivered by a single regulated provider," says Starr, "but customers will be free to buy their electricity and contract for energy services from their supplier of choice."

Other changes in the industry call for fewer and larger utilities (which can expand beyond what Starr calls "historical accident" boundaries), an "electricity marketplace" that creates competition in generation, and regulatory reforms that eliminate the situation where Ontario Hydro is at once a regulator, supplier and potential competitor.

Technician Mark Chin demonstrates the ability to review and download data stored within technologically advanced Time of Use meters.

"For our customers, we want the lower rates which will flow from a more competitive environment," says Starr.

Customer choice is good news for an efficient operation such as Hydro Mississauga's. With competition, Starr foresees the utility moving from 142,000 customers to a much larger critical mass of 500,000, and perhaps more.

In a more competitive future, Starr realizes utilities may find themselves in bidding wars for their most valuable customers. To prepare for this, Hydro Mississauga is differentiating the requirements of its customers.

"We're aware our customers want different things," says Starr. "By catering to their desires we make them more loyal and preserve our margins. The most loyal customers are those who come to rely on the unique convenience of dealing with a firm that knows and remembers them."

The goal is to build integrated customer relationships. That means meeting with customers and learning about how electricity relates to the success of their operation. It means building a database of what was learned, as in the Customer Intelligence System, and becoming interactive with the customer.

And it means using the customer's feedback to customize services and pricing options, maximizing the customer's satisfaction. Starr talks about distinguishing Hydro Mississauga's "product-service bundle," and expanding the number and complexity of "velcro bonds" that integrate the utility with the customer.

Ultimately, all of that promises to increase value to customers even further. By providing dependable and affordable electricity, and helping customers use it wisely, Hydro Mississauga plays an active role in the economic development of the city. ⓜ

Computer-based technology, which Engineer Michelle Cody is using here, has become indispensable. Automated mapping systems allow Hydro Mississauga to design services and model situations for maximum system efficiency.

Metering Supervisor Jim Butler monitors a display linked directly to a customer site.

*M*any factors may have sparked the growth of Mississauga, but a blue flame has played a key part in making it an energetic community. It is the blue flame of Consumers Gas, the largest natural gas distribution utility in Canada.

More than 1.4 million residential, commercial, industrial and transportation-service customers

Consumers Gas

depend on Consumers Gas for the reliable delivery of natural gas.

The company's pipeline network extends over 22,000 kilometres, delivering more than 11 billion cubic metres of gas a year. Consumers Gas serves a market that encompasses Eastern Ontario, Metro Toronto, parts of Central Ontario up to Georgian Bay, the Niagara Peninsula, and Mississauga.

"As a supplier of clean-burning and cost-competitive natural gas, we help fuel the Mississauga economy," says Ron Munkley, president and CEO. "Where natural gas fuel

Mississauga offices of Consumers Gas. The company is also Canada's largest retailer of natural gas appliances, and continually offers the latest in energy-saving equipment.

and technology is available as part of an energy mix, you end up with productivity and development that generates jobs, profits and new enterprises."

A few milestone years highlight the company annals. One was 1848, the year Consumers Gas was founded in Toronto.

Its first shareholders consisted of people who were dissatisfied with the gas supply and quality of another supplier. The Consumers' Gas Company of Toronto, as it was then known, lit the street lamps in that Victorian era and provided gas for five miles of cast iron mains.

Another key date was 1954, a true turning point in the company's history. That year saw the start of the construction of the TransCanada Pipelines system. Completed in 1959, this massive transmission system made possible the conversion from manufactured gas to natural gas. The system linked the gas field of Western Canada with the distribution facilities of Eastern Canada.

Consumers Gas has kindled the community spirit as a strong supporter of a wide range of local charities and institutions. Shown here is the flag-raising during the Heart and Stroke Campaign.

For the people of Mississauga, yet another notable year was 1978. That was when Consumers Gas opened an office here to serve the company's western region. The company had first obtained a franchise in the region in 1931, to supply Port Credit with manufactured gas. Almost five decades later, the increasing demand for natural gas services in this fast-growing area made it logical to establish a local presence.

"Mississauga was and still is a significant market for us," says Ron Munkley, who himself

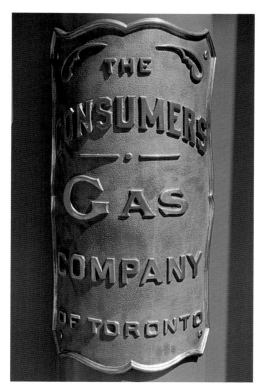

The Consumers' Gas Company of Toronto, as it was then known, lit the street lamps in the Victorian era and provided gas for five miles of cast iron mains.

is a resident of the city. In fact, two of the last three company presidents have lived in Mississauga.

Mr. Munkley is presiding over a Consumers Gas that does much more than deliver natural gas, even while adding many towns and communities to its market. This is a company whose stated mission is to become "the best energy supplier and services company" in the entire country.

Consumers Gas is a leader in research into new natural gas technology, and has contributed to the development of equipment such as high-efficiency furnaces.

The company is also Canada's largest retailer of natural gas appliances, and continually offers the latest in energy-saving equipment.

In the effort to create fuel systems that cost and pollute less than gasoline or diesel, Consumers Gas has become a leader in Natural Gas for Vehicles (NGV). The company has already helped spur a Canadian market for NGV by developing natural gas fuel systems for commercial fleet vehicles and buses. This is a promising area, as the federal government has said that by the year 2005 three-quarters of its fleet vehicles must run on alternative fuels such as natural gas.

Throughout Mississauga you'll also find Consumers Gas advisors working closely with government, builders, engineers and industry, helping customers improve the energy efficiency of buildings and reduce operating costs.

With its efficient, safe and economical performance, no wonder natural gas is the fuel of choice for 99 per cent of all new urban housing units in Mississauga.

Along with providing comfort to residents, Consumer Gas is a leading supplier to numerous public buildings and gathering places across the city. Among the diverse facilities who rely on the advantages of natural gas for space heating and hot water are the Mississauga Civic Centre, the Public Library, Square One Shopping Centre, Terminal 3 at Lester B. Pearson International Airport, and Stage West Theatre.

Consumers Gas supplies and services scores of major office complexes, and provides natural gas for cooking facilities at the city's popular restaurants and hotels.

Within local industry, natural gas is used for plant and water heating, various manufacturing and industrial processes, and make-up air systems (which preheat fresh air for building ventilation after stale air has been exhausted).

Not only is natural gas equipment a cost-effective choice, but it also provides precise temperature control without producing corrosive byproducts during combustion. Natural gas drives industry by firing the kilns that bake building bricks at Mississauga's Canada Brick, by producing steam used in dehydrating pet foods at the local Ralston-Purina plant, and in countless other industrial applications.

"We see ourselves as helping large industries compete," says Ron Munkley, "which benefits not only the companies but the Mississauga community as a whole."

Consumers Gas has become a leader in Natural Gas for Vehicles (NGV). NGV buses serve the city of Mississauga.

He says that Consumers Gas' role in Mississauga extends beyond being a supplier of natural gas, to embrace community participation.

"Our employees not only serve Mississauga, but live here as well, and we feel a strong commitment to help meet the community's goals," he says.

The company has kindled the community spirit as a strong supporter of a wide range of local charities and institutions, including the United Way, Mississauga Hospital, Erindale College, the Living Arts Centre, and the Mississauga YMCA.

Corporate philanthropy isn't the only form of support. For years Consumers Gas has given community groups use of the Blue Flame room at the Mississauga office. The room was formerly used to teach classes on cooking with natural gas. Today dozens of organizations and thousands of residents a year use it for meetings, banquets and fund-raising events.

"Community groups are always looking for suitable space, and our company and employees are proud to share the Blue Flame room with the people we serve."

Care for the community, low rates, innovative natural gas products, customer-driven services—they're all examples of how that blue flame helps energize the city of Mississauga. Ⓜ

QUIK X Transportation Inc.

*F*ounded in Mississauga, Ontario in December 1989, QUIK X Transportation Inc. has, in a few short years, become Canada's recognized leader in expedited, less-than-truck-load transportation services.

From its early days as an over-the-road carrier operating between Ontario, Quebec and western Canada, QUIK X has continuously sought out new markets where its particularly high level of service could benefit its growing customer base. Service was initiated to Atlantic Canada and Thunder Bay, Ontario to add those important regions to its list of Canadian service offerings. It opened service centres in Chicago, Illinois; Los Angeles, California and Detroit, Michigan to service those major international markets. Through strategic alliances formed with highly recognized regional carriers in the United States, it further expanded its service capabilities to capitalize on the rapidly changing realignment of the North American market brought about by the implementation of the North American Free Trade Agreement.

In January 1997, QUIK X Transportation Inc. opened its state-of-the-industry service centre, fleet maintenance centre and corporate offices on 12 acres in the Dixie and Derry Roads area of Mississauga, just west of Pearson International Airport.

Today, QUIK X Transportation Inc. services every major market within Canada, and between Canada and the United States with a standard of excellence that has come to be expected by its ever-growing base of loyal customers. QUIK X customers benefit from the company's cost-effective solutions, including reduced warehousing costs, reduced inventories, reduced order cycle times, reduced delivery times, increased emergency response capability and improved cash flow.

The QUIK X company slogan emphasizes its commitment to its customers: "Never satisfied…until you are!"

QUIK X maintains exclusive marketing partnerships with Southeastern Freight Lines, Inc., Silver Eagle Company, ANR Advance Transportation Company and West Ex.

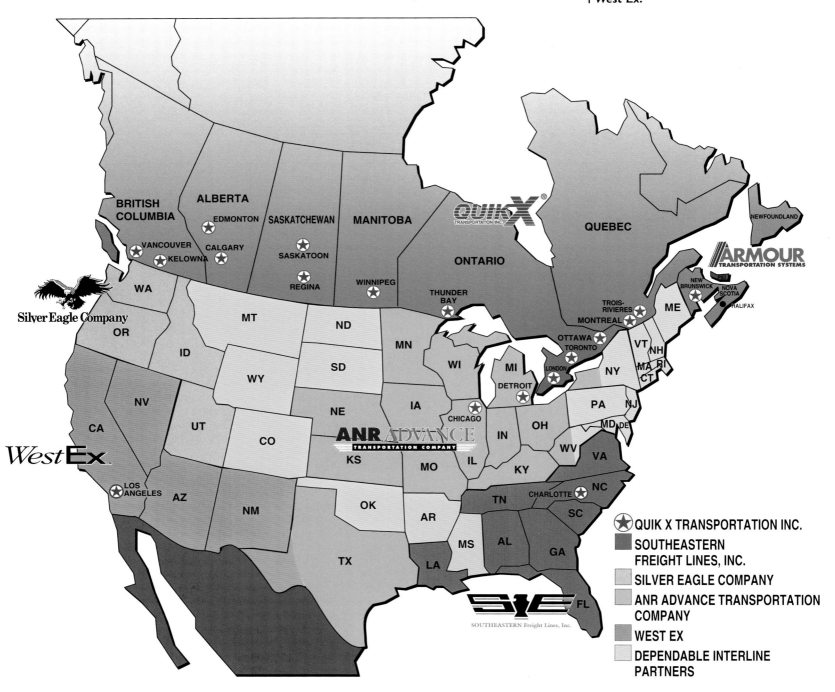

★ QUIK X TRANSPORTATION INC.
■ SOUTHEASTERN FREIGHT LINES, INC.
□ SILVER EAGLE COMPANY
■ ANR ADVANCE TRANSPORTATION COMPANY
■ WEST EX
□ DEPENDABLE INTERLINE PARTNERS

| QUIK X of Mississauga

In its determination to fulfil that promise QUIK X retains top-of-the-line equipment and technology along with experienced professionals dedicated to satisfying customers' expedited transportation needs. QUIK X can provide for just about any equipment need imaginable with its fleet of temperature-controlled "Air Ride" "Sleeper" tractors and High Cube trailers. QUIK X technology is second to none and features integrated on-line information systems, satellite tracking, mobile communications and document imaging.

It should come as no surprise that QUIK X is Canada's leading expedited carrier considering the company's track record for specializing in high-tech, high-value shipment handling. Delivery of high-quality service ranks foremost with QUIK X and is reflected in the following areas of distinction:

• LTL and TL service throughout Canada
• Canada's premier trade show carrier
• 99.7 per cent claims-free shipment handling
• Committed to error-free customer invoicing
• Committed to service perfection

QUIK X is the international transportation specialist. In fact, the company lists over 175 transportation centres throughout the United States and Canada. QUIK X streamlines the transportation challenges faced by customers by providing amenities such as no "break bulk" operations, non-stop over-the-road "expedited transportation and post audit privileges. QUIK X is bonded by both Canada and U.S. Customs and is skilled in customs clearance procedures.

QUIK X Transportation Inc. stands ready to meet the needs and exceed the service expectations of each and every transportation customer. Ⓜ

| Quik X tractor-trailer units

Standing, left to right: **Jeff King, controller; Dave Murray, vice-president, Sales; Bill Kimmel, vice-president, Marketing.** Seated, left to right: **Gary Babcock, president and CEO; Ed Powers, vice-president, Operations.**

*T*wo couriers meet in the middle of the night at their designated site, halfway between their home bases in the provinces of Ontario and Quebec. They quickly exchange packages, then return back the way they came to deliver the shipments to their customers.

Purolator Courier Ltd.

From such humble beginnings in the 1960s, Purolator Courier Ltd., then known as Trans Canadian Courier Ltd., now has over 11,000 dedicated employees across the country.

Tony Slade, one of the early employees of the company, is currently the senior vice-president, linehaul and fleet services. He has watched the company's ongoing growth and expansions over the last 29 years. "With our extensive network and wide range of services, we have established ourselves as the top Canadian courier," claims Slade. "As well, with the number of people working for us, we have also become one of Canada's larger employers."

The people at Purolator don't take this responsibility lightly. And they don't forget who helped make them become number one—a combination of hardworking employees and loyal customers.

"We value the loyalty of our customers," explains Ray Pedersen, senior vice-president, human resources and customer service centres, "but the loyalty of our employees is equally important. In such a changing market, we pride ourselves on the fact that our employees have stayed with us through the ups and downs. We have service anniversaries that range up to 30 years."

One of the great strengths of Purolator is its culture that encourages operations and sales personnel to customize services to meet the needs of customers. This has enabled the company to grow its business to a level that is twice that of the nearest competition.

Purolator also builds partnerships with fellow service providers. For example, in an important strategic move, Purolator introduced same-day delivery service nationwide in a partnership with Dynamex Courier. This was aimed at expanding Purolator's range of services to meet all the needs of its customers.

But it doesn't end there. This relationship building extends to the community, where Purolator has been involved with annual United Way campaigns, food and toy drives at

Purolator prides itself on its Canadian heritage and expertise. The company is 100-per cent Canadian owned and operated.

Purolator employees are committed to making shipping the easiest part of their customers' day.

Christmas, as well as supporting many other local groups and charities.

Proud to Be Canadian

Purolator also prides itself on its Canadian heritage and expertise. The company is 100-per cent Canadian owned and operated. "In many ways, along with some other outstanding Canadian corporations, we are a 'true Canadian treasure,'" declares Fred Manske Jr., president and CEO. "Let's face it—who else knows Canada better than its largest courier? We know the country, the people and the businesses."

The size of its operations network makes it possible for Purolator to help its customers better serve their customers. Whatever their shipping needs, customers can count on Purolator for ultra rush same-day messenger service within the same city, to overnight and even worldwide shipping to 180 countries.

"We try to work with our customers in whatever way is easiest for them," says Maurice Levy, senior vice-president, marketing and sales. "That means staying on top of technology, and offering a wide range of choices to our customers."

To that end, Purolator has developed services and deliveries that meet and exceed its customers' expectations, as well as outstanding technology to deliver on those promises. These features include Purolink shipping software, a leading-edge Web site, bilingual customer service and an extensive network of shipping centres and drop boxes.

Services for Every Need

Since its inception, Purolator has been committed to innovative, efficient ways to service

In addition to its air fleet, Purolator operates more than 2,900 courier vans and 600 highway trailers.

its customers. To meet this commitment, Purolator offers next-business-day delivery within Canada by 9 a.m. or 10:30 a.m. to more locations than any other courier, as well as next-day delivery by noon to all major locations across the country. Next-business-day delivery by noon to major cities in the U.S. is available with Purolator's USAM service.

In addition, Purolator is one of Canada's most experienced carriers of dangerous goods, providing safe and reliable transportation for many regulated materials within Canada and to the U.S.

Half a Million Packages Each Night!

Some people might wonder how Purolator can handle and track the amount of shipments that pass through their systems daily—over half a million packages each night.

In order to track all these packages, Purolator boasts Canada's most extensive bar code scanning system. "Packages are typically scanned five times from pick-up to delivery," states Jean-Francois Boyer, senior vice-president, national ground operations and hubs, "and this data is fed into the national computer mainframe. By calling customer service or accessing the company via the Internet or our Purolink software, tracing information is readily available from the date of pickup

Purolator offers next-business-day delivery within Canada by 9 a.m. or 10:30 a.m. to more locations than any other courier, as well as next-day delivery by noon to all major locations across the country.

right through to the final delivery. Once delivered, it even provides all the details regarding who signed for it and when."

Key components of this shipping process are the sortation facilities, as well as the planes and trucks that move the shipments.

To keep up with their growing demand, three new major air/ground facilities located at the Moncton, Winnipeg and Vancouver airports are nearing completion. Additional new facilities are planned for the Montreal area. This will ensure further capacity for Canada's largest courier.

Meanwhile, to satisfy its expanding air line-haul requirements, Purolator Courier Ltd. charters a dedicated fleet of 44 aircraft.

In addition to its air fleet, Purolator operates more than 2,900 courier vans and 600 highway trailers. Nearly 3,300 couriers, working from 81 regional terminals, pick up and deliver more packages than any other courier in Canada.

Purolator's mission is to continue to provide world-class service and innovative distribution solutions for its customers, now and into the next century. Employees are committed to making shipping the easiest part of their customers' day. ◍

$\mathcal{W}$ithin Canada, North America… And Everywhere There's a Roadway.

Backed by more than 26,000 transportation professionals, today's Reimer Express Lines Ltd. continues its tradition of quality. The year 1997 was an eventful one. It saw the friendly acquisition by Roadway Express result in a fully

Reimer Express Lines Ltd.

integrated seamless transportation system like no other in the world. Reimer's wide-ranging transportation services now include Canada, the United States, Mexico and 65 countries around the globe. That's a long way from the humble beginnings dating back to 1952.

Dr. D.S. Reimer's father and grandfather began by operating a general store and feed business in the small southern Manitoba community of Steinbach. They also purchased packing house by-products, used in animal feed production, in Winnipeg and sold them in the United States. The transportation of these products marked the beginning of Reimer Express Lines Ltd.

Today the founder, Dr. D.S. Reimer, remains as chairman.

Mississauga plays an important role in the Reimer system. It's home to approximately 250 employees and is the terminal for the Greater Toronto Area. Expansion of the Shawson Drive facility is a certainty due to recent sales growth.

Reimer Express Lines Ltd. is not a traditional trucking company. Its motto, verse and mission statement are well displayed in every facility across Canada. For many years Reimer Express Lines Ltd. has employed a full-time chaplain to offer counselling to any staff member. The chaplain and his wife are based in the Winnipeg head office but travel across the country visiting Reimer Express Lines Ltd. employees.

Reimer Express Lines Ltd. prides itself in offering quality service to its customers. It defines quality as meeting and exceeding customer requirements through continuous process improvement. Obviously, it has succeeded, because Reimer Express Lines Ltd. received the Canada Award for Business Excellence in Quality, the only company in the transportation sector ever to be so recognized. The award, given by the federal government, acknowledges the unmatched high level of superior performance of every Reimer Express Lines Ltd. employee.

Since 1982, Reimer Express Lines Ltd. has set the pace for Canada's expedited service through its Fast-as-Flite service. Reimer's direct-to-customer service helps major manufacturers and retailers eliminate costly interim warehousing. Reimer Express Lines Ltd. is so proud and confident of its efficient expedited service that it offers an On-Time-or-Free guarantee on major westbound lanes.

The Reimer Express Driver Training Institute Inc. is also a vital part of Reimer Express Lines Ltd.'s overall transport improvement. The school is a stand-alone entity and was initially created in the early 1970s to provide superior training for drivers at Reimer Express Lines Ltd. As the program expanded, the training institute matured to its current stature, whereby it provides driver training to the entire trucking industry.

It offers three programs—Earning Your Wheels, the Professional Driver Recognition Program, Certification Workshop, the Skills Upgrading Series of Modules for experienced drivers and the Business Skills Course for Owners-Operators. The institute has been so successful it has been accredited to deliver the driver training programs by the Canadian Trucking Human Resources Council (CTHRC).

There's an exciting new chapter being written at Reimer Express Lines Ltd. But through it all, the players haven't changed. And neither has their drive to succeed in every aspect of the transportation services they offer here in Mississauga, within Canada, the United States…and everywhere there's a roadway. $\mathbf{M}$

$\mathcal{B}$ML Leasing, founded in 1975, is one of Canada's largest fleet management firms, serving companies with a handful to a thousand vehicles of all makes and models and providing those companies with the trouble-free fleet operations they require to run their businesses effectively.

BML Leasing Limited

Some of Canada's biggest corporations are served from BML's head office, relocated two years ago to Mississauga to take advantage of a very welcoming business environment and the benefits that accrue in a well-run city, and from its regional offices in Montreal and Calgary. For clients with international interests, BML provides the highest level of service through partnership in a "best in country" association of fleet management companies.

As a subsidiary of Commcorp Financial Services, which has more than $2 billion in assets, BML boasts an enviable financial stability and strength.

Doug Leith, BML's founder, president and CEO, says it's not only the company's size that benefits customers. He notes that BML is also the only Canadian-owned leasing company with the ability to provide the full range of fleet management services on a national basis. "We've developed specifically to address the needs of the Canadian market, with continuing input from our clients, and can quickly adjust priorities to respond to our clients because the systems and managerial control are here."

BML's head office is located in the Airport Corporate Centre, with excellent access to the airport and to the network of freeways which service the total Metropolitan area.

BML was formed to capitalize on the need for what Leith calls a "high-touch, high-tech" fleet management firm. "We offer personalized service by knowledgeable, experienced service-minded people, who are supported by the most advanced technology."

Every service and software program is designed in-house to address each client's information and management needs, creating an unparalleled data resource that maximizes efficiency and minimizes costs.

The company pioneered computer access in the 1970s as the first fleet management company to offer on-line communication, a facility that allowed customers to have direct access to all their fleet data, e.g. maintenance history, vehicle inventory, vehicles on order, vehicles for sale, and has since become an integral facet of corporate fleet management. BML can, for example, maintain a full current history of every driver, can communicate directly with drivers through their laptops, and can transmit billing information to a client's cost centres in moments. In turn, clients can access any BML data and create their own reports on-line. BML also places, monitors and expedites vehicle orders through its on-line links with auto manufacturers.

BML innovations include the Fleet Kit Instruction Cassette, which accompanies the Fleet Card issued to drivers for all operating requirements. The company's service specialists provide advice to drivers, fleet managers and repair facilities directly, ensuring low-cost solutions to vehicle problems.

Through the card's usage, BML can also give clients the detailed statistical reports needed for fleet management, budgeting and long-range planning.

About 25-30 per cent of clients outsource their

BML finds, hires and keeps the best people in the business because the company believes experience, dedication and consistency are essential to the long-term relationships it has with its customers.

total fleet administration to BML. This option is becoming increasingly popular as companies get back to their core businesses.

Other imaginative BML services include an employee lease program and a lease again program where clients' staff can take advantage of preferential pricing and leasing expertise, or can personally take over off-lease corporate vehicles. A safety program was developed and introduced in 1988, and a claims control service handles accident management and reporting, through to prompt repair at controlled costs.

You might say that with all its "high-touch" services, BML is a fleet management company that's driven...customer-driven. **Ⓜ**

John Crawford Sr. dreamed that one day his son, John Jr., would someday work with him in his business. John Sr. started the company in 1985 as J.S. Crawford & Son Transport Inc., even though John Jr. was just 19 at the time. His dream became a reality. John Jr. now handles the day-to-day operation

than four years old. I'd match our fleet and the professionalism of our drivers with any competitor in North America."

J.S. Crawford & Son services the LTL (less than truckload) market for shipments to and from the U.S.A. within a 1,500-mile radius of Mississauga. The core business is to the

J.S. Crawford & Son is a fully licensed and bonded carrier in both Canada and the United States and hauls everything from confections to computers, furniture to machinery. It was the first Canadian company to utilize satellite tracking technology, equipping its entire fleet in 1991. The company operates 24 hours a

J.S. Crawford & Son Transport Inc.

day and has a modern, fully equipped M.T.O. Certified maintenance facility at its Mississauga yard.

"Mississauga is perfectly situated for our purposes," says John Crawford Jr. "It has immediate access to Ontario's major highways and is conveniently located within the Greater Toronto Area. We are very comfortable here. Our slogan is 'Large enough to serve you, small enough to care.' We never lose sight of our roots. We're proud to be Canadian, proud to be truckers and proud to put the Crawford name on our equipment. Our two biggest assets are our people and our fleet."

His father's dream has come true, and John Jr., the fourth generation of Crawfords to bear the name John Sinclair, also has a son named John. It's not difficult to visualize another Crawford carrying on the family dream. Ⓜ

Left to right: **John Crawford Jr. and John Crawford Sr.**

of the company, while John Sr. enjoys semi-retirement in the Florida sunshine during the long Canadian winters. When at home in Mississauga, John Sr. can still be found chatting with the company's drivers at a local coffee shop.

The company has always operated on a personal, open-door policy. Many of the company's original drivers are still with the company, as are many of its original customers, a tribute to the high level of service provided.

"Dad started this business with 3 trucks and 5 trailers," says John Jr. "I started out on the loading docks, then went out on the road for several years before joining the rest of the family in the office. We now have 65 tractors and 125 trailers, and more than 100 employees, but we haven't lost touch with our 'family of employees.' Our employees aren't just numbers. We treat everyone with respect and always focus on the positive. When drivers hire on with us, we hope they are hiring on for life. Drivers are paid higher than average wages, and are provided with top-of-the-line equipment. None of our power units is more

Chicago area and along the U.S. northeast seaboard, ranging from Baltimore, MD, to Boston, MA, with direct service to the New York City area a specialty. Satellite terminals are maintained at Perth Amboy, NJ, and Chicago, IL, with plans to make both locations full terminals within five years.

"Large enough to serve you, small enough to care": The J.S. Crawford family of employees

CHAPTER 12

High Tech, Biotech & Info Tech

Ⓜ

Photo by Michael Scholz

It was 1967, and the first minicomputer had just been introduced, when Rod Coutts, then 27, got together with fellow engineering colleague Lawrence Cragg to form Teklogix.

Working from the basement of Cragg's home in Mississauga, the two soon attracted three other colleagues, Peter Halsall, Clifford

Teklogix International Inc.

Bernard and Al Vanderburgh, to spearhead the development of automation technology.

Three decades later, Teklogix is a global leader in the design and manufacture of wireless data communication systems. And Coutts, who became the company's chairman, president and CEO in 1992, now oversees a company of about 500 people worldwide, 250 of them in Mississauga.

Teklogix's headquarters at 2100 Meadowvale Boulevard houses manufacturing, research and development, and administrative functions.

"We were one of the pioneers in the wireless field," said Coutts. "The company began focusing on developing wireless data communications equipment in the early 1980s, but it wasn't until the early 1990s that sales started to take off."

In 1992, revenue was $16.6 million. By fiscal 1996, sales had jumped fivefold to $92.5 million.

Today, *Fortune* 1,000 companies worldwide, including General Motors, Georgia Ports Authority, Mercedes-Benz, Nippon Express, Estee Lauder and Hertz Corp., look to Teklogix's wireless data communication system to reduce their distribution costs, increase efficiencies and enhance customer responsiveness.

Teklogix's wireless system is designed for organizations with a mobile workforce and a need for real-time interactive data communications. Typically used by manufacturing, retail, service and transportation sectors, the system consists of a radio frequency-based network that incorporates bar code scanners, hand-held

Teklogix wireless data terminals serve the intermodal industry.

and vehicle-mount computers, base or repeater stations and network controllers. The system is controlled by the company's network management software.

For example, when Nippon Express, the world's largest private freight agency, needed a cost-effective inventory tracking system to keep thousands of shipments on the go and to inform its customers about the status of their merchandise, it turned to Teklogix. Employing Teklogix's wireless system, which included vehicle-mount communication terminals, Nippon Express was able to quickly scan bar-coded shipments as they arrived, then transport and ship them out of the warehouse. Teklogix's wireless technology ensured real-time communications between staff on the warehouse floor, the host computer and the end customer.

At the Georgia Ports Authority (GPA), the challenge was to develop an accurate method for tracking and recording the contents and location of the more than 30,000 containers that arrive via ship, train or truck each day. The GPA also looked to Teklogix.

The GPA installed Teklogix's narrow-band wireless data communication system that provided coverage over the 853-acre site. Wireless terminals were installed on all toplift equipment, yard trucks and supervisory vehicles. Staff working at the container port were also equipped with hand-held units. The terminals provided direct communication access to the mainframe computer system, which verifies and records all port activities in real time.

And when Hertz was looking for a quick and easy way for customers to return rental vehicles, Teklogix was there to create an "instant return" program for the company. As a customer drives up to Hertz, an employee using a Teklogix hand-held unit would be able to greet the customer and produce a receipt for him or her on the spot. There is no need for the customer to return to the counter.

With a leadership position in the design, production and implementation of wireless data communications solutions, Teklogix is well positioned to capitalize on the burgeoning

logistics management market, estimated to be worth some $3 billion worldwide.

Thus far, Teklogix's system has been installed in more than 40 countries. That number is expected to rise to more than 50 in the near future. Almost 96 per cent of Teklogix's sales are now generated outside of Canada.

To fuel its growth and raise funds for a new $9-million state-of-the-art world headquarters at 2100 Meadowvale Boulevard in Mississauga,

"We are a results-driven company. We believe in team building, finding the right people, placing them in the right jobs and then giving them the freedom to run the business as they see fit. For example, the American company looks like an American company, and our German division is headed by a German national."

Success was also driven by the company's decision to concentrate its product development on wireless data communications for commercial applications.

units are already in use by the Tampa Police Department.

"The Teklogix wireless technology," Coutts pointed out, "is relatively stable in terms of where we're going. We are going to see more and more wireless applications in the next few years."

Although international business will account for the majority of Teklogix's revenues in the next few years, Coutts is determined to maintain the company's roots in Mississauga.

"The fact that we spent $9 million on a new world headquarters here in Mississauga is indicative of our commitment to the city, to our employees and to the economic climate here," Coutts said. "It's hard to beat Mississauga for its quality of life. We will be here for the long term. It's our home." **Ⓜ**

A Rite Aid worker uses a Teklogix vehicle-mount terminal for warehousing and distribution activities.

Teklogix went public in September 1995, raising $47.5 million. A significant number of the company's outstanding shares are owned by its employees.

The headquarters, which were completed in the summer of 1996, house manufacturing, research and development, and administrative functions. Its boardrooms bear the names of the five company co-founders and names of Teklogix's past street addresses.

Having grown beyond Mississauga, the company now has sales offices in Cincinnati, Chicago, Santa Rosa, Tampa, Atlanta and Wilmington, as well as international offices in London, Paris, Dusseldorf, Goteborg, Milan, Mexico City, Sao Paulo, Buenos Aires, Santiago and Singapore, and a network of independent distributors in the Middle East, Europe, the Pacific Rim and Australia.

Coutts attributes the company's strong growth to a number of reasons, one of which is acquiring good people.

"Teklogix has developed a global reputation for leading virtually every major technology development in our wireless niche," Coutts said.

Teklogix also received the prestigious ISO 9001 registration in early 1996, further indicating its adherence to quality in the design, manufacture and service areas. The ISO standards are the most comprehensive in the world and are recognized in more than 60 countries.

To further enhance its competitive position and maximize its future growth potential, Teklogix acquired Badger Computers, a division of Tampa, Florida-based Group Technologies Corp. The acquisition provided Teklogix with "rugged" mobile notebook computers which can communicate data wirelessly over a wide-area network. They were manufactured for use by transportation companies as well as field service and police and ambulance services.

The move paid off almost immediately when Teklogix was awarded a contract to supply more than 1,100 of the mobile computers, docking stations, technical support and service to the Chicago Police Department. The

A Tampa police officer communicates wirelessly through Teklogix's rugged notebook computer.

*O*verall, DiverseyLever has a physical presence in 60 countries, with a combined workforce of over 12,000 and annual global sales of $2.5 billion (Canadian dollars). In Mississauga, DiverseyLever has a dual presence. It is headquarters for the Canadian operating company (located in Clarkson) and is

DiverseyLever

Corporate Headquarters for the global Food and Beverage business unit (an office near Mississauga's City Centre). This office also houses two groups with global responsibility in the Institutional and Laundry Group. These are the Business Development of Health Care, Hotels, Restaurants and Quick Service market sectors and the International Account Group responsible for managing relationships with major global customers.

"The average person may not know about DiverseyLever because we're not a consumer products company," says David Hull, country manager and senior vice-president, Food and Beverage. "But to our customers, we are critical to their ability to maintain standards of cleanliness and hygiene."

DiverseyLever brought together two of the industry's most respected research and development resources and expanded its distribution networks and international coverage.

Customers ranging from a small restaurant to Coca-Cola, Holiday Inn and McDonald's realize their reputation rides not only on what they sell but also on the integrity of their processes—their kitchen, their laundry, and the inside and outside of their production equipment. The aim is to develop products and systems that give the restaurant, hotel, hospital or food producer end-users "peace of mind."

It's no exaggeration to say that cleanliness can be a life-and-death issue. Imagine what would happen, for example, to a food processor and its consumers if a product line suffered bacterial infection because of a shortcoming at the plant. DiverseyLever's traditional strength comes from using global resources to develop top-quality cleaning and hygiene processes, with service and customer care focused at the local level. "However, in the new global marketplace, our value proposition goes a long way beyond supplying chemicals," says Steve West, vice-president, Business Development-Food and Beverage. "We are now in the business of working with the totality of our customers' process and finding ways to optimise and improve their overall plant performance and create value through a total service offering."

For instance, DiverseyLever employs application experts, familiar with their customers' manufacturing processes, who are able to ensure protection of client brand integrity through superior microbiological results.

DiverseyLever markets products and systems critical to maintaining standards of cleanliness and hygiene in the restaurant, hotel, hospital and food-producing industries.

Complementing the company's products and advice are total support packages, which include hygiene audits, user training and even software that helps users schedule operations for the best results at the lowest cost.

Though DiverseyLever only officially came into being in 1996, the company has a rich tradition on both sides.

In 1885 in England, William and James Lever formed Lever Brothers, and introduced the world's first packaged and branded laundry soap. Called Sunlight, it was marketed as an alternative to the "wash day evil" of other soaps that took their toll on a woman's skin.

The soap business can be seen as the basis for the company's eventual expansion into cleaning products for industrial and institutional customers. But that represents just one aspect of an incredibly diverse company, which in 1930 changed its name to Unilever.

Through intensive product development and shrewd acquisitions, Unilever now markets over 1,000 brands, from ice cream (Good Humor) and cosmetics (Calvin Klein), to spaghetti sauce (Ragu) and detergent (All). Unilever employs over 300,000 people worldwide in over 90 countries, has sales in another 70, and is ranked near the top of the *Fortune* 500 list.

The company's Diversey roots go back to 1923, when Diversey Corporation was born in Chicago as a subsidiary of the Victor Chemical Company. The new company, which took its name from a local street, aimed to sell specially formulated chemical cleaning and sanitizing products. An important early innovation was Diversol, a dry crystal which didn't freeze in the Midwestern winter, and was used to sanitize dairy equipment.

Diversey incorporated a Canadian operation in 1937, and in 1950 commissioned a plant in Port Credit—the beginning of its history in Mississauga. Three years later, Diversey bought 22 acres of land in Clarkson for a factory to formulate products and produce raw material.

Aggressive expansion and acquisitions turned Diversey into an international force. Interestingly, market penetration in Canada was higher than anywhere else in the world. In 1978, Molson acquired Diversey Corporation and four years later moved its corporate world headquarters from Chicago to Mississauga.

It was Molson's sale to Unilever of most of Diversey that created DiverseyLever. The coming together of Diversey and Lever Industrial International made perfect sense. Unilever is a European-based company, with greater strength on the cleaning and hygiene side of its business in that continent than in North America. Conversely, Diversey, though active worldwide, was dominant in the industry in Canada.

As a unified entity, DiverseyLever brought together two of the industry's most respected research and development resources, combined cleaning and product systems for an even more complete range, and expanded distribution networks and international coverage.

Canadian operations now include more than 10,000 customers across the country, with plants in Vancouver, Edmonton, Winnipeg and Montreal, as well as in the home base of Mississauga.

"Global hotel, catering and restaurant chains value the consistently high cleaning standards and staff training we provide. That fuels our growth in every country," says Dr. Susan Quinn-Mullins, director of Business Development for Lodging and Health Care.

As a driver of DiverseyLever's growth, she cites rapidly expanding markets in the developing world, where improving economic conditions are raising the standards of hygiene. Meanwhile, as DiverseyLever's multinational customers enter these emerging markets, they look to existing suppliers to maintain their established standards. A beverage-maker, for example, would want precisely the same hygienic environment in its bottling plants, wherever those plants operate.

With a commitment to providing the highest quality products and systems, DiverseyLever is making a clean break into an even brighter future. Ⓜ

The DiverseyLever floor-care system is just one example of the company's commitment to providing the highest quality products and systems.

*T*he first thing that strikes you about Pharmacia & Upjohn is its logo—a stone bearing the symbols of a hand, a star and a bird. Resembling the markings you might find on a cave wall, the casually drawn symbol is not what you would normally associate with the precise and scientific world of pharmaceuticals.

Pharmacia & Upjohn Inc.

Then again, Pharmacia & Upjohn strives to stand apart in its industry. Consider the logo's meaning, which the research-based company says "crosses time and all cultural boundaries."

The stone signifies strength, durability and permanence. The hand denotes human inventiveness, friendship and communication. The star stands for inspiration that stimulates the human imagination to wonder what is possible. And the bird implies challenge and hope.

Left to right: **Dr. Nicola Di Pietro, vice-president, Medical & Pharmacaoeconomics, Colin R. Campbell, vice-president, Finance & Administration, and Robert J. Little, president. In the background is the new company logo which symbolizes humanity, innovation and aspiration within strength.**

As for the company's strength, you don't have to look any further than its name. The result of a 1995 merger between Swedish firm Pharmacia AB and United States-based The Upjohn Company, the combined company has revenues of $7 billion U.S.

That makes Pharmacia & Upjohn, now based in London, England, one of the top 10 pharmaceutical companies in the world. While that's impressive, the company's stated goal is to become one of the top 5 in the industry.

The company sells products in more than 100 countries and cooperates with thousands of hospitals, universities and research centres. In Canada, you'll find Pharmacia & Upjohn's national headquarters on Spectrum Way in Mississauga. Opening in late summer 1997, this four-floor, custom-built facility houses all head office departments, as well as a clinical research division.

"Our goal is to become a very significant contributor within the Pharmacia & Upjohn

| **The Canadian headquarters, located at Spectrum Way, Mississauga**

corporate world," says Robert Little, president of the Canadian operations.

While the Pharmacia side of the business was already located in Mississauga, The Upjohn Company of Canada had been based in North York (where a distribution centre remains). When it came time to find a new location after the merger, Mississauga was a natural choice.

"Mississauga is good to business," states Colin Campbell, the company's vice-president, Finance and Administration.

He cites the significant tax savings of locating here, and says it didn't hurt that a stretch of Mississauga is known as "Pill Hill" because of the prevalence of pharmaceutical companies. That provides what he calls an "excellent" local talent pool for the entire industry.

Though Pharmacia & Upjohn as a combined entity is young, the company's roots go back to 1886. That's when Dr. William Upjohn formed the Upjohn Pill & Granule Company in Kalamazoo, Michigan.

His patented pill, which disintegrated easily after being swallowed, formed the company's early success—some pills of the day wouldn't crumble even when hit by a hammer. His company established a Canadian office in

biotechnological research and production, with an operation in Montreal).

Little calls Pharmacia & Upjohn "compassionate and caring." He is referring to the company's corporate culture, its support of health care charities (and its matching of staff's donations) and, of course, its products. The "hand" of Pharmacia & Upjohn, its human inventiveness, is countless prescription and non-prescription products that make a critical difference in people's lives.

Most consumers may be familiar with Pharmacia & Upjohn through the company's over-the-counter brands—names like Motrin IB (an analgesic), Dramamine (anti-motion sickness), Nicorette (nicotine replacement) and Rogaine (hair loss treatment). Some prescription drugs are also well known, like Ansaid (arthritis) or Provera (hormone replacement).

Yet many other breakthrough products are best known only within the medical community and by the patients who benefit from them. These are the drugs that are used to treat cancer (Adriamycin), AIDS (Rescriptor), glaucoma (Xalatan), heart disease (Kabikinase), diabetes (Glynase) and much more.

Getting products to market requires two things: innovative research ideas, and the funding to back up these efforts. Pharmacia & Upjohn is committed to both, boasting a $1 billion-plus annual R&D budget and more than 4000 researchers worldwide.

In Canada, approximately 13 per cent of 1996 sales went back into R&D, more than the 10 per cent level the Canadian pharmaceutical industry is mandated to spend. The result is imaginative products that fill a vacuum in medical science— symbolized by the inspirational star in the company's logo.

"We won't come out with 'me-too' products," says Campbell. "Our vision is to create value through generating products that satisfy unmet medical needs."

Research is focused mainly on five therapeutic areas: infectious diseases, metabolic diseases, central nervous system diseases, oncology, and inflammatory diseases. Other areas of R&D include thrombosis, critical care, women's health, nutrition, opthalmology, and urology.

"Everything we do has to translate into patient benefits, not just relating to survival but to a fuller life, a life with enjoyment and satisfaction," says Nicola Di Pietro, vice-president, Medical Affairs and Pharmacoeconomics.

Drug development is a lengthy process, taking perhaps 10 to 15 years from a research spark to a finished product. The total R&D expenditure for a new, original medicine, including clinical trials, can be upwards of $500 million.

Pharmacia & Upjohn coordinates its R&D resources globally to reduce development time, getting products into the hands of patients with a minimum of delay. Other development initiatives focus on identifying new applications for existing products, or testing whether a product can treat a wider range of diseases.

It's an effort that promises a healthier future for patients worldwide as Pharmacia & Upjohn, like the bird in its logo, challenges itself to reach new heights. "Our mission is to save lives and improve the quality of life," says Little, "to bring people hope." ⓜ

Pharmacia & Upjohn's mission is to help people live longer and fuller lives by meeting medical needs through innovative research and development.

1935, one year before launching a notable product that's still on the market: Kaopectate.

Today, Pharmacia & Upjohn ensures a steady flow of new products through its Pharma Product Centres. Each one is responsible for research, development, production and strategic marketing in one or more therapeutic areas. A network of market companies— Pharmacia & Upjohn Inc. in Mississauga being one—are then responsible for sales and contacts with pharmaceutical authorities.

The company also consists of a Consumer Healthcare Unit (non-prescription pharmaceuticals) and several affiliated businesses: Animal Health (pharmaceuticals and feed additives, with a Canadian presence in Orangeville, Ont.), Diagnostics (allergy testing), Pharmaceutical Commercial Services (pharmaceutical chemicals), Pharmacia Biosensor (biomolecule analysis) and Pharmacia Biotech (chemicals and systems for

Robert J. Little, president of Pharmacia & Upjohn Inc.

*T*he name Xerox has been synonymous with the photocopying of documents since production began on the first commercial copier, the Xerox 914, in 1959.

Today, Xerox is no longer just a manufacturer of photocopiers. Its range of products includes analogue and digital copiers, digital

The Document Company—Xerox

colour laser printers and copiers, electronic printers, facsimile terminals and network systems, professional workstations, scanning systems and engineering/graphic and work-flow management software products. Xerox also provides all the supplies its customers need to run their office equipment. Beyond hardware and software solutions, Xerox offers consulting expertise in document management.

This focus on the document resulted in the 1994 name and logo change to better reflect

| The Xerox Document Centre

what it is and what Xerox does. The new name, The Document Company—Xerox, reflects this philosophical change and the new logo includes a red digitized X symbol. These alterations follow the company's change from being a traditional copier manufacturer to the digital pioneer and document-based consultant it has become.

The new corporate signature underscores a commitment to provide the industry's most comprehensive document services—products, systems, solutions and support—that enable printing, scanning, faxing and colour in addition to copying.

Xerox Canada plays an integral role in the overall Xerox structure. The first Canadian office opened in 1953 with just 116 employees. Today, Xerox Canada employs more than 4,000 people across the country and services its customers through sales offices in most major Canadian cities as well as through selected alternate channels such as retail stores, sales agents and value-added resellers.

During the 1970s, Xerox felt that it was necessary to increase the Canadian content of its products marketed in this country. Thus evolved the Canadian Value Added program which was established to manufacture photocopying equipment, to conduct research and to procure parts and components from Canadian suppliers for Xerox companies around the world.

As a result, the first photocopier manufactured in Canada came off the Xerox Canada production line in January 1974. Later that same year, the Xerox Research Centre of Canada opened in Mississauga. This benchmark facility has a worldwide mandate to conduct research in the design and development of materials for Xerox document processing products and is home to some 100 scientists and technologists. Ongoing work is currently being done on such materials as transparencies, inks, toners, specialty chemicals, developers and photoreceptors.

Xerox Canada manufactures document handler devices and colour toner for Xerox worldwide. To support these efforts, Xerox purchases parts and components for the manufacture and servicing of Xerox equipment from more than 30 Canadian-based suppliers. The company has received numerous national and worldwide awards for its ongoing commitment to protect the environment through the recycling of packaging materials, toner cartridges, major components of used machines and recycling of waste materials.

Both the current and the future goal of Xerox is to be the preferred vendor in the document services industry, offering customers total solutions to meet their business needs. It will achieve this goal through customer satisfaction.

The company has also made Leadership Through Quality the basis of its corporate culture. Three key pillars of this strategy include:
- a dedication to understanding customer requirements;
- a work culture and ethic which makes every employee responsible for quality improvement;
- a management style that encourages employees to reach their maximum potential.

Xerox recognizes that the workplace of tomorrow will be profoundly different from today's. A greater number of employees work outside the traditional office framework—either from a customer location or from home. All Xerox sales and service representatives use the latest laptop computer technology to manage their business. Their office is where it needs to be—in front of the customer.

The key element for the company's future success lies in providing customer satisfaction through immediate response to service problems or inquiries. As a result, a National Call Centre was set up in Saint John, New Brunswick, in 1995. The centre's 170 full- and part-time employees handle more than 9,000 calls a day—every day of the week, every week of the year.

Xerox helps customers, both large and small, manage the shift in office technology towards the digital document. One solution that addresses this requirement is a new family of Xerox digital document products that combine copying, laser printing and faxing throughout a distributed network. These Document Centre Systems offer businesses a quantum leap in workplace technology, delivering immediate and tangible benefits in terms of office productivity.

In addition, colour has become the new standard for business communications. Xerox is committed to making this technology more accessible (and affordable) for more customers through a wide range of colour output devices from desktop printers to production colour systems.

Other customers find it strategically important to outsource their document services to Xerox Business Services (XBS). XBS can manage any aspect of the document life cycle: printing, publishing, office equipment and technology management, mailroom and distribution services, archiving and more. Xerox has helped government agencies, private corporations and small businesses improve productivity, free up resources to focus on core services and avoid heavy capital investments in equipment.

Canadians are embracing the power of change and adopting technology and innovation in order to capture opportunities. The result, Xerox believes, will be a Canada that is more competitive and productive.

In order to give back to the community, as well as, support this vision of a more prosperous Canada, Xerox has redefined its Corporate Contributions Program to support projects and

initiatives which will help Canadians acquire Information Technology Literacy (ITL). ITL represents the skills knowledge and ability an individual requires to use information technology comfortably.

As Canadians face the challenges and opportunities presented by our fast-changing world, The Document Company—Xerox will continue to offer innovative and unique solutions to meet and exceed their needs. **Ⓜ**

Scientists at the Mississauga Research Centre have a mandate to conduct research in the design and development of materials for Xerox document processing products.

The Document Company—Xerox Research Centre opened in Mississauga in 1974 and is home to some 100 scientists and technologists.

*I*f you associate laboratory equipment only with medical science, think again. In settings ranging from beverage manufacturers to educational institutions, VWR Canlab products are helping some 44,000 customers meet their research needs.

"We serve all disciplines, anywhere something has to be tested," says Pete Forrest, general manager for VWR Canlab.

VWR Canlab

The company is Canada's largest national distributor of lab equipment, chemicals and supplies, from simple beakers to solvents for analyses to the most sophisticated scientific instrumentation.

VWR Canlab's customers include those in the clinical field—i.e. hospital and medical labs, university and government laboratories. But the company sells more equipment and supplies to industrial customers than any other segment.

These customers are involved in such diverse

VWR Canlab sources and distributes over 5,000 scientific supplies and instrumentation under their own brand label.

industries as pharmaceuticals, biotechnology, food and beverage, forestry, chemicals, cosmetics, pulp and paper, mining and metals, aerotechnology, petroleum and much more.

All VWR Canlab customers benefit from the widest selection of lab products in Canada, the diverse scientific backgrounds of their sales and customer service associates and the top shipping service levels in the industry. The company distributes more than 350,000 products from over 2,000 quality manufacturers, and offers another 5,000 products under its own brand.

"Our VWR brand private label gives customers the same high quality at a much more competitive price," says Forrest. "For us, another advantage is that it gets the VWR name out in front of people, raising our brand awareness."

Because laboratory needs are always changing, VWR Canlab also actively and continually monitors the market for new and innovative products.

Their product portfolio and market share rose dramatically in 1994, with the purchase of Baxter Canlab by VWR Scientific.

Peter Forrest, vice-president and general manager of VWR Canlab believes the company's VWR brand label offers its customers a more competitive price for the same high-quality products.

The combined company is a wholly-owned subsidiary of VWR Scientific Products Corporation, a multinational firm that boasts 130,000 customers and well over $700 million (U.S.) a year in sales.

After the acquisition, VWR Canlab established itself in Mississauga. Both companies have served the scientific research field since the early 1900s, and have a rich tradition in Canada.

In fact, Canadian Laboratory Supplies, which evolved into Canlab, played a supporting role in one of the country's greatest medical achievements. Back in the 1920s one of their first customers was researchers Frederick Banting and Charles Best, who used the lab products in their Nobel Prize-winning discovery of insulin.

VWR itself discovered and embraced what is now called "partnering," long before the concept was in vogue. Today the company, which also has offices in Montreal and Edmonton, adds value to customer relationships by helping them reduce costs through reviews of their purchasing and logistics practices.

"A number of firms have selected us as their primary vendor or sole supplier," says Forrest. "Because of our breadth of product, and the fact we operate coast to coast, they can reduce the suppliers they deal with, and drive costs out of their system."

You don't need a lab to confirm that that's a formula for success. **Ⓜ**

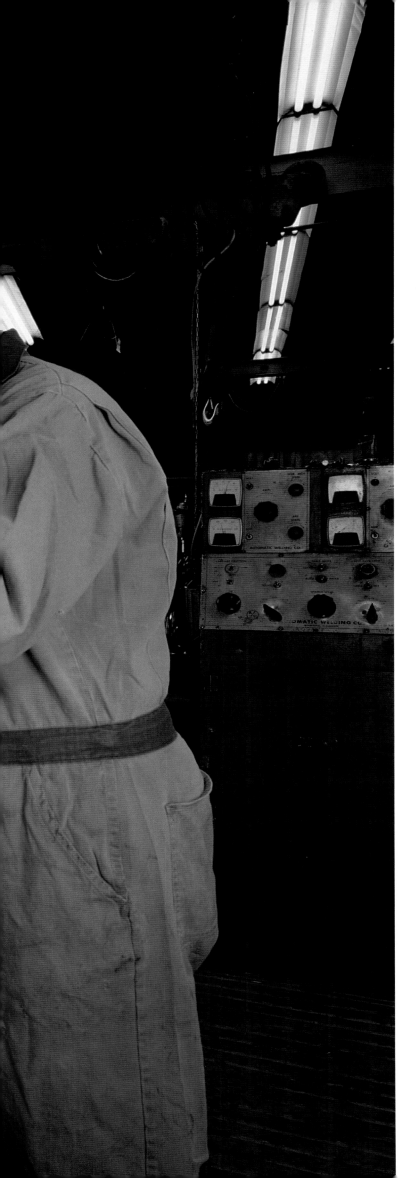

Manufacturing & Distribution

Ⓜ

Photo by Michael Scholz

$\mathcal{W}$hether you drive on the highways of Ontario, depart the runways of Pearson International Airport, ride an elevator in an office high-rise or play with your children at the local playground, St. Lawrence Cement has likely played a part in the construction.

When the St. Lawrence Cement (SLC)

St. Lawrence Cement

Mississauga plant opened in 1956, it took more than 4 million labour-hours to complete, becoming one of the largest and most modern cement plants ever built. Over the more than 40 years since, St. Lawrence Cement has improved and upgraded its operations, maintaining this proud distinction.

It currently produces about 23 per cent of the total cement needs for all of Canada. Holderbank Financiere, the largest cement manufacturer in the world, is St. Lawrence Cement's largest shareholder (58 per cent). Canadians own about 39 per cent of SLC. Holderbank has more than 75 years of experience in the business and conducts operations in 25 countries.

Originally, the plant housed two wet process kilns with a capacity of 1,700 tonnes per day

St. Lawrence Cement's Mississauga Plant is home to more than 200 employees.

(tpd). In 1968, the size of the plant increased dramatically with the startup of a 3,000 tpd preheater kiln, then the largest kiln ever constructed in North America. In 1971, further cement grinding capacity was required, and a 3,500-horsepower mill was moved to the Mississauga plant from St. Lawrence Cement's Beauport, Quebec, plant.

In 1974, Cement Mill No. 7 was installed. It was one of the largest cement mills in North America and featured an 8,700-hp ring motor. Today, total plant capacity approaches 2 million tonnes of cement per year.

However, improvements to the Mississauga plant extend well beyond the grinding process. In 1988, the addition of a precalciner increased the capacity of kiln No. 3 to 4,300 tonnes per day. Other operating features include the large storage hall, housing the coal and clinker used in the cement manufacturing process.

While we routinely refer to various types of substances as "cement," there are a variety of cements designed for specific purposes. One of the more common forms is Portland. Other

SLC's Kiln Exhaust Gas Baghouse was constructed in 1996 as part of the company's ongoing efforts to maintain a clean local environment.

types include mobile cement, High Early cement, HSF cement, masonry and slag. Cement is a powder that reacts with water to form a rock-like material. It is used as the binding ingredient in concrete. Cement, itself, is made up of earth materials such as limestone, clay, sand and shale.

"Natural" cement (burnt limestone) has been with us for thousands of years, and many early cement structures, such as the Roman Pantheon, built in 138 A.D., still remain. In 19th-century England, a bricklayer named Joseph Aspdin registered his patent for creating "artificial stone" by pulverizing lime and clay materials. Resembling a type of stone quarried on the Isle of Portland off the English coast, he named it "Portland" cement.

The first rotary kiln was invented back in 1885, and Thomas Edison, better known for his breakthroughs in the use of electricity, was one of the pioneers in improving Aspdin's process, providing a more efficient means of burning the raw materials for producing cement.

Toronto's SkyDome and CN Tower; Hibernia, off the coast of Newfoundland; the Fixed Link to Prince Edward Island; the Sunshine Skyway in Tampa, Florida and the Sears Tower are examples of modern concrete structures.

The Mississauga cement manufacturing process actually starts at SLC's Colborne quarry, located 160 kilometres east of Toronto. This large geological formation is known as "Trenton

Visitors listen to an explanation of plant procedures during a tour at SLC's 40th Anniversary Open House held in September 1996.

Limestone" and represents more than 200 years of resources in reserve.

The limestone face is drilled with holes 18 metres deep by drills specifically designed to reduce dust emissions. Thirty-six thousand tonnes of rock are loosened with each blast. The free stone is then transported via quarry trucks to a crusher, from where it is moved on a conveyor to a dock for loading onto lake ships. Lakers have a single-load capacity of 18,000 tonnes and make four trips per week to ensure company production needs.

The limestone is unloaded at the Mississauga dock and carried on a 1.6-kilometre covered conveyor to a limestone stockpile. Stone is drawn from the bottom of this pile into the Aerofall Mill, where it is ground to a powder at a rate of 280 tonnes per hour. This process ensures that the resulting powder, known as raw meal, is uniform in size and chemistry. The raw meal is tested and transported by conveyor belt to storage silos at the feed end of the kiln.

The second step is kiln processing. A pre-heater, pre-calciner system is used to swirl the raw meal down a series of cyclones against the stream of hot gases from the kiln. The intense heat is necessary to effect chemical changes in the raw meal. The raw meal enters the huge, rotating furnace known as the kiln, where temperatures exceed 1,450 degrees Celsius. As raw meal tumbles through the kiln, it becomes partially molten, causing molecular changes that result in new minerals—calcium silicates—forming.

These calcium silicates have special hydraulic properties, allowing them to react with water to form a hard mass (clinker)—the distinguishing component of cement. The white-hot clinker is air-cooled, sampled, analyzed and moved by conveyor for storage in silos with a total capacity of 150,000 tonnes.

The final step is called cement grinding, whereby a blend of clinker and five per cent gypsum is ground into cement in the cement mills. The gypsum, mined in Nova Scotia, is used to control the set of the cement. Clinker must be ground and mixed with the gypsum to required particle size, depending on the strength of cement required. Steel balls cascade within giant rotating drums, resulting in 150 tonnes per hour of the fine powder known as Portland cement being formed.

About 30 per cent of SLC's annual production is exported to the United States by cement boat, rail or truck. Within Canada, the majority of the cement is transported by truck.

St. Lawrence Cement continuously monitors and controls the environmental conditions at all its facilities. The entire manufacturing process, beginning with the raw materials and ending with shipping, is monitored for environmental, process and quality parameters.

Every process within SLC's Mississauga facility is monitored in the central control room. Information is fed into, and recorded by, a sophisticated computer system. The entire kiln production line is monitored and controlled by a Linkman computer—a state-of-the-art, high level supervisory system that analyzes every stage of the burning process. The chemical and physical composition of the cement is controlled in the testing laboratory. In the chemical lab, a "fluxer" is used which fuses cement powder into glass discs. These discs and pressed powders are measured using modern x-ray spectroscopy.

In the concrete lab, the performance of the cement is measured in concrete—the customer's

At trade shows, technical sales representatives meet with customers to discuss St. Lawrence Cement products.

end product. The concrete lab also provides technical service to SLC customers.

St. Lawrence Cement has always taken a proactive approach to environmental issues and in 1996 commissioned two new baghouses at a cost of $16 million. The start-up of the baghouse units was the culmination of several years of work by SLC and the Ministry of Environment & Energy.

The Mississauga facility can now operate at permitted production capacity and maximize kiln utilization, while maintaining emission levels within increasingly stringent environmental regulations and, at the same time, meeting area citizens' demands for a clean local environment.

St. Lawrence Cement agreed to install baghouses on the clinker cooler and on the kiln gas exhaust systems by January 1, 1996. Holderbank Engineering Canada was responsible for the design and retrofitting details of the two baghouses, which replaced the clinker cooler gravel bed filter and the kiln exhaust electrostatic precipitator. As the baghouses were to be an integral part of the overall plant upgrading plan, their design throughput reflected the maximized plant production levels.

The kiln exhaust gas baghouse is a reverse-air type, designed and supplied by Wheelabrator Inc., located in Milton, Ontario. It consists of 12 individual compartments containing 2,592 woven fibreglass filter bags, and is made of steel-welded panels forming the exterior walls, roof, hoppers and internal partitions. The bags are suspended from steel hangers and secured to an airtight cell-plate floor of carbon steel.

From the cooling tower discharge ducting, the dust-laden gases enter the baghouse and flow up through the modules. The dust is captured on the inside of the bags, while the "cleaned" gases flow through the bag filters and exit through the outlet plenum on top of the baghouse.

The dust captured on the bags is removed when a compartment is isolated from the plenums and air is directed in a reverse

flow through the bags. The dust falls into a hopper at the bottom of the compartment and is returned to the cement-making process.

The second baghouse is called the clinker cooler baghouse. The hot dusty air from the clinker cooler is conveyed via a large duct to an air-to-air heat exchanger. The materials flow down through the heat exchanger tubes and are cooled by a series of fans. A hopper at the bottom of the heat exchanger collects a large percentage of particulate as does a settling chamber connected to the side of the hopper. The final particulate is then captured in the clinker cooler baghouse. The process of removing the particulate from the air stream is the same as the kiln exhaust gas baghouse—the air flow is directed through the bag filters and the dust is captured on the surface of the bags.

However, the particulate in the clinker cooler baghouse is removed by pulsing a jet of air through the bag. A rotary screw system then gathers particulate from the heat exchanger hopper, the settling chamber and modules and

conveys it back to the process system.

The cleaned gases exit the baghouse to the clinker cooler baghouse process fan. The gases then exit the fan to the clinker cooler stack where the cleaned gases are finally discharged.

Originally scheduled to take a year to complete, St. Lawrence Cement was able to have the new baghouses up and running in just seven months, attributing the reduced construction time to the dedication of its employees and the co-operation among government officials, consultants, contractors and suppliers.

During 1997, another major upgrading was taking place—the implementation of SAP, a multimillion-dollar integrated business system designed to enhance St. Lawrence Cement's current information systems and business practices. It links SLC's many divisions throughout North America. The Mississauga facility is home to more than 200 employees and is the base of operations for the Ontario Marketing Department, which includes sales and technical service staff in addition to millwrights, electricians, engineers and administrators.

The year 1996 was a year of celebrations for St. Lawrence Cement. In May, the company won the Corporate Fit & Fund Challenge, an annual fund-raising event. Then, in September, more than 400 employees, customers and members of the community attended an Open House in celebration of SLC's 40th anniversary in Mississauga. Experienced staff provided displays, tours and a barbecue lunch.

Located on the Mississauga-Oakville border, the company is a leader in providing support to both communities. Through financial and volunteer support, SLC has supported such organizations as Foodshare, the Oakville Arts Council, Operation Lookout, the Mississauga Living Arts Centre and the Mississauga YMCA. SLC was awarded the 1995 Mayor's Award for Business & the Arts from the town of Oakville for its continued support of the Oakville Centre for the Performing Arts.

The employees, through their loyalty and commitment, have helped to ensure that the future of St. Lawrence Cement's Mississauga plant is as strong as the cement they produce. ℳ

Every process within SLC's Mississauga facility is monitored in the central control room.

*C*onsidering that the sprawling Central Reproductions' facility is filled with the most advanced printing, image scanning and bindery equipment you could assemble, it seems odd to hear the way that the two owners describe the company.

Central Reproductions Ltd.

"We're more of a consultant than a printer," says Doug Snow, who, with partner Ward Spencer, founded Central Reproductions in 1983. "We're not order takers. The actual printing is secondary. What we do is ask questions, assess a situation and the material, plan what the client needs and see it through from start to finish. We provide total service."

It's a philosophy that has served Central well, making it one of Mississauga's 10 fastest growing companies according to *Profit* magazine, and one of the country's fastest growing printers according to *Canadian Printer.*

Clients have come up with their own honours, giving Central their "Supplier of the Year" awards, not to mention increased business.

If Central has a secret, it's the ability to combine a commitment to customer service with years of printing expertise and the latest equipment.

Central's name stands out in the printing field, as it is one of Mississauga's fastest growing companies.

It all goes hand in hand. In a technology-intensive industry, the company is constantly looking to upgrade its equipment and the abilities of the people who make it work. Central is adept at anticipating the needs of the market, and offering customers the most current technological options to meet their changing printing requirements. Sitting still is the only option that's out of the question, and that's what keeps Central so focused on service.

The formula must be working, for Central has achieved a phenomenal pace of expansion—an annual averaged sales growth rate of 15-30 per cent, and departments that are each running 18 hours, at least, every day.

While those figures are impressive, Snow and Spencer are careful not to grow too fast. "We want to make sure that we're doing the job right."

Central takes pride in its versatility. That means the ability to handle brochures and newsletters, posters and training manuals, letterhead and labels, and any other type of material you can imagine.

It means the proficiency to take over a client's entire printing operations, with Central acting as their outsourced "printing department."

Ward Spencer and Doug Snow, partners and founders of Central Reproductions. A relationship driven by energy, positive attitudes and competitiveness.

Most important, versatility means offering an astonishing variety of printing competencies and methods. Central works on the single source premise, offering clients everything they could possibly need all in one place.

From creating concepts or editing customer files, to typesetting and printing, to warehousing and distribution—Central does it all at a single location, under rigid controls. "This range of services places us in an enviable position," says Snow. "Our customers, whether corporations or print brokers, realize the advantage we have in the marketplace. We are actually able to present our customers with four distinct printing methods and prices, and let them decide which method, timing and cost is right for them. Customers want choices, and that's what we offer."

Unlike the practice in most, if not all, printing companies, Central has combined instant and commercial printing under one roof.

"We carry a diverse range of instant print equipment designed for different types of print requests," says Spencer. "It's important to remember that there's a large market for smaller, more focused print."

New equipment carries much greater printing capabilities, which lets Central move a number of printing jobs away from the larger pieces of equipment. Spencer says: "This allows us more printing flexibility in a market that demands such flexibility." Central's commercial printing department handles small, medium and large print requests, from four-colour processes to five-, six- and seven-colour

jobs. This department has grown out of the instant-print department, with the demand from customers pushing Central into greater capabilities.

An expanding Xerox department—with high resolution digital scanning, digital print and laser imaging (from disc or originals); colour laser copying from disc, e-mail or originals; and the ability to mass-produce personalized material—is demonstrating the ever-increasing capabilities of printing technology.

"Our philosophy since we opened our doors has been to accept any challenge," says Spencer. "That attitude has definitely played a major part in our growth." Being able to do it all was Snow and Spencer's original concept. It evolved from their astute observations of the market when the future partners were still working for Xerox Canada Inc.

"This was a spot market when we started," says Spencer. "Companies specialized in specific types of printing, but there wasn't a full-service printing company in the west end of the city. Our idea was to combine it all."

At Xerox, Snow worked in sales, and his territory included the west end. The rapid expansion of business that Xerox was witnessing demonstrated a definite demand for a full-service printer, beyond Xerox's range of services.

While Snow had the sales and marketing expertise, Spencer had extensive experience on the printing side, working as production

"An array of technology." These words are typical of customers' observations. Central takes great pride in hearing these comments. Telling customers is one thing—showing them hits home!

manager of the Xerox Reproduction Centres. The two men had talents that perfectly complemented each other, and quickly agreed to form a partnership.

"We're both very hard-working, competitive, driven people," says Snow. "We really didn't have to talk for very long about doing this. And we had also seen how some other individuals from the Xerox Reproduction Centres had broken off to form their own companies. If they could do it, so could we, but we would do it full scale."

Though they had the background, the determination and the plan, Snow and Spencer said that getting financing was still tough. This was at the tail end of the 1980-82 recession, new business was scarce and the existing business centres of the region were still largely downtown Toronto, Don Mills and Scarborough.

"But we saw where the potential growth area was, and noticed the gap in the marketplace for our services," says Snow. "We put a lot of thought into where we should be located. It was almost a frontier town mentality."

Although their objective was to be a full-service printer, there was no way they could afford to start off with all of the equipment and staff needed to turn that vision into a reality.

At the beginning, it was just Snow and

Spencer in a modest, 1,900-square-foot office in Etobicoke. They had a two-colour press, a Xerox copier, and a cutter. The plan was to sell by day and print by night.

They actually landed their first job before they even opened their doors. The job was due in July, and the only two problems were that Central's equipment was still on order,

People with lots of talent and an aggressive attitude for technology provide constant change and progress.

and the company was licensed but wasn't planning to open until August. "But it was too good a job to turn down," recalls Snow. "We said we could handle it, and arranged to print it somewhere else. That got us some cash flow." Spencer can still remember renting a trailer to cart off the finished product. That was an uncommon occurrence, as the company likes to retain control of its projects, to ensure the quality and confidentiality and to keep costs down for the client. If requests start coming in for new types of work, that's Central's cue to obtain the equipment in-house, hire the personnel to meet that client need and even expand the space to make it all work.

Most of the industry, for instance, sends out its finishing work. Central bucked the trend by deciding that bindery had to be part of their equation. It eventually got a second building just to house a bindery department, which handles specialized finishing, packaging and assembling.

Back in 1983, Central established itself on the ground floor of an office tower. The location was great for attracting clientele, a large percentage of which, Spencer happily reports, still do business with the company.

As sales began to climb, Central started to hire staff and purchase more and

Central's buildings house a unique array of equipment, technology and warehousing—a combination that provides for very informative tours.

more equipment. While having specialized gear was critical, Spencer says that one of the keys to Central's success has been the expertise of the employees. "Our staff have a phenomenal knowledge base," he says of the current 85-person team. "People aren't just hired like that. They go through numerous interviews. We look for positive attitudes, abilities and energies. We have a solid energy drive at this place. That's what really grows Central."

Central believes in literally repaying that dedication, with the entire staff involved in a profit-sharing program. The company holds quarterly meetings with all staff, where performance, profitability and any new directions are all outlined. Each quarter, employees receive part of the profits based on the performance of the company as a whole and by the individual's performance.

"We get a big kick out of seeing our team develop and grow," says Snow. "We place a strong emphasis on education and cross-training, and because of this attitude and our continued technological drive, staff really benefit."

Back in 1986, enough of that staff had joined the company—not to mention the equipment additions—that the company had outgrown its first site. Central relocated into a space with more than twice as much square footage.

Soon, Central was running day and night shifts, and found itself in the fortunate predicament of running out of space yet again.

In 1989, Central moved its head office, printing and bindery operations to 4520 Eastgate Parkway in Mississauga, while maintaining a separate Xerox division. This new location had 17,000 square feet—almost 10 times the size of Central's first office. The Mississauga location was also convenient because of the proximity to the airport. Many a client has picked up or dropped off material on the way to or from a business flight, confident that the job would be ready in time.

The Eastgate facility seemed to provide ample space for growth, which it did for five years. By 1994, Central had grown to the point where it had to take over a neighbouring building, 4524 Eastgate. Two years later, the company expanded to the adjoining unit. Now, the only way to add any space is to take over the giant postal plant to the west! Snow and

Spencer say that their industry has changed tremendously since 1983. Because of the way that information is transmitted, their market is now North America. A lot of clients appreciate that Central is just a few minutes away, but many others are based throughout Canada and the U.S., and communicate with Central electronically. To provide total service, Central maintains its own fleet of delivery vehicles in and around the Greater Toronto Area, and can use carriers for North American destinations.

The company also created an elaborate

Central operates its own fleet of cellular-equipped company vehicles and still provides free pick-up and delivery, a practice that it instituted once its doors opened in 1983. Shipping is also performed throughout Canada and the U.S. via carriers.

computer system to track the variety of processes that occur daily. An integral part of the business, the system allows instant access to the status of every order—even to a signature and the precise moment of delivery.

Staying on top of the technology edge is a huge challenge. From the day it opened, Central has always looked at the technology on the horizon and made sure that it was equipped to handle its clients' needs in more complete and efficient ways.

"Doug and I, along with our managerial staff, spend approximately 25 per cent of our time on R&D," says Spencer. "We do this through focus groups, which consist of 3-4 staff members who are working on very specific technical fields and applications."

"This technique lets the groups define and interpret technology trends and review current methods of production. Our staff bring forward the ideas for technological expansion, and that kind of involvement is in itself a vital component for growth. We review and prioritize the ideas and fit them into the overall picture. This takes a lot of planning, time and energy, but it's all worth it."

Central's partners say they still find the business exciting and always changing, filled with even greater opportunities than when they started. The company is growing both by adding new services and through strategic

Focus groups are a major strategy at Central, utilizing small groups of staff to explore existing systems, technological advances and applications within the company to ensure that Central remains on the leading edge.

acquisitions, though the fit has to be just right.

"We're always looking to add peripheral services, building on ones that are already in place, such as warehousing and fulfilment," says Snow. "We envision huge potential in those kinds of services."

"Right now, if a client sends orders to us, for instance, we can print on demand, or warehouse, or handle any combination. It really lets us take over areas that are not part of the client's core business, and that we can accommodate better."

In a business built on the concept of reproductions, where the goal is to produce precisely the same final product multiple times, Snow and Spencer say the appeal of the business is actually its variety.

"This is a hugely demanding business, where every project is different," says Snow. "We're never doing the same thing twice, and we're never sitting idle. You have to continually be progressive with incorporating technology and building the team."

"What is always interesting is to look back and view the distances that Central has travelled in technology, equipment and services," adds Spencer. "The goal is to see how much farther we can move for the client—and how far the client can go with us." Ⓜ

Current technology and staff education go hand in hand at Central. This combination provides benefits for customers and staff alike.

*N*ot many manufacturing plants talk about their romance, but to the folks at McDonnell Douglas Canada Ltd. there is nothing like looking skyward and seeing the fruits of your labour winging through the clouds.

"You get attached to the aviation business," says Wes Morris, a principal specialist at the

McDonnell Douglas Canada Ltd.

plant. "Even after all these years, people are still in awe of flight. There's the romance of flight—I've never heard of anyone building, say, a model refrigerator."

One of Mississauga's leading industrial employers, McDonnell Douglas Canada fabricates and assembles wings for commercial aircraft. A wholly-owned subsidiary of the McDonnell Douglas Corporation, the facility consists of 1.8 million feet of plant and office space, on a 113-acre site bordering Pearson International Airport.

Since the introduction of the DC-9 in 1963, this plant has been the sole supplier of transport wings for Douglas Aircraft. Today the plant's 1,800-plus workers turn out wings for

the company's family of Twin Jets, the MD-80, MD-90 and MD-95; and the Wide Body Tri-Jet MD-11, shipping them by rail on a 2,300-mile journey to Long Beach, California.

"Every Douglas aircraft since the DC-8 is on Canadian wings," proudly says Ray Rogers, manager of projects and communication.

It can take as long as 32,000 hours to assemble a set of wings, in the case of the MD-11 Tri-Jet, and Rogers says the work is meticulous. He describes the challenge in words usually associated with a fine craftsman.

"Our people are artisans, working to very close tolerances. This is very precise work, dealing with parts that vary in size from something you could lose in your shirt pocket to something you have to pick up with a crane," he says.

In fact, McDonnell Douglas operates one of the largest spar milling facilities in North America. It has eight 5-axis, 3-spindle Gantry machines operating on 90- to 120-foot beds, for the precise machining of the long, complex parts required to build the wings. The plant is capable of processing parts as big as 95 feet long, 13 feet deep and 5 feet wide.

No wonder, when you consider the final product. The wings for the MD-11, for instance, weigh 22,500 pounds apiece, with a fuel capacity of 33,000 gallons. Each wing half

is 97 feet long and a wing set contains more than 10,000 parts.

"Our quality controls ensure that each wing is manufactured to the same specifications and tolerances as the wing that was originally designed and tested," says Morris.

Nowadays, he explains, aircraft are designed not on a drawing board but in a computer environment. This ensures less variability in the fabrication process, making the assembly of

Gantry Mills at McDonnell Douglas Canada operate on 90- to 120-foot beds for the precise machining of the long complex parts required to build aircraft wings.

One of Mississauga's leading industrial employers, McDonnell Douglas Canada fabricates and assembles wings for commercial aircraft.

newer wings easier and more automated.

The Douglas wings were designed in the analog age, in the 1960s, so the assembly operations are more labour intensive. However, Morris says the durability of the wing points to the effectiveness of its design.

"The Douglas wing design is unique, and is generally considered to be the Rolls Royce of wings," he says. "It has a good use life, and the basic structural design is strong."

When the average passenger looks out the window of a plane, a wing is a wing is a wing. But Morris says there's a distinct visual difference between a McDonnell Douglas wing and those of other manufacturers.

"If you look at the top surface of other wings, you often see little `vanes.' These are called vortex generators, and they're there to improve the air flow over the wing. Our wings don't need them because of their superior aerodynamics. The wing is clean."

Under the McDonnell Douglas Canada banner, the plant can take pride in an outstanding track record. But this facility has played an even longer and storied role in Canada's aviation history.

It opened in 1939 as National Steel Car, producing Westland Lysanders and Avro Ansons. In 1943 the Canadian government assumed control, changed the name to Victory Aircraft Ltd. and shifted production to Avro Lancasters. The plant built almost 1,500 aircraft during the World War II years, making it an integral part of the war effort on the domestic front.

At the end of the war Hawker Siddley of the U.K. purchased the facility and renamed it A.V. Roe Canada Ltd. Eventually, the company was split into an engine division (Orenda Engines) and an aircraft division (Avro). From 1949 to 1959, Avro designed and produced a number of historic Canadian aircraft, such as the CF-100 Canuck all-weather fighter and the C-102 Jetliner—the second commercial passenger aircraft in the world to fly, only two weeks after Britain's De Havilland Comet.

The plant's best known aircraft was the CF-105 Avro Arrow, a spectacular feat of engineering. The cancellation of the Arrow program in 1959 was a blow to the local aircraft industry.

De Havilland Aircraft of Canada took over the facility, and in 1963 won a contract to manufacture the wings for Douglas Aircraft's new DC-9.

In 1965 Douglas itself bought the facility, which was renamed again, to Douglas Aircraft of Canada. Douglas merged with McDonnell Aircraft Company in 1967 to create McDonnell Douglas Corporation, though it wasn't until 1978 that the Mississauga operation became known as McDonnell Douglas Canada.

In the years since the plant has been part of Douglas Aircraft and McDonnell Douglas corporation, it has manufactured nearly 3,000 wing sets, with a total value of more than $7 billion.

Building on the successes of the past, today's McDonnell Douglas Canada has made a lasting commitment to continuously upgrade its employee skills, improve quality processes and reduce cycle times. Management is looking at not only extending its support of current Douglas Aircraft programs, but also to playing a key role in future programs.

"We have a focused management team, which is dedicated to a continuous improvement thrust," says Rogers.

Techniques may change. But throughout the plant's history, McDonnell Douglas personnel have been linked by a singular challenge—building one of the most complex and advanced "components" in any industry, an airplane wing.

Under the McDonnell Douglas Canada banner, the plant can take pride in an outstanding track record.

"An awful lot of people are drawn to this industry because the end product is so sophisticated," says Rogers. "And there's very real pride of workmanship in each and every wing set that leaves the plant." **Ⓜ**

The wings for this MD-11 weigh 22,500 pounds apiece, with a fuel capacity of 33,000 gallons.

*T*wice, before he was nine years old, Konosuke Matsushita witnessed first hand the failure of a business—first his father's and, later, a company he had gone to work for to help his family.

He vowed, even at that young age, that he would never be involved with a business that

Panasonic Canada Inc.

failed. And how right he was!

His name probably isn't familiar to a majority of consumers, but the brand names of the products his company sells certainly are: Panasonic, Technics and National. In 1918, at age 21, Konosuke took his entire savings of $50 and started Matsushita Electric Manufacturing along with his wife and brother-in-law.

Konosuke was a genius at taking discarded parts and turning them into such things as attachment plugs for cords that enabled people to safely transfer electricity from the original source to other parts of the house. By 1922 the company had grown to include 300 employees. Konosuke was hailed as a financial success.

As Matsushita developed new, innovative products, its fortunes continued to rise in Japan. But the Depression devastated the economy of Japan and led Konosuke to proclaim, on May 5, 1932, that the mission of his business from then on would be to fill the world with products, thereby eliminating want. That

| Panasonic Canada Inc.

date is still recognized by the company as Spiritual Foundation Day.

Konosuke set a 250-year mandate for this mission with each generation responsible for a 25-year time span, further divided into segments geared toward achieving specific goals.

"The first 25-year time span is for us who attend the meeting today," Matsushita said at the time. "The second period will be followed through by the people of the next generation, who will adopt the same method and policy, so that a very prosperous paradise will be achieved within 250 years."

Over the next four years, Matsushita established Seven Objectives to coincide with his visionary plan. More than 60 years later, the company still follows the objectives: 1) National Service through industry; 2) Fairness; 3) Harmony and cooperation; 4) Struggle for betterment; 5) Courtesy and humility; 6) Adjustment and assimilation and 7) Gratitude. The seven objectives set the course for all aspects of the company, from whether a certain product would be developed to how much a commodity would sell for. Konosuke wanted everyone to be able to afford Matsushita products.

In 1951, after a visit to the United States, Matsushita returned to Japan determined to bring the prosperity he witnessed there to his people. In 1960 Matsushita tested the U.S. marketplace with a few radios. However, it soon became apparent that if the company to was to be successful in America a name change was in order. So Matsushita electronic products

Shunzo "Steve" Ushimaru, President of Panasonic Canada Inc.

became Panasonic just at the time colour television was catching on in North America.

It wasn't until Canada's Centennial Year that Matsushita established a permanent presence here. First-year revenues hit $495,000 and have continued to climb every year, with sales now exceeding one-half billion. The company's Mississauga headquarters houses more than 400 of Canada's 550-plus employees.

True to its founder's philosophy of *sunao* which, translated from Japanese, means "untrapped mind," the 1980s brought new challenges and successes for Panasonic.

Sunao frees the individual of rules and regulations when considering a course of action. Employees are encouraged to put tradition and socially accepted processes aside, temporarily, and approach all situations with an open (or untrapped) mind. As a result, Panasonic has become known for its unique applications of new technology, as well as its innovation when developing emerging technologies.

Thus, Panasonic began a number of initiatives that included its head office assuming all marketing functions, integrating Quasar with Panasonic and introducing revolutionary new products such as videocassette recorders, microwave ovens and more sophisticated colour televisions.

During the same decade, the Industrial Division launched a new cash register system for the fast food sector, with McDonald's Restaurants and Mr. Submarine the first national chains to implement the system. Not to be outdone, Panasonic won a $3-million contract from Bell Canada in 1986 that saw its products sold through Phonecentres.

As Panasonic approached its 25th anniversary in 1992, Canada was in the midst of a recession, and consumers began demanding more for less. As a result, Panasonic entered its second 25-year cycle with a new emphasis on providing excellent customer service and top-quality products.

The resulting "Customer Care" program is the basis for how Panasonic does business. So critical is it to the overall philosophy of the Canadian company, that it has its own annual report. The 1995 edition pointed out, in part, "to succeed today, we must ensure our customers feel good about doing business with us.... The act of caring for the customer is a task infinitely more difficult than simply producing quality products at reasonable prices."

As part of the "Customer Care" philosophy, employees are encouraged to volunteer their time in the communities in which they live and work. Employee-driven initiatives are given support by senior management, and annual awards are handed out to recognize outstanding contributions.

Panasonic Canada Inc. plays an integral role in a program in the Peel Region called "Breakfast for Kids." The purpose of the program is to link schools with sponsors so that no child starts the school day hungry.

Continuing its outreach to children, Panasonic has been able to provide state-of-the-art video equipment to teach communications and organizational skills to "at risk" school children. This program lends video editing equipment to selected schools and allows

Founder, Konosuke Matsushita

student participants to demonstrate their abilities and creativity through video production. The video clips created by the students represent their own Panasonic Kid Witness News broadcast efforts. The student videos feature current events, news reports, public service announcements and interviews with prominent individuals, along with topics relevant to today's youth.

With its outstanding record for growth and extensive commitment to Mississauga's overall well-being, it's certain Konosuke Matsushita would be very proud of what has been accomplished. Ⓜ

*I*f you were looking to decipher the reasons for NSK-RHP's success, consider the construction of the pyramids.

No, the company wasn't established in ancient Egypt. Here in Canada, NSK-RHP was officially formed in 1994. The roots of one of its forerunner companies go back to 1928 in

NSK-RHP Canada Inc.

this country. And parent company NSK Ltd., which has 17,000 employees worldwide, was founded in 1916. But the principles behind the company were in use 4,500 years ago.

Egypt's pyramids were engineering feats, but forget for a moment about how they were built. Consider how the workers moved the massive stones. The hieroglyphics of the time show us—the stones were placed on logs and rolled forward, much easier than dragging them.

Moving parts. They're the essence of anything you can possibly define as a machine. Possessed with the same vision that led to those early rollers—the equivalent to modern bearings—NSK-RHP makes the parts that make machines work.

The company is one of the world's foremost manufacturers of bearings, selling over 1 billion a year—that's 13 per cent of the world's rolling element requirements—and is a leader in motion and control technology.

"Virtually any machine that has a moving part requires a bearing," states Terry Quinn, president and chief operating officer, NSK-RHP Canada Inc. "The applications for NSK-RHP products range from VCRs and computer hard drives to dentist drills and tunneling machines such as the one used to bore under the English Channel."

Working from a head office in Mississauga, NSK-RHP Canada ensures meticulous mechanical movement for its customers' applications. Major customers include resource industries (pulp and paper, mining, steel) automotive manufacturers, aerospace engine manufacturers and a host of other diverse industries.

NSK-RHP acts as a commercial distribution company, purchasing products from its 28 bearing plants around the world, and selling them under the NSK and RHP brands. Along with the Mississauga corporate and distribution office, the company has distribution and sales sites in Vancouver, Edmonton, Winnipeg and Montreal that support a coast-to-coast network of outside distributors.

Figuring out the company's evolution is an alphabetical challenge. The "NS" in NSK

Moving parts. They're the essence of anything you can possibly define as a machine. Possessed with the same vision that led to those early rollers—the equivalent to modern bearings—NSK-RHP makes the parts that make machines work.

Along with the Mississauga corporate and distribution office, the company has distribution and sales sites in Vancouver, Edmonton, Winnipeg and Montreal.

stands for Nippon Seiko, the original name of the Japanese-based parent company. (The word *seiko* means precision.)

That company's founder, by the way, started off in the metalworks industry—this was at a time when the level of Japanese technology was so low that the country couldn't even produce nails of adequate quality. How times have changed!

As for the "RHP," the initials stand for three British-based companies that eventually merged: R&M Bearings (which opened a Montreal office in 1928), Hoffman Manufacturing Company and Pollard Ball & Roller Bearing Company. RHP Bearing Canada Inc., the Canadian subsidiary, had its national head office in Montreal.

NSK bought RHP Bearing Canada's parent company in 1990, and in 1994 merged the Canadian operation with Mississauga-based NSK Bearing Canada Ltd. to form NSK-RHP Canada Inc.

If you think of a bearing as just a steel ball, that conception has no, well, bearing on the industry's reality. The ball is only part of a bearing, the rolling element, and these products come in every size and shape imaginable. History records that it was Leonardo da Vinci who gave bearings a scientific definition. In his notes on the subject of friction, he explained

NSK-RHP offers one of the most diverse product ranges available, with some 100,000 configurations of bearings, automotive components and linear motion products.

why rolling friction is less than sliding friction. Alas, manufacturing techniques of the day had not caught up with the great designer's dreams.

Five hundred years later, NSK-RHP is realizing those dreams in ways even da Vinci couldn't conceive, extending the abilities of this technology to reduce friction and control motion.

Some bearings have bore diameters as tiny as one millimetre, while others have outside diameters as large as five metres. In some bearings, the conventional balls or rollers have been replaced by a cushion of air or a magnetic field. Others are made of unique materials such as ceramics for special applications.

In fact, NSK-RHP offers one of the most diverse product ranges available, with some 100,000 configurations of bearings, automotive components and linear motion products.

These products are so precise—with submicron accuracies—that NSK-RHP has to invent much of the equipment used to make them. (To gain an appreciation for this level of accuracy, consider for a moment that a human hair is 40 microns thick!)

NSK-RHP is also the only bearing company in the world to offer a comprehensive package of mechatronic products. These incorporate bearing and motion and control technology to provide movement, and are controlled from electronic and software technology. "We are constantly developing new products and technologies to meet the ever-evolving needs of industry," adds Terry Quinn. Bringing together these areas of expertise helps NSK-RHP customers achieve market leadership in areas such as automation in their plants.

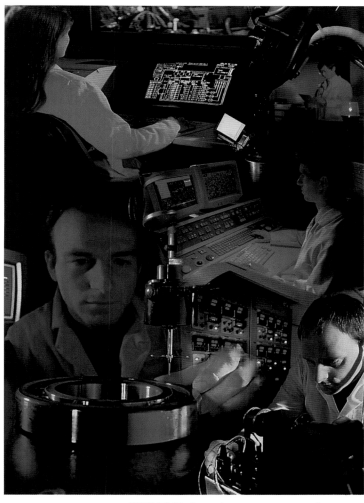

NSK-RHP Canada ensures meticulous mechanical movement for customers in diverse industries, including, but not limited to, pulp and paper, mining, steel, automotive manufacturers and aerospace engine manufacturers.

By tapping the skills, intelligence, cultural diversity and abundant experience on a global scale, NSK-RHP is ready for the next era and poised to challenge the future head-on. **Ⓜ**

*I*TL Industrial Tires Limited started operations in July, 1958. With two people, a service truck and 100 square feet of space, the company imported solid tires and provided sales and service to fork lift truck users in the Mississauga area.

ITL Industrial Tires Limited

From Mississauga to Moscow—Award-Winning Firm Achieves World-Class Status

In 1978, ITL designed and produced a non-pneumatic tire for use on a track-propelled vehicle imported by the State Agency located in Moscow for use in geophysical exploration in the U.S.S.R.

By 1997, ITL's Mississauga continually expanding headquarters operation occupied 100,000 square feet and housed the industry's most complete library of manufacturing technology and marketing know-how.

Some 500 people worldwide are involved in the manufacturing and marketing of ITL brand products. This year the company's sales will approach $60 million with forecasts at $100 million by the year 2000.

A Mission Statement

A visionary company from the outset, the start-up of Canadian manufacturing in 1965 created the requirement to author a mission statement.

Export Sales Fuel Dramatic Growth

The industrial portion of the tire business is a mature and well-serviced niche. Recognizing that the total Canadian requirement for industrial tires at all trade levels would not support economies of scale, volume purchasing or new product development, ITL turned to export opportunities. In fact, although ITL enjoys a 70 per cent share of the market in Canada, today 80 per cent of the company's sales are to dealers, distributors and O.E.M. accounts in export markets. ITL's focus on export began in 1975 and by 1979 the company's achievements were recognized by the Province of Ontario with an award of their coveted "A" banner.

Outstanding Achievement

ITL leads the industry in the design and development of new products and applications research. As a result, the company's non-pneumatic tires are now supplied to an ever-expanding list of O.E.M. and aftermarket customers worldwide.

ITL specializes in the design, manufacture, and distribution of solid rubber tires, also known as "resilient" tires, for a wide variety of industrial applications. In line with ITL's strategy of horizontal expansion, the company's technology can be found on airport dolly carts, aerial platform equipment, construction and mining vehicles, and virtually every make of forklift truck.

ITL's performance was recognized by the Ontario Chamber of Commerce with its prestigious Outstanding Achievement Award 1984.

The mission of ITL is to achieve and sustain the premier position as a manufacturer and marketer of industrial tires on a world scale.

A Leader in Technology and Quality

One other North American industrial tire manufacturer, and only one other in the entire world, has achieved the stringent and coveted ISO 9002 status for manufacturing and quality excellence. ITL qualified its operations in 1994.

Marketing and Entrepreneurship

ITL is a market-driven company and its adventuresome and aggressive campaign to capture increased market share worldwide was recognized by the Government of Canada in 1989 with separate Canada Business Awards for Entrepreneurship and Marketing.

A Mississauga Success Story

Tom Buckley, the founder, chairman and CEO of Industrial Tires Limited, credits part of the firm's success to the pro-business environment created by the inimitable Mississauga Mayor Hazel McCallion. This provided the foundation on which ITL grew and prospered. Over the years there have been seven expansions to ITL's original Mississauga plant of 15,000 square feet opened in 1964.

Tom Buckley was recognized as Mississauga's Businessman of the Year in 1983.

The Future

The planning and priorities are in place to continue to maintain ITL's momentum and to earn increased market share worldwide. ITL products are now manufactured in Mississauga, Mexico and Sri Lanka, and in March 1996, a world-class plant officially opened in Yantai, China. ITL's technology and marketing skills are now in place to support the company's growth plan to the year 2000 and beyond.

Mississauga's ITL—a very bright future indeed! Ⓜ

The book you are holding represents 304 more pages in the success story of Transcontinental Printing.

Transcontinental Printing is extremely proud to have been selected to print this important book on the vibrant city of Mississauga. There are two reasons for this:

Transcontinental Printing

first, it has given the company the opportunity to demonstrate the quality of its craft to a very important audience—you, the reader—and second, it provides an overview of a true company success story. A success that ranks Transcontinental among the top 10 printers in

Transcontinental Printing's people are its greatest resource.

the world and Canada's second largest printer overall. And that's only the beginning!

A company culture with a long-standing commitment to quality and customer service has been responsible for the wide and diverse line-up of important companies with whom Transcontinental works. The duration and diversity of many of these relationships stand as a testimony to the success of the company's business philosophy.

From leading retailers such as The Bay, Zellers, Home Hardware and Oshawa Foods, to consumer publications such as *Saturday Night* and *Hockey News*, the names of the customers who rely on Transcontinental Printing are plentiful enough to fill a telephone directory—and

Skilled personnel with strong technical capabilities power Transcontinental Printing.

Transcontinental produces several of those too. In fact, the average Canadian likely touches some piece of paper printed by Transcontinental every day.

Transcontinental's traditional focus on high-end, high volume and high-quality printing—flyers, catalogs, magazines, directories, books, brochures, annual reports and newspapers—has evolved through acquisition and emerging technologies to encompass other complementary communications sectors: distribution, publishing and technologies such as the manufacture of audio CDs and CD-ROMs. The CD-ROM technology was made possible through the 1993 acquisition of Americ Disc, one of the largest independent manufacturers of audio CDs and CD-ROMs in North America. Thanks to Americ Disc's presence within Transcontinental, the printing sector's customer catalogs and the publishing sector's newspapers and magazines can also be made available on CD-ROM.

In publishing, Transcontinental Publications is a leader in specialized and "new trend" publications. This division has evolved from a magazine and newspaper publisher into an overall information provider, expanding into areas such as direct marketing and electronic publishing. Publi-Home Distributors Limited is a division renowned for revolutionizing home distribution of flyers, using delivery methods such as the Ad-Bag and Ad-Stand. It has also provided value-added services such as targeting (Ad-Target) and database management, as well as publishing community newspapers.

Printing is a technology-intensive business, and Transcontinental has always been at the forefront in incorporating the latest equipment

to make the printing, binding and distribution processes more efficient. The Printing Division also encompasses electronic prepress (for direct output to plate-ready film) with printing, finishing and shipping services available across North America from more than two dozen plants.

Transcontinental continues to expand rapidly through a balanced combination of internal growth and acquisition. The strategy can be summed up in one word—integration. In concert with vigilant customer services, growth has come by creating complementary new services or sectors, buying businesses that complement or extend the range of operations within a sector, purchasing businesses that link two or more sectors and developing strategic alliances.

Efficiently utilizing this network drives Transcontinental's success. Each plant and division has its own areas of expertise. By producing work in the plant or plants that are best suited to the customer's requirements, whether in the Mississauga area or elsewhere, Transcontinental can better control costs and turnaround. This approach also offers customers a full range of printing and communications-related services at the local, regional or North American-wide level.

Transcontinental Printing is proud of its people, its capabilities and its success in working with its clients to help them to fulfil their diverse and evolving communications needs. **Ⓜ**

Transcontinental continually invests in advanced technologies and press systems.

Transcontinental Printing is a proactive partner in the preservation of the environment.

*T*o many Canadians, the name Inglis is associated primarily with home appliances such as refrigerators, dishwashers, ranges (stoves) and washers and dryers.

Anyone born before 1945, however, is likely to recognize Inglis more for its contribution to Canada's efforts during the First and, especial-

Inglis Limited

ly, the Second World War (when its gunmaking and general engineering divisions were put at the disposal of the federal government).

The company was founded in 1859 in Guelph, Ontario, by John Inglis and an associate to manufacture machines for grist and flour mills. In 1881, the operation was moved to downtown Toronto, on Strachan Avenue.

In 1898, William Inglis, one of five sons of John, took over the company when his father died, and in 1902 switched production to marine steam engines and waterworks pump-

One in every two Canadian households contains an Inglis Limited supplied clothes washer.

ing engines. During the same period the John Inglis Company Limited built the main engines for the Canada Steamship Lines passenger steamers *Hamonic* and *Huronic,* the first such engines manufactured in Canada.

During the First World War, Inglis produced shells and shell forgings as well as more than 40 steam marine engines for freighters ordered by the government. By 1933, the company was building tugs, including the Toronto Island Ferry, named the *William Inglis* in recognition of Inglis' contributions to the city's industrial and cultural progress.

In 1938 the federal government awarded Inglis a contract for the manufacture of Bren guns, and the British government followed suit. During this period, the company increased its heavy manufacturing facilities and its plants provided work for over 17,000 employees, most of whom were women.

During the Second World War, Inglis produced marine engines, Scotch marine boilers and Inglis-Yarrow water tube boilers for Corvettes, boilers for cargo vessels, plus a variety of pumps, pressure vessels and other equipment. It also manufactured and installed the machinery for four Tribal Class destroyers.

When the war ended, Inglis turned its attention to producing stationary boilers, marine turbines, marine boilers, condensers, evaporators and many other kinds of pumps. It also built a mill for the manufacture of fine paper from bamboo in Ballapur, India, and another paper mill in Chile, South America, in 1961.

At the same time, Inglis took advantage of the postwar economic boom and a pent-up consumer demand for major appliances, building its first wringer washer in 1946 and adding the automatic washer in 1950.

The Inglis Administration Centre is located in Mississauga, Ontario.

Today, Inglis Limited is Canada's largest marketer of major home appliances supplying under the brand names of Inglis, Whirlpool, Admiral, Roper, KitchenAid, Speed Queen and Estate. Inglis is the primary supplier of Kenmore branded appliances to Sears Canada.

Inglis has a head office in Mississauga, Ontario, sales and service locations across Canada and a manufacturing facility at Montmagny, Quebec, which produces electric ranges for the Canadian market and export to the United States.

Inglis Limited is a wholly owned subsidiary of Whirlpool Corporation, the world's leading manufacturer and marketer of major home appliances. As Inglis moves toward the 21st century, the company looks to its past with pride and the future with confidence. ⓜ

How do you pay tribute to a company whose airplane engines cost upwards of $250 million to research, design and test? Forty-five cents will cover it. That's the cost of a Canadian stamp issued in 1996 to honour aerospace technology. The image chosen to grace the stamp was a PW305 turbofan, built by Pratt & Whitney Canada.

Pratt & Whitney Canada personnel celebrate the company's ISO9001 approval status.

"Everyone was excited to see the work recognized," says John Blackie, Vice President of Engineering Operations and Design Engineering.

Pratt & Whitney Canada designs, develops, manufactures and markets an array of turboprop, turboshaft and turbofan engines. Customers include the corporate, commercial, military and regional aviation markets, making

Inspecting an accessory gearbox installation on a JT15D Turbofan Engine is just one part of the quality-assurance process for which P&WC is known.

Pratt & Whitney Canada the world's largest producer of small aircraft gas turbine engines.

Using that technology, Pratt & Whitney has expanded into the industrial and marine markets, manufacturing gas turbines and related systems for power generation and pipeline compressors.

A subsidiary of United Technologies Corporation, Pratt & Whitney Canada was founded in 1928 in Longueuil, Quebec. Back then, the company serviced a growing number of U.S.-built Pratt & Whitney engines used by the Canadian Armed Forces and bush pilots exploring the Far North.

The company's history in Mississauga goes back to 1979, when it opened an engineering operation here. Situated on the western edge of Pearson International Airport, Plant 22 employs more than 850 people. They're involved in gas turbine research and development, and in assembling and testing various Pratt & Whitney Canada turbofan engine families.

"The opportunity to tap into Ontario's aerospace experience and attract skilled personnel drew us here," says Blackie. To maintain its global leadership, Pratt & Whitney Canada invests heavily in research and development. In fact, it's the second-largest R&D investor in Canada's private sector.

"We constantly strive to improve the performance of our engines," Blackie says. "The ability to produce more thrust, be more fuel efficient, have better power-to-weight ratios and accomplish this in ever-reducing lead-times—these all give us a competitive advantage."

Pratt & Whitney Canada

The Mississauga operation is credited as one of the leaders in computer modeling techniques for combustion and compressor design which enables the engineers to gain a more comprehensive understanding of the design's performance and functionality. It eliminates a lot of rig testing and enables higher quality initial design results.

It takes about three years to design and test a new engine and acquire the coveted certificate of airworthiness from Transport Canada. That only comes after a series of strenuous structural, environmental, test cell and flight tests that puts the engine through its paces for all operating conditions.

After all that time, Pratt & Whitney personnel build and test the actual airplane engine in a few days, during which they inspect and test all aspects of engine performance and operability before package and shipping to the customer.

The result of all of this focus on quality? Engines that earn the "stamp" of approval. **M**

*N*issan Canada Inc. has come a long way since its humble beginnings in British Columbia 30 years ago when it sold a couple of hundred cars and pickup trucks under the Datsun banner. Now, more than 4,000 Canadians depend on Nissan for their employment, and the company has sold more than

Nissan Canada Inc.

1 million vehicles and is the world's fifth largest automaker, with more than 70 per cent of vehicles sold in North America being made on this continent. North American content in these vehicles ranges as high as 74 per cent and continues to climb as more local suppliers are identified.

Nissan's Canadian operations were first incorporated in Vancouver in January 1965. At that time, the company imported and distributed budget-priced cars and pickup trucks.

In 1982, the company moved its national head office to a building on Argentia Road in west Mississauga and, in 1989, Nissan moved to new, custom-designed headquarters in east Mississauga, just across Highway 401 from Pearson International Airport—just in time to celebrate its 25th anniversary.

Now, Nissan offers Canadians a broad variety of award-winning economy, family and sports cars, pickup trucks, 4X4s, the Pathfinder sports utility wagon and the Quest minivan. And the Infiniti Division offers a range of vehicles ranging from the sporty 130 to the plush Q45 and the upscale QX4 sport utility.

Across Canada, a typical Nissan dealership sells between 400 and 500 new and used vehicles per year and offers parts and service, leasing, financing and body shop repairs—all under the same roof.

Best known as a Japan-based automaker, Nissan is actually one of the world's most widely diversified and geographically dispersed manufacturers of transportation, aerospace, textile, industrial and marine equipment. It has plants in Japan and 21 countries on 6 continents and markets its products to more than 150 countries.

It also builds buses, heavy trucks, industrial pumps and generators, air and water-jet textile looms and is a pioneer in Japan's aerospace technology.

Nissan has received worldwide acclaim for recruiting local designers, engineers and staff to help it create imaginative, quality products that meet local market tastes and needs.

Two prime examples of that philosophy at work are the highly successful Altima family sedan and Quest minivan, both of which were designed by North Americans, in North America, for the North American market.

The Canadian company has also been a leader in tackling environmental issues. For example, Nissan was the first automaker to pledge support to the Montreal Protocol on the Environment. Nissan was also the first car company to support Canada's Globe 1990 environmental conference.

In 1988, Nissan pioneered the recycling of CFC (chlorofluorocarbons) air-conditioning refrigerants—doing so as vehicles entered Canada in Vancouver. In 1990, Nissan Canada made the recycling of CFC refrigerants mandatory at all its dealerships and, the same year, made the capture and recycling of new refrigerants mandatory at all its dealerships.

The company and its dealers also place great emphasis on being good citizens in their communities. In 1993, the company incorporated the Nissan Canada Foundation, an independent philanthropic organization. The Foundation has chosen to focus its resources on the needs of Canada's senior citizens. In partnership with local dealers, it has provided more than 50 minivans to Meals on Wheels and other social agencies across the country.

Since 1990, most Nissan head office employees, including the president, have taken turns delivering Meals on Wheels, while other staff members have given up their free time to provide breakfasts to local school children who would otherwise go hungry. Each spring, Nissan staff spend at least one Saturday refurbishing the Scott Mission's Caledon-area camp for inner-city children.

Nissan's motto, "think locally and act globally," certainly works in Canada and is a key reason for the company's success here. **ⓜ**

| Nissan Canada headquarters in Mississauga

*T*he expression "walk a mile in my shoes" could be the rallying cry for the Munnings family, which has owned and operated Industrial Safety Equipment Co. Ltd (ISECO) since 1938, when George Munnings founded the company. At that time George sold leggings, coats, first-aid kits and head, eye and ear protection.

It was the "Dirty Thirties"; jobs were at a premium and only those with entrepreneurial instincts prospered. Munnings saw a need for specialty industrial safety clothing and products. It wasn't until a few years later that safety footwear was added to the product lineup.

Industrial workers of all kinds are the primary ISECO customers, with many workers paying for their footwear through payroll deduction. The steel, forestry, electrical, automotive, railway, lumber, construction and airline industries depend on ISECO products. So, too, do the hospitality and food industries as well as hospitals, municipalities and school boards.

ISECO is a family business. George's brothers Ted and Bob joined him after the Second World War, and younger brother Vic signed up in the late 1940s. Since then, second and third generations of Munnings have joined the company, carrying on the tradition of the Munnings families.

ISECO originated the concept of mobile trucks for selling shoes and now has 32 mobile vans and 17 stores across Canada. The first mobile store, launched in 1946, was a Mainstream Trailer pulled by a car. Now, each of ISECO's mobile vans costs about $60,000 to convert and is leased rather than purchased. A

ISECO

typical mobile store stocks from 1,000 to 1,200 pairs of shoes in about 75 styles, as opposed to a permanent location which stocks 100-plus styles.

Among the unusual product lines available from ISECO are antistatic-soled shoes for workers in the aircraft and computer industries, where a static shock could purge valuable files or even cause a general network crash. Police forces' riot squads like ISECO's puncture-proof shoes made of ballistic nylon. ISECO sells Brooks running shoes, a complete line of hiking boots and steel-toed dress shoes. You can even get the popular Doc Martens™ with safety toes.

Recently, ISECO introduced a new line of non-slip footwear made especially for the food service industry. It has become very popular in fast-food restaurants, and ISECO is now a major supplier to such large chains as Scott's, KFC and Wendy's.

There are two permanent locations in Mississauga: the Dunwin Mall, and the head office at 2640 Argentia Road. **M**

ISECO's head office is one of the most modern buildings in Mississauga.

ISECO was the first company to use mobile trucks to service customers at their place of work. There are now some 32 trucks on the road, along with 17 retail stores, 3 of which are in Mississauga.

George died on September 10, 1996, but his legacy in the company continues through his son Garry, who is president, while Bob is chairman of the board. Nephew Randy is secretary-treasurer and general manager, George's grandson Devin is director of marketing and national sales manager and Kimberley McDonald, George's granddaughter, is manager of human resources, benefits and payroll.

ISECO, originally based in Etobicoke, moved to Mississauga in 1979. "When we were looking for a new facility, we looked west to Mississauga," Garry Munnings said. "It was a young city on the rise and was attracting young couples and businesses. We were a growing company, too. It was a natural fit for us."

$\mathcal{A}$lthough corporate executives do their best to plan companies' futures, sometimes it is only by looking over our shoulders that we can understand the reasons for a company's success. Over the course of the past 45 years, Garland has grown from a one-man distributor into a globally recognized leader in

Garland Commercial Ranges Limited

quality commercial cooking and ventilation equipment through dedicated attention to customer service.

The Patterns of Success

Russ Prowse was selling radios in his native Winnipeg after the Second World War when he decided a better living could be made in the sale of appliances to the fast-growing Canadian consumer market. Russ moved to Toronto and began working for Moffat. Once there, he recognized even greater opportunity in the supply of commercial cooking equipment to the growing restaurant business in Canada. Garland, a name well known in the United States as a maker of commercial cooking equipment, was struggling in Canada. Prowse decided that if he could out-service his competition he could carve out a successful business in the growing restaurant market. In 1952 he incorporated Garland, and business opened from a converted storefront on Eglinton Avenue West, in central Toronto. From the front of the 1,000-square-foot facility Prowse managed a traditional sales

Garland Commercial Ranges Limited first moved to Mississauga in 1975 and to its current location in 1980. The building has been expanded and a second facility opened a few blocks away for Vent Master.

operation. It was, however, from the rear basement of the facility that he built his competitive success by reducing delivery times with local warehousing of key parts and reducing down time with an improved service capability.

Within a year he moved to larger facilities nearby, began manufacturing and hired key executives George Attridge, Wally Beech and Phil LaMantia, who were to stay with the company for over 30 years. Success in Canada and expansion to the United Kingdom in 1964 forced further manufacturing expansion.

In 1975, Garland moved to its current site on Kamato Road in Mississauga. In 1980, 4,000 square metres were added to house a porcelain enamel facility. In late 1984, a second plant, three blocks away, was built to accommodate Vent Master.

Service Service Service

Garland's current president and chief executive officer is David McCulloch, a 10-year veteran. McCulloch and his new management team have emulated the service lessons provided by the former management team's success and extended the company's international service reputation. In 1992, McCulloch orchestrated the acquisition of Vent Master, based in Houston, Texas, and moved the operation from the U.S. to Mississauga, a reversal of the usual north-to-south transfer of companies' head offices. The Mississauga facility designs,

Garland Commercial Ranges Limited founder Russ Prowse, right, and David S. McCulloch, president and CEO of the Garland Group. Prowse still has an office at Garland's Mississauga head office and drops in regularly, even though he's in his 80s.

manufactures and sells commercial equipment, such as ranges, ovens and ventilation hoods, to customers worldwide, through 65 international distributors. Plans are in place for further expansion in South America, China, India and Eastern Europe.

Garland Commercial Ranges Limited has over 300 employees, has recorded 50 per cent growth in four years and plans to double again by the year 2000. Both Garland Commercial Ranges Limited and Vent Master are divisions of the Garland Group of Companies. The group itself is a subsidiary of Welbilt of Stamford, Connecticut, and Welbilt, in turn, is owned by Berisford PLC of London, England. **ⓜ**

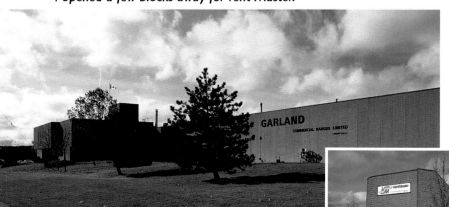

Since its founding in 1934, Fujifilm has pioneered a variety of technologies and brought diverse products to the world marketplace with the objective of popularizing photography—for both the amateur and the professional.

Now, more than six decades later, Fujifilm continues to offer an advanced line-up of products for the manipulation of still and moving images—from photographic films, film-with-lens products, cameras and magnetic tapes to electronic imaging equipment.

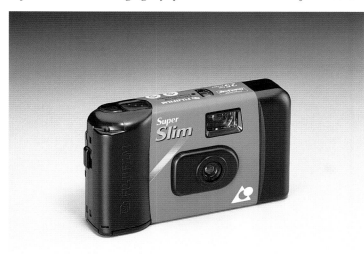

Fujifilm's QuickSnap SuperSlim, the film and camera all-in-one, uses the new Advanced Photo System. It's compact, convenient and foolproof.

Fuji Photo Film Co. Ltd. annually reinvests a significant percentage of total sales in research and development. Many of these initiatives result in exclusive patents. There is a direct benefit to consumers through the introduction of unique technologies.

For example, in April, 1996, Fujifilm launched its first products for a revolutionary new system of photography called the Advanced Photo System (APS). In accordance with its goal of providing products that make photography fun and easy, Fujifilm launched a full line of film, print paper, cameras, photofinishing equipment, image scanners and photo players.

APS seamlessly combines the benefits of conventional photography with the unlimited capabilities of digital image processing and printing technology, thus expanding the application of photographs.

Fujifilm is aggressively applying its expertise in colour management and reproduction to the world of digital imaging. It has developed products such as digital card cameras, with highly precise colour and contrast input, and full-colour digital printers, which make possible a range of colour reproduction by

using a hybrid electronic printing method that applies electronic printing technologies to silver-halide photography.

The Motion Picture, Magnetic and Computer Media Division encompasses a wide variety of different products—including motion picture positive and negative film, professional video and audio products, data storage media and a full line of consumer video and audio tapes.

Fujifilm continues to strive for excellence in all phases of its business. All four Japanese manufacturing facilities have received ISO 14001 certification from the Japan Quality Assurance Institute. This certification recognizes excellence not only in manufacturing but also indicates Fujifilm has achieved international standards for quality assurance and environmental management systems.

Certification recognized the environmental management systems instituted at the factories on a total basis, from waste reduction and energy and water conservation to the screening out of substances harmful to the environment and the procedures to minimize environmental damage in times of accidents and natural disaster.

In the end, however, consumers judge the value of Fujifilm's products by the actual prints they receive from the photofinisher. That's why Fujifilm has developed a complete range of sophisticated photofinishing processing equipment designed for the one-hour service providers. Fuji uses only the highest

Fuji Photo Film Canada Inc.

quality recyclable photographic papers available to produce prints from both colour negatives and colour transparencies.

Fuji has programs to assist all Fuji equipment owners with chemical handling information, and the Fuji Green Box recycling program provides dealers with collection tools to aid in the reuse and recycling of Fujifilm packaging and QuickSnap cameras.

Fuji first entered the Canadian marketplace in 1964 with the sales of Fuji's film brand and Fuji cameras sold through R&H Products of Montreal. The company established its head office in Mississauga in 1987 under the banner of Fuji Photo Film Canada Inc. and now has regional offices in Montreal and Vancouver.

FUJI FUJIFILM. *Simply More Advanced.* Ⓜ

While the company maintains regional offices in Montreal and Vancouver, the majority of Fuji Photo Film Canada's 220 employees work at the head office on Britannia Road in Mississauga.

*M*anufacturers and industrial producers have been turning to Henkel as their Canadian source for specialty chemicals and intermediates for more than 25 years. And as we approach the 21st century, Henkel Canada Limited continues to provide innovative chemistry while improving and expanding its

Henkel Canada Limited

products and services to meet the changing needs of Canadian industry.

Fritz Henkel started a detergent company, Henkel & Cie, in Aachen, Germany, in 1876, and a member of the Henkel family was at the helm of the firm, overseeing day-to-day operations for more than 100 years. Today, global Henkel Group's network encompasses more than 200 companies worldwide.

Henkel Canada's first office was in Montreal in 1971. A Toronto office was established in 1972, and the Mississauga head office opened in 1990 and includes administration, sales and marketing, consumer service, finance, regulatory affairs, distribution and human resources. Three manufacturing sites in the Greater Toronto Area each serve one of the company's divisions. There are more than 400 employees across Canada.

Henkel Canada Limited understands the special needs of Canadian manufacturers, their need for products that meet international quality standards. That's why it pursued and received ISO 9002 certification.

In a recent three-year study of 50 of the world's largest chemical and pharmaceutical groups, the Hamburg Environment Institute, an independent research group, rated Henkel second in environmental performance.

Ultimately, Henkel's products improve consumer goods—by simplifying their manufacture, by functioning as a more ecologically sound alternative to a current ingredient, or by improving performance or durability of the consumer product.

The Chemical Division consists of an Oleochemical business unit which is a fatty acid and glycerine manufacturer and a market leader, serving a wide range of industries—personal care products, cosmetics, soaps, pharmaceutical, plastic and coatings.

The Cospha business unit markets a full range of surfactants, emollients, bases, emulsifiers and bioactive ingredients for the personal care industry, as well as surfactants for household cleaning applications.

Henkel's Fine Chemicals business represents the full range of natural vitamin E, antioxidants and natural beta carotene products, aimed at the Canadian nutritional market.

The Performance Chemicals Group has a close-working relationship with all markets it serves—including business units for coatings and inks, textile chemicals, syn lubes, ozone acids, agricultural chemicals, plastic additives, polymerization and oilfield chemicals.

Henkel Surface Technologies, which includes the former Parker Amchem and Novamax organizations, is the leader in surface treatment chemicals and services. This division provides specialty chemicals and support services to the metalworking and plastic fabrication industries. Its products and services provide surface treatment that improves paint adhesion on metal and plastic substrates and improves the corrosion resistance of painted metal.

The Consumer Adhesives Division was formed in 1995, when Henkel Canada purchased LePage and, a year later, Canadian Adhesives. LePage is the leading Canadian manufacturer and marketer of adhesives, sealants and decorative products for the retail home improvement and professional markets, which include lamination and woodworking,

transportation and building components and manufactured housing construction. In 1996, Loctite Specialty Adhesives with its head office in Mississauga, was added to the Henkel Group.

After more than 25 years of doing business in Canada, Henkel believes that its vision—to be first on the choice list of major enterprises—and its strategic objectives to be leaner, greener and keener, will keep it focused on practices that will achieve its goal of serving its customers with ever-improving products and services. **Ⓜ**

Occasionally, a brand name becomes so linked with a particular product that it is treated as a generic term. Kodiak is one of these rare brands. Think of the work boot, and the name Kodiak comes to mind, evoking an image of durable and dependable footwear.

Kodiak boots were born from the requirements of some of the toughest people anywhere—Canada's construction crews and steel workers, loggers, miners and Arctic explorers.

Greb International, Kodiak Division continues to incorporate the latest footwear technology, ensuring an ever-increasing array of lightweight and functional, anatomically designed, waterproof leather boots and shoes.

Kodiak currently offers a complete range of footwear to suit both work and safety environments as well as the expanding outdoor rugged market.

Mississauga is presently home to the head office of Greb International. Like the word "Kodiak," the name Greb stands out in the history of the Canadian footwear industry.

In 1912 brothers Charles and Edwin Greb purchased the Berlin Shoe Company located in Little Berlin, Ontario. Four years later, the firm changed its name to the Greb Shoe Company, the same year the town became known as Kitchener. The brothers' ground rule through their years of growth was "function first."

During the Second World War Greb was active in producing army boots, along with its range of dress and casual shoes. Greb continued to supply combat boots to the armed forces in the 1950s, and became the first North American footwear manufacturer to produce shoes utilizing a high-pressure vulcanizing process.

This process enabled the company to bond a rubber sole directly and securely to leather uppers, thus creating North America's first truly waterproof boot.

Greb developed a worldwide reputation for high-quality work and hunting boots. The company experienced a key expansion in 1959 with the purchase of Canada West Shoes and the Calumet Shoe Co., both of Winnipeg.

That expansion made Greb the first Canadian manufacturer in both eastern and western Canada. More important, along with Canada West came the Kodiak line of work and safety boots, and the licence to manufacture Acme boots.

Other great names are part of Greb's history. For decades, Greb manufactured and distributed Hush Puppies® shoes in Canada. For decades Greb owned the Canada Skate Manufacturing Co., Bauer Canadian Skate, the Tebbutt Shoe & Leather Co., Collins Safety Shoe and the Industrial Footwear Co.

In 1974 the Greb Shoe Company was purchased by Warrington Inc., and in 1980 moved its head office and distribution centre to Mississauga. After several corporate reorganizations, Greb International's Kodiak brand remains synonymous with quality craftsmanship that is distinctly Canadian.

Today Kodiak means more than a pair of tough leather boots, much more. Through a licensing program covering clothing to sport bags, the company has positioned itself to increase its international sales, with the Kodiak image so associated with Canada's own for the rugged outdoors. After all these years, Kodiak remains Canada's Boot®. ⓜ

Greb International

Kodiak currently offers a complete range of footwear to suit both work and safety environments as well as the expanding outdoor rugged market.

*U*ddeholm is a worldwide leader in the production of high-quality steel and precision cold rolled strip steels, with a marketing network that spans the globe.

Since establishing itself in Canada in 1953, Uddeholm has maintained its presence in Ontario. For nearly 30 years now, the head

Uddeholm Limited

office and main service centre has been situated in Mississauga—with additional service centres in both Montreal and Vancouver. You will also find four specialty steel stores strategically located throughout Southern Ontario, catering to the urgent needs of local toolmaking companies.

Most of Uddeholm's steel is imported from and manufactured at its mills in Sweden, home of the parent company (Uddeholms AB). This Swedish company, which services more than 100,000 customers worldwide, is owned by Austrian-based Böhler-Uddeholm AG, a world leader in specialty steel.

In 1990, Uddeholm purchased a heat treatment facility (Uddeholm Heat Treatment Limited) located in Newmarket, Ontario. The Heat Treatment Division is responsible for

Uddeholm's technical representative supporting one of the company's many customers

first-class thermal processing and ensuring that tool and die steels are treated to give customers optimum tool life and performance. In 1996, Uddeholm Heat Treatment Limited received certification for both QS 9000 and ISO 9002.

Uddeholm produces a complete range of high-quality tool steels, including powder metallurgy grades for improved tool performance and lower tooling and production costs. Uddeholm has a long-established reputation for introducing new grades and services, while adopting the latest production techniques to ensure that product quality is of the highest order. Uddeholm's mills are ISO 9001 (tooling) and ISO 9002 (strip) registered.

Uddeholm Limited distributes top-quality steel to tool and die makers, as well as mould makers, who specialize in the creating of metal stamping, plastics moulding, die casting, extrusion and press forging. Almost any plastic product you can imagine must be shaped, pressed, cut or moulded during production. In turn, these processes form products ranging from automobile dashboards to CDs to Tupperware products.

Selling specialty steel may be Uddeholm's primary business, yet its concept is customer service—service in exacting specifications from

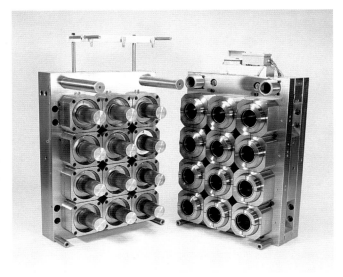

A 12-cavity mould constructed from Uddeholm's mould steels. Courtesy of Tradesco Mold Limited.

the most modern type of metal cutting saws and milling machines to qualified metallurgists. In fact, wherever tools are made or used, Uddeholm is there to ensure readily available tooling materials backed by strong technical support. ⓜ

*T*he first order that Upper Canada Forest Products ever received was for $5,000 worth of red oak lumber, used by a woodworking company to manufacture doors. They've been opening doors in their industry ever since.

UCFP's management team *from left to right:* **Brin Langmuir, Sales Manager; Michael Dabner, Director of Operations; Andrea Moore, Controller; Mark Mah, Vice-President; Warren Spitz, President**

Founded in 1986, the company is a wholesale distributor of hardwood and softwood lumber. Their customers include the manufacturers of countless wood products, from furniture to flooring, millwork to mouldings, and cabinets to cribs.

President Warren Spitz says Upper Canada's edge comes from raising the level of excellence in the industry, through quality people, service and products.

Upper Canada's head office in Mississauga, Ontario

The company focuses on hardwood lumber, providing premier domestic and imported products, as well as specialty softwoods.

Along with their Mississauga head office and distribution centre, Upper Canada has sales offices and warehouse facilities in Vancouver and Kelowna, British Columbia. They also wholesale their products throughout Canada.

In the U.S., Upper Canada does business through sister company Sierra Forest Products Inc. Its office is located in Salt Lake City, Utah, with a sales office in San Francisco. Sierra also carries a full line of hardwood and softwood products, in addition to a full line of high-quality sheet goods.

Upper Canada's sales group view themselves not merely as sales representatives but as lumber consultants, working to see how their range of products can best meet their customers' requirements.

"We never say, 'Here's the product and the price,'" says Mr. Spitz. "Our goal is to add value to their business, by learning more about their market, products and processes. That way we are better able to meet their needs. We want to be their business partner."

The strategy is working. Upper Canada has at least doubled their size every three years, and is among the fastest-growing hardwood lumber companies in North America.

In 1997 the company moved into their new head office and warehouse facility in Mississauga, a 68,000-square-foot complex, which will enable them to maintain their unparalleled level of customer service. Upper Canada also has their own fleet of curtain-side trucks to ensure prompt deliveries and rapid off-loading.

The son of a successful British Columbia logging entrepreneur and no stranger to logging camps while growing up, Mr. Spitz dismisses suggestions he was destined to end up in the wood business. "I was encouraged by my family to go to university and graduated with a degree in business administration.

Upper Canada Forest Products Ltd.

However, it was pure coincidence that I ended up in the lumber business."

Just 28 when he founded the company a decade ago, he describes Upper Canada as highly entrepreneurial, full of young, yet experienced staff with a core group of managers that has remained intact for years.

Upper Canada staff are given a thorough education and hands-on experience in all the company's products and service practices. New sales and operations trainees learn the business of buying and selling lumber from the ground up, beginning their employment at Upper Canada by working in the warehouse. The company is firmly committed to ongoing staff education and training.

Today Upper Canada Forest Products stands as an example of excellence in the lumber industry, as durable and admired as a finely crafted piece of wood. Ⓜ

Photo by Jeff Chevrier

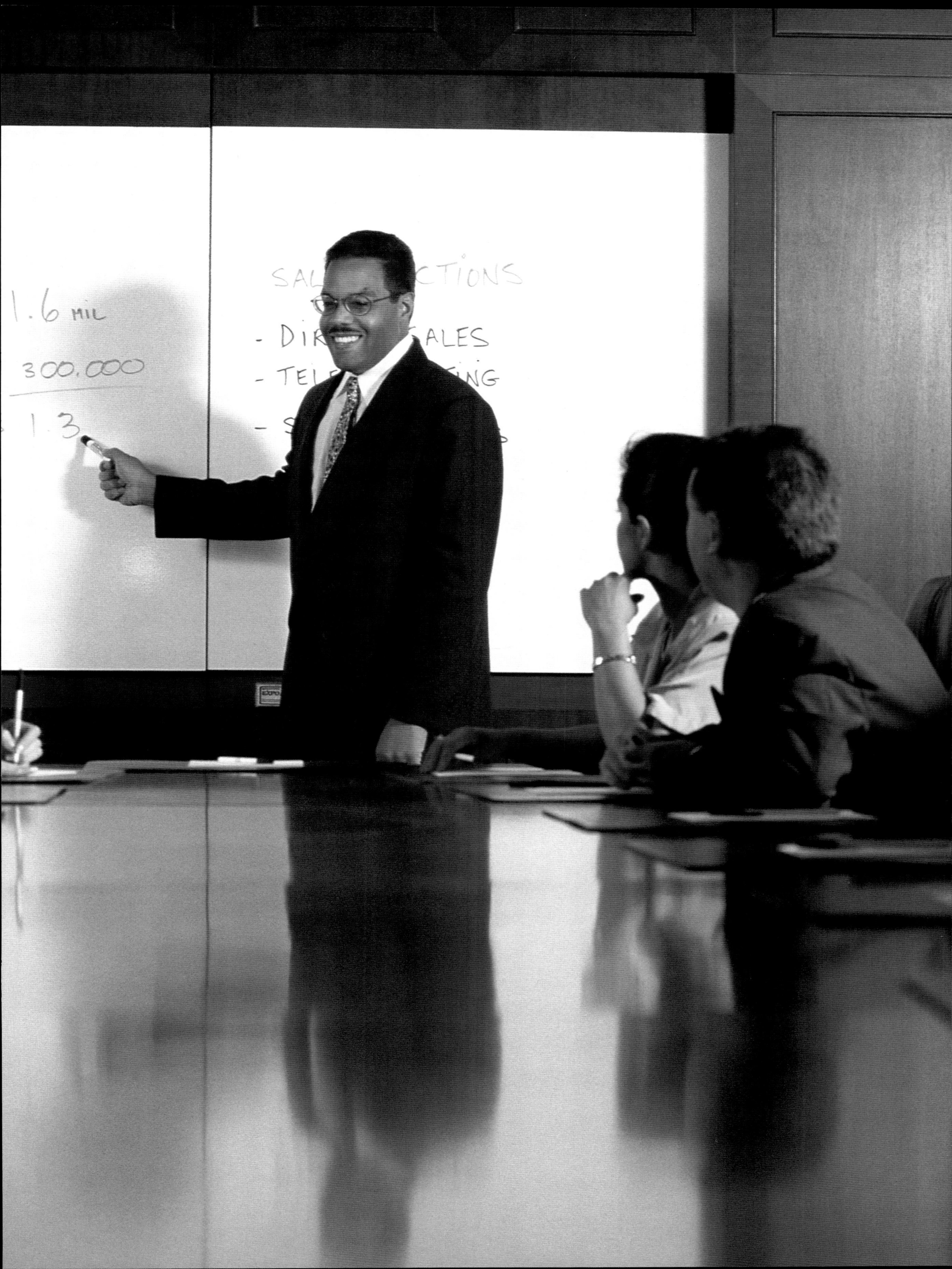
1.6 MIL
300,000
1.3

The time has long since passed when a company's accounting firm did little more than undertake a financial audit verifying financial statements.

In the 1990s, companies such as Price Waterhouse are as much business advisers as they are Chartered Accountants. They must

Price Waterhouse

offer clients a wide range of business advisory skills, which now include information technology, change integration, pension advisory and corporate finance services.

The Mississauga office of Price Waterhouse is among the leaders in the changing business world, one of the major reasons it has increased its staff from 25 when it opened its doors in Mississauga in 1977 to more than 175 professional staff. PW, as it is known in the industry, recognized the potential business growth of the city and has been a major contributor to it.

When the Colleges of Applied Arts & Technologies wanted to take its capital out of the Ontario Municipal Employees Retirement Fund, it turned to Price Waterhouse. The result was that PW staff assisted in the negotiated settlement that saw the more than 22,000 members' $2.7 billion assets transferred to a new pension fund.

Price Waterhouse set up the infrastructure, assisted with the fund's governance structure and assisted in managing a $750-million global equity liquidation.

The project wasn't unique or unusual. It's all part of the extensive services Price Waterhouse offers clients in Mississauga and around the world. PW staff in the Mississauga office can communicate by way of e-mail with thousands of other consultants in any one, or all, of the 110 countries where Price Waterhouse is located.

As PW's services have become more varied, so, too, has the type of person joining the firm. While Chartered Accountants still handle about 50 per cent of all PW's business, it's just as likely that a lawyer, systems analyst, pension consultant, computer programmer and tax specialist will be part of the team assigned to major clients to provide depth of resources. In addition, the traditional auditing, accounting and business advisory services are provided to a wide range of clients in Mississauga.

Evolving technologies such as the Internet, World Wide Web and high tech demand new expertise and are proving to be major growth areas for Price Waterhouse's Mississauga office. Mississauga is quickly becoming a major centre for the high-tech industry and PW is well positioned to offer a full range of services in that area. At the same time, though, Price

Waterhouse hasn't neglected the traditional range of services expected of it. It provides integrated advisory services to a number of the leading companies, public sector organizations and pension plans.

The Advisory Business Service group offers complete auditing, accounting, financing, initial public offerings and restructuring services, and PW has worked closely with a number of major firms to make acquisitions.

Susan Allen, a partner in the Mississauga office and a director on the Living Arts Centre Board, received a Civic Award of Merit for her contributions to the community during the years leading up to the Centre's opening.

The Information Systems Risk Management group assists in the evaluation of controls over computer systems, disaster recovery procedures, as well as assisting companies in special security considerations relating to the Internet.

The Management Consulting Services group assists in the selection and implementation of various financial and manufacturing systems, data warehousing and custom system development.

The Pension Services group provides corporate and public sector clients with plan design, executive pension arrangements and pension plan conversions.

The Corporate Recovery group is responsible for implementing reorganizations or, where necessary, the liquidation of assets, as was the case with the Bargain Harold stores and Bramalea, a major industrial land development firm.

Like so many other employers in Canada and around the world, Price Waterhouse has had to deal with the growing importance of women in the workplace. With 23 offices from Halifax to Vancouver employing more than 2,000 men and women full time, there remained the issue of lack of career opportunities for female staff.

The company realized as long ago as 1988 that a disproportionate number of women left the firm before becoming partners. In response,

Staff of the Mississauga office of Price Waterhouse

PW established a task force on Family and Lifestyle Programs and Policies to address the problem.

As a result of the task force's report and implementation of its recommendations, the firm improved its maternity benefits and introduced two flexible work programs in 1989: part-time, under which professional staff at the managerial level and above could work as little as 60 per cent of a full-time schedule, and core hours, which allowed staff to limit their office hours to 10 a.m. to 4 p.m., while doing the balance of their work from home.

While more than 100 women seized the opportunity, the firm continued to lose a significant number of talented women. It hired outside consultants to interview and run focus groups for those who had quit.

The result was a new three-year plan that saw PW launch a child and elder care referral service; a new staff appraisal program that links every employee with a development counselor; gender awareness and sensitivity training; providing guidance to managers on how better to work with flexible work options; developing better procedures and policies for dealing with sexual harassment and conducting annual staff opinion surveys to monitor the program's progress.

Having more women in management positions, especially as partners, has led to a significant change in attitude, not only among females,

but also among male employees, who are coming to realize that women have a valuable contribution to make to Price Waterhouse and its clients, many of whom are now also women.

This commitment by senior management to flexible lifestyles and women's initiatives has helped Price Waterhouse to be recognized as one of the best companies to work for in Canada.

While Price Waterhouse has a genuine concern for its employees, it plays a leading role in the community, as well. Many employees participate in, and contribute to, a wide sphere of civic endeavors, including The Credit Valley Hospital, Junior Achievement, the Canadian Cancer Society and the Mississauga Board of Trade.

Susan Allen, a partner in the Mississauga office, was president of the Mississauga Arts Council and a director on the Living Arts Centre Board during the years leading up to the Centre's opening. She received a Civic Award of Merit for her contributions to the community.

The ambition of Price Waterhouse is to be "the leading global consultants, committed to solve complex business problems" for its clients. To help achieve that goal, the Mississauga office recently added two new partners in the Advisory Services group and another to oversee its Canada-wide MCS practice.

| **The Mississauga office of PW**

Both moves were in response to the significant growth opportunities in the local economy, once again proving Price Waterhouse is well positioned to be a leader in Mississauga—and around the world. **𝕄**

| **Monty Baker, senior partner**
| **Price Waterhouse, Mississauga**

nsuring yourself against risk is a concept as old as recorded history. Back in 1700 B.C., the Code of Hammurabi in Babylonia provided that a borrower could pay extra to forego a debt, if personal misfortune made repayment impossible—an early form of credit insurance.

Kingsway Financial Services

Kingsway Financial Services has a staff of 250, and is served by over 3,000 brokers across Canada.

In ancient Rome, the Collegia gave its members disability insurance (as well as old-age pensions and a burial). And in more recent times, three centuries ago, underwriting emerged at Lloyd's coffeehouse in London, when people willing to share the risk of insuring a ship's freight would sign their names under the statement of cargo.

"A good spread of risk" is the foundation of the insurance industry, says industry veteran William Star, founder and CEO of Kingsway Financial Services. But any risks taken in building the firm have been "calculated." Kingsway prefers to talk about its steady rise as "a logical progression."

It's a progression that has made Kingsway Financial Services one of the fastest growing group of property and casualty insurance companies in Canada. The group consists of Kingsway General Insurance Company, York Fire & Casualty Insurance Company, Transit Insurance Company and Jevco Insurance Company.

Kingsway was launched in 1986 out of a rented 800-square-foot office. By the time the company celebrated its 10th anniversary, it was operating from a 73,000-square-foot space

in its own building, and trading on the Toronto Stock Exchange.

Few Canadian insurance firms are public companies, but Star felt the initial public offering would give Kingsway the capital needed to support continued expansion.

"For every dollar in capital, we can write $2.75 in premiums," he says. "The whole idea is to be financially strong to look after the risks we take, and create a solid base of insurance companies. I also thought it was important that people view the insurance industry as a sound investment."

That has certainly been true in the case of Kingsway, which has had a proven record of profitability and returns on equity that are well above the industry average. The company's strategy includes careful underwriting, good pricing, stringent claims management and specialization.

Its main business is non-standard automobile insurance. Kingsway covers drivers whose driving records don't satisfy the underwriting criteria of standard insurers, mainly due to accidents or traffic violations.

The company also operates in the commercial automobile, property and other specialty markets, and through Jevco is the largest writer of policies for motorcyclists in Canada. One intriguing plan, from York Fire & Casualty, is aimed at policyholders who abstain from alcohol, much as policies that offer a break to non-smokers.

Growth areas include surety bonds, marine

cargo, pleasurecraft and long-haul trucking (the specialty of Transit Insurance).

Kingsway moved to Mississauga from its original home because of lower taxes, better highway access, and the proximity to the airport—handy now that the company has offices in Montreal and Calgary.

The company has a staff of 250, and is served by over 3,000 brokers across Canada. Kingsway uses an "open market" approach, which means no contracts, no minimum volume commitments and higher commissions to attract the kind of business Kingsway wants.

Kingsway has been able to prosper by pursuing niche markets where limited competition allows above-average returns.

At the same time, the company refuses to sacrifice underwriting profitability to increase volume, operates at a lower expense ratio than the industry average and rapidly terminates unprofitable lines of business.

The company doesn't even try to seek traditional lines of business, feeling that, despite its growth, Kingsway is still too small to compete that way. Instead, the Kingsway group has gone after lines of business that other companies simply don't want. Handling bonding for Canada Customs work is a prime example. Kingsway aggressively sought the business and has managed to capture over 50 per cent of the market. Company officials say that most insurance companies don't even bother with that particular line.

In its first full year, Kingsway wrote $8 million in business, not bad for a fledgling insur-

William Star, founder and CEO of Kingsway Financial Services, welcomes the mayor to the opening celebration.

Mayor Hazel McCallion cuts the ribbon during the opening celebration of Kingsway Financial Services.

ance firm. A decade later, the company wrote 20 times that amount, and the figures continue to rise.

To investors, the company is attractive because of its high profitability. Star notes that unlike most insurance companies, Kingsway actually makes money on its underwriting.

"We're one of the few insurance companies in Canada to consistently have an underwriting profit," he says. "Other companies rely on investment income to make their profit."

That emphasis on profitability is not just a corporate strategy; it's the corporate philosophy. Most insurers don't take in enough premiums to cover their losses and expenses, resulting in an underwriting loss. This loss represents the financing cost of the float of money—available from the time the premium is collected to the time the claim is paid—that insurers have available to invest.

In Kingsway's case, their float is essentially free. That's strictly because the company has achieved underwriting profits. This access to "free money" significantly boosts Kingsway's performance.

The company plans to accelerate its growth by continuing to focus on profitable specialty insurance markets, and through strategic acquisitions. Buying other insurers is actually made easier by being a public company, as Kingsway has the ability to issue shares as part of the purchase.

Another advantage of being public is the opportunity to give employees a stake in the company through share ownership. Kingsway enables payroll deduction to let staff buy shares, with the company kicking in part of the price.

Because staff can directly benefit from the company's success, Kingsway features a sense of teamwork, ambition and excitement in seeing the company evolve.

"People are buying two things when they get insurance," says Star, "protection and service. We provide good products and good service, and that's the main thing that's allowed us to grow." Ⓜ

Guests join in the opening-day festivities at the new office of Kingsway Financial Services.

Since 1978, Mississauga has been home to Mary Kay Cosmetics Ltd., a subsidiary of Texas-based Mary Kay Inc. The company's success story began in 1963 after Mary Kay Ash "retired" from a long and prosperous career in direct sales. She dreamed about a company of her own which would give women unlimited

Mary Kay Cosmetics

opportunities for career advancement and personal and financial success. She already had the

An informal skin care class is conducted by a beauty consultant and attended by approximately three to five guests. The consultant teaches her guests a personalized regimen of good skin care with Mary Kay's five-step program.

perfect product—skin care products she had been using for years. She purchased the formulas, providing the basis for her initial product line, and opened a small storefront in Dallas, Texas.

Since the company's inception, Mary Kay has used the Golden Rule as her guiding philosophy. She encourages employees and sales force members to prioritize their lives: God first, family second, career third. Mary Kay also believes in praising people to success. The company's incentive and reward programs are world renowned. With special promotions, prize programs and the famous career car program, beauty consultants and directors are recognized for every career accomplishment. Undoubtedly, the pink Cadillac is one of the most sought-after career rewards!

The beauty consultant often begins her career with Mary Kay as a customer. At an informal skin care class conducted by a consultant, she is taught a personalized regimen of good skin care. Classes are held in the home of a "hostess" who has invited approximately three to five friends to participate in a smoothly paced two-hour session. The consultant teaches her guests about proper skin care through Mary Kay's five-step program, and guests can return home and start their new skin care and color cosmetic routines immediately.

The class is where brand loyalty begins and long-term consumer buying relationships are established. It is also at the skin care class that a customer is first introduced to the Mary Kay career opportunity—one that has become a serious career choice for thousands of women. Each

Since 1978 Mississauga has been home to Mary Kay Cosmetics Ltd., a subsidiary of Texas-based Mary Kay Inc. The current office, a 76,000-square-foot building built in 1994, is located at 2020 Meadowvale Boulevard.

beauty consultant is self-employed, not an employee of the company. Only one wholesale distributor exists between the company and the consumer—consultants buy directly from the company on a wholesale basis and sell to customers at retail.

Beauty consultants set their own schedule and advance at a pace they set for themselves. When the consultant begins sharing the Mary Kay career opportunity with others, she can work towards becoming a sales director by building a unit of consultants.

Every independent Mary Kay beauty consultant is in business for herself, but never by herself. With the support of staff at the Mississauga corporate headquarters in departments such as sales development, product marketing, service support and fleet administration, career guidance and product information are just a phone call away. In addition, the company continually provides education, sales aids and advertising support, and conducts meetings and special events to help consultants build their business.

The Canadian headquarters is based in a 76,000-square-foot building built in 1994. Decorated in soft pastels and neutrals, the building houses an impressive collection of Canadian art, an ongoing venture that began when the subsidiary opened in 1978. Dedicated to providing the best possible service to consultants, hundreds of orders are processed, picked and shipped in the 50,000-square-foot warehouse each day. Each employee at Mary Kay strives to maintain the company's high standards and dedication to service. It is no surprise that Mary Kay Cosmetics Ltd. has twice been recognized by the *Financial Post* as one of the 100 best companies to work for in Canada.

The *Mary Kay*® product line includes more than 200 products in nine categories: basic skin care, skin supplements, color cosmetics, nail care, hair care, body care, sun protection, fragrances and men's skin care. All products, imported and locally produced, are distributed through the warehouse in Mississauga, assuring that consultants and their customers receive their products in an efficient and timely manner.

Mary Kay is also a company with a conscience. Since 1989, Mary Kay has not engaged in animal testing—the company neither conducts nor causes testing of its products or ingredients on laboratory animals. The company is an active participant in programs to develop alternative testing methods. Mary Kay also consistently works to preserve the environment through such steps as using recycled packaging materials and eliminating unnecessary packaging. *Mary Kay®* products, too, are environmentally friendly.

Mary Kay Cosmetics Ltd. is a founding member of the Look Good…Feel Better Foundation, a program dedicated to teaching beauty techniques that enhance the appearance and boost the self-esteem of women undergoing cancer treatments. The company has rallied behind the program and annually donates products for use in patient workshops, while many beauty consultants donate their time and expertise at local workshops, helping cancer patients "look good and feel better."

In June of 1989, Mary Kay Cosmetics introduced a sun care public awareness program called *Skin Wellness®*. The program is designed to educate the public about the dangers of sun exposure and how to best protect themselves and their family members.

Mary Kay has some of the most loyal customers in the cosmetics industry, thanks primarily to the company's unwavering commitment to offer products that consistently meet the highest standards of quality, safety and

performance, all backed by the company's 100-per cent customer satisfaction guarantee.

As Mary Kay Cosmetics enters its third decade of success in Canada, its primary goal hasn't changed: to offer women of all cultures and backgrounds a real career alternative that allows increased time with their families, recognition and rewards for their efforts and financial independence.

When Mary Kay Ash started the company back in 1963, she did so with the fulfillment of

Mary Kay believes in praising people to success. The company's incentive and reward programs are world renowned. With special promotions, prize programs, and the famous career car program, beauty consultants and directors are recognized for every career accomplishment.

a dream in mind. Today, Mary Kay Canada is the outgrowth of Mary Kay's clear vision of a better economic opportunity for women. As Mississauga Mayor Hazel McCallion noted during the grand opening of the new Canadian headquarters in 1995, "Behind every great corporation is a woman." **Ⓜ**

The company continually provides education, product marketing and advertising support, and career guidance. The company also conducts meetings and special events to help consultants build their business. Here, sales directors attend a workshop at the company's annual conference in Toronto. The conference is attended by close to 2,000 beauty consultants from across Canada each year.

*I*n any business, there are many more ways to measure success than the dollars and cents of transactions—even when your business is literally dollars and cents.

Royal Bank Financial Group knows that having more customers than any other Canadian bank is an achievement. But even

Royal Bank Financial Group

more important than the volume of customers is the extent to which they are satisfied and appreciated. That is a standard of success which will inevitably lead to customer loyalty and increased business.

Which brings us to the bank's Metro West Business Banking Group, serving Etobicoke and Mississauga from its location at 33 City Centre Drive, across from Square One in Mississauga. In an organization that is driven to ensure customer satisfaction, the Business Banking Groups across Metro West have had the distinction of attaining the very highest overall customer satisfaction ratings.

That's often the sign of a motivated and knowledgeable staff, and the Business Banking Groups possess that too; measured against other Royal Bank units, employee satisfaction levels across Metro West are also the highest in the country.

These high ratings, on both the customer and employee side, come from an ability to truly serve the distinct needs of entrepreneurs and corporations.

The Business Banking Organization is a model concept, comprising about 100 staff who are split into three market segments: commercial, small and medium-sized enterprises and growth markets known as Knowledge-Based Industries.

This last category was created specifically to meet the needs of fast-growing companies in the areas of information technology and life sciences, which are so prevalent in Mississauga. With fewer accounts per account manager and specialized industry knowledge and training, the team will be able to add more value and spend more time with each customer.

Segmenting the business client base gives all of the bank's account managers the opportunity to build their understanding of the various industries, and avoid a "one-size-fits-all" approach.

| **"Royal Bank Financial Group" members**

Teams of account managers are positioned at seven locations across Mississauga and Etobicoke. An in-house credit approval team ensures quick turnaround of loan requests, while other support groups—including administration, cash management and technology—make the entire unit extremely productive and virtually self-sufficient.

Royal Bank has a strong presence in Mississauga. In addition to the Business Banking staff at 33 City Centre Drive, this location includes offices for Royal Trust (investment management, trust and custody services), RBC Dominion Securities (investment advice), and Private Banking (wealth management for the complex needs of high-income customers).

While this unique building offers customers "one-stop shopping," the Group has continually added branches to Mississauga as the city has grown. It now boasts 29 branches throughout the community.

Mississauga is also home to a Royal Direct call centre that serves not only the city's bank customers but also the entire Ontario market. In itself, the call centre is a key area employer.

Royal Bank Financial Group's breadth and depth in Mississauga simply underlines its position as Canada's premier financial institution. Consider its scope and track record:

- Royal Bank Financial Group's 55,000 staff provide and support financial products and services to nearly 10 million consumers and business customers in 35 countries.
- The bank's delivery network includes nearly 1,600 branches and offices, more than 4,200 automated banking machines, more than 500 self-service account updaters, and some 50,000 point-of-sale merchant terminals.
- In Canada, Royal Bank has the leading market share in residential mortgages, consumer loans, personal deposits and Canadian dollar business loans.
- The Group is the largest money manager, and the third largest in mutual funds (first among bank-owned funds).
- The Group owns the biggest and most profitable full-service investment dealer (RBC Dominion Securities), and offers the largest and most lucrative global banking operation.
- The Group's discount brokerage operation, Action Direct, is the second largest in Canada, while in insurance Royal Bank ranks among the top generators of life insurance premiums (first among Canadian banks).
- Internationally, Royal Bank is a leader in corporate and investment banking, trade finance, correspondent banking and treasury services for business customers.

With the intense competition among financial institutions, Royal Bank understands that the ingredients for continued success are no mystery: quality service, and innovative products leading to customer value.

At the branch level, the bank builds stronger relationships through proactive financial advice and effective problem resolution. A major emphasis on training ensures that front-line employees have the sound investment knowledge that today's customers demand.

One measure of the focus on ongoing education is the registration figures from the Institute of Canadian Bankers. They show that members of Royal Bank Financial Group have almost twice as many registrations for courses as the next leading financial institution.

With a well-trained staff, it's no surprise that Royal Bank Financial Group has received excellent service ratings (based on independent research) in several key markets and product areas.

To maintain its leading position, the Group also continually strives to introduce products, new areas of business (thanks to re-regulation) and new ways of doing business that extend value and convenience to the customer.

That could include anything from a new Visa card offering instant retail discounts to a personal investment "boutique," Internet banking to insurance options, and financing programs to integrated trading units.

Any responsible bank helps build communities not only through sound financial products and services, but also through community involvement. That is certainly true for Royal Bank in Mississauga.

Just mull over the list of causes to which the bank lends its financial and volunteer support, either corporately or through the efforts of staff: United Way of Peel, Mississauga Hospital, Credit Valley Hospital, the Living Arts Centre, Mississauga Symphony, the Mississauga Crime Prevention Association, Peel Children's Safety Village, Carassauga, the Bread and Honey Festival, the Mayor's annual gala, the Mississauga Shrine Circus, Peel Junior Achievement, the City of Mississauga Economic Advisory Council and numerous local sports organizations.

This and other support helps enrich the fabric of the community immeasurably. The strong commitment to the people of Mississauga complement Royal Bank Financial Group's imaginative products and superior services. Together, it all illustrates the Group's greatest characteristic: the ability to exceed expectations…and deliver satisfaction its customers can bank on. Ⓜ

The movie *Field of Dreams* has a famous line: "If you build it, they will come." In many ways, that has been the reality of Mississauga's business growth. With a top-notch infrastructure, accessible highway system, prestige business parks, Canada's largest international airport and among the lowest

Mississauga's Economic Development Office

taxes in the Greater Toronto Area (GTA), countless companies have found their city of dreams in Mississauga.

Just as businesses must market their products and services, so too, the City must sell itself to the business world. That's the job of the Economic Development Office (EDO). Its vision: develop a dynamic, competitive business environment that fosters economic growth and prosperity for the citizens of Mississauga.

"Every EDO markets its city as a good place to do business while reflecting the particular image of that city," says Karen Campbell, director of Economic Development. "In Mississauga, we strive to attract and retain investment by creating awareness of Mississauga as a superior business community. Our corporate slogan reaffirms our progressive image: leading today

The Economic Development Office works closely with realtors to ensure that business clients find the best location in Mississauga to fit their needs.

for tomorrow. We pride ourselves in delivering quality services at a lower cost, so we keep taxes down. The business-like attitude of our City is a real asset."

For companies considering a move, the EDO helps find the best location—whether an existing industrial building, office space or serviced land for a custom-designed facility—and guides them through municipal regulations and procedures, allowing a smooth business transition.

The EDO touts Mississauga's benefits through its brochures, advertising, newsletters, trade shows and the City's Web site on the Internet. It also uses aggressive strategies, such as targeting high-growth sectors including information technology, biomedical and automotive. "Important leads also result from realtors familiar with what the City can offer," states Campbell.

EDO activities touch on businesses of all sizes, from top 500 companies (Mississauga is Canada's fifth largest head office centre according to the *Financial Post*) to new start-ups. "Every type of business is vital to our economy," says Campbell. The Small Business Self-Help Office located within the EDO, for example, handles approximately 20,000 inquiries and 500 individual consultations annually and runs a series of popular business-related seminars.

Mississauga's downtown boasts more than 3 million square feet (300,000 square metres) of office space, eastern Canada's largest shopping centre, lots of entertainment, great restaurants and a substantial high-rise residential community.

Along with gaining valuable advice, businesses benefit from the EDO's connections with municipal, provincial, federal and industry-specific bodies. These links help local companies access the right government programs, influence senior levels of government on business issues and "plug in" to networking groups.

To support a company's business plans, detailed information and statistics are also available on topics including demographics, market conditions, taxes, labour and employment, services and utilities and transportation. As well, the EDO produces an annual business directory with detailed information on Mississauga's manufacturing, wholesale and service industries.

"Through our diligent efforts, we have successfully attracted many blue chip Canadian and foreign-owned businesses to the city," says Karen Campbell. "Companies have done extensive research before locating their businesses here, so they know that Mississauga offers them an environment of excellence in which they can succeed." **Ⓜ**

Keyser Mason Ball, situated in the heart of Mississauga, has developed over the past 20 years through amalgamation, diversification and planned expansion. Today, this firm of over 60 lawyers and staff is the largest full-service law firm in Mississauga.

The founding partners of the firm, John Keyser, Colin Mason and John Ball, have each imparted unique qualities to the firm's evolution, but all three have always emphasized the vital importance of responding quickly and effectively to each client's needs. In the day-to-day pursuit of the law, this penultimate operating principle has motivated the firm to make comprehensive changes as the firm has grown, not only in the ways of interpreting and applying the law, but also in the growing number of people and technologies the firm employs to practice it.

Traditionally, law firms have organized themselves into departmentally structured divisions consisting of experts practicing in distinctly specialized areas of the law. In today's competitive marketplace, however, such a configuration often does not respond quickly or effectively to a client's overall requirements. The fact that no client exists within a vacuum mirrors the certainty that no lawyer should function in one either.

The practice group approach advocated at Keyser Mason Ball is essentially the marriage of like disciplines, best aligned to provide clients with the maximum benefit of the collective skills and expertise the firm has to offer. Tailored to each client's individual situation, this inspired teamwork approach enables innovative solutions to complex legal problems and helps clients determine creative strategic planning for the future.

The firm's structure of related practice group areas allows them to provide clients not only with the benefits of a personal lawyer-client relationship, but also with access to the myriad of legal skills and expertise which the teamwork approach embraces.

Experienced executives administer the firm's day-to-day operation, and an exceptional professional support staff proficiently expedites routine matters, conserving time and money for lawyers and clients alike.

What distinguishes Keyser Mason Ball from its competitors is the firm's demonstrated commitment to meeting the increasingly sophisticated legal demands of both the city and its growing business base. Apart from valuable people resources, the firm also draws from a vast reservoir of state-of-the-art technology. A complete and current library, professionally

maintained and computerized, a sophisticated computer network including voice-activated computer technology, direct on-line service and Internet access have all significantly reduced the time and costs traditionally associated with the practice of law.

Responsive to the increasingly global

Keyser Mason Ball

demands of business today, Keyser Mason Ball offers clients the expertise of legal associations throughout North America, Europe and the Far East. These international affiliations augment the scope of legal service available to clients of the firm.

With Mississauga's population expected to double over the next 10 years, Keyser Mason Ball is ready to meet the challenge of providing legal expertise to both domestic and international companies in an ever-changing economic and regulatory environment. Ⓜ

$\mathcal{W}$hat do Red Skelton, Whirlpool and Algoma Steel have in common?

On the surface, not much. Behind the scenes, however, is the legal firm of Barrigar & Moss, which represents all three in Canada. Barrigar & Moss, with offices in Mississauga, Ottawa, Vancouver and Victoria, is one of the

Barrigar & Moss

larger and more influential intellectual property law firms in the country.

The firm was established by Robert H. Barrigar in Ottawa in March 1974. Separately, W. Dennis Moss opened an office in Mississauga in 1977 and the two firms merged in 1990. Lawyers in the firm include members of the Ontario, British Columbia and Alberta bar associations.

Barrigar & Moss restricts its practice to patents, trademarks, copyrights and designs, as well as trade secret law, computer law, technology transfer and licensing, franchising, unfair competition and anti-combines (antitrust) law and related litigation. All lawyers in the firm are registered patent agents or registered trademark agents, or both.

So, where do Skelton and Whirlpool fit in? Barrigar & Moss handles both Red's copyright affairs and Whirlpool's patent matters in Canada. So, for example, should someone reproduce tapes of Red Skelton shows without his permission, or copy the patented dual-action agitators in Whirlpool's washing machines, Barrigar & Moss is called upon to take whatever steps are necessary to protect their interests.

Left to right: **Adrian Kaplan, Dennis Moss, David Greer, Peter Hammond and Eric Devenny**

Front row, left to right: **Peter Hammond, Michelle Bonsteel, Kathleen McGill, Ursula Roman and Katherine Lam.** Rear row, left to right: **Erin Dyke, Dennis Moss, Marcela Vleck, Adrian Kaplan, David Greer and Eric Devenny.**

In addition to its international reputation of providing high-quality service and technical expertise in such areas as mechanical, electrical and chemical engineering, Barrigar & Moss has hundreds of local clients who like the idea of dealing with a local company, a firm that has business and personal roots in the community.

Coincidentally, most of the firm's partners are also qualified engineers in addition to having their degrees in law. Robert Barrigar obtained his Bachelor of Applied Science degree from the University of Toronto in engineering physics; Dennis Moss has a Bachelor of Applied Science degree in mechanical engineering from the University of Waterloo; and Peter Hammond studied civil engineering at the University of Toronto.

Thus, Barrigar & Moss is well qualified to handle intricate cases relating to patents, trademarks, copyrights and industrial designs in a broad range of industries.

Under the direction of Peter Hammond, the Mississauga office has been responsible for obtaining patent protection for a local inventor of games, including a baseball board game and a hockey board game, both of which were successfully licensed to a major Canadian toy manufacturer. Dennis Moss has obtained patents for inventors of everything from fishing lines and waterbeds to automotive radar and nuclear power plant equipment.

Long Manufacturing Inc., a Mississauga-based multi-national manufacturer of many of the automotive radiators and heat exchangers found in most of the automobiles we drive today, is also a long time client of Barrigar & Moss.

Among the more unusual inventions Barrigar & Moss has handled are a goalie stick with a big bend in the handle, permitting the goalie to get a better grip, and a pair of sunglasses with a mirror coating on the inside of the lenses so you can see someone coming up from behind you.

The phenomenal success of the Trivial Pursuit game brought board game inventors swarming into the offices of patent attorneys such as Barrigar & Moss, but that craze has died out with the new emphasis on computers, the Internet and electronic gadgets.

These current crazes should keep Barrigar & Moss occupied well into the next century. Ⓜ

Established as a Canadian-chartered bank in 1981, Banca Commerciale Italiana of Canada (BCI Bank) is a wholly owned subsidiary of Banca Commerciale Italiana, a leading global institution represented in 49 countries.

BCI Bank is a full-service bank ready to meet the needs of individuals, businesses and corporations alike through a wide range of products and services. These include competitive interest rates on mortgages and personal loans, savings and chequing accounts, high-interest RSPs and the BCI Bank MasterCard. BCI Bank also offers a wide range of commercial and corporate loans. Reliability and dependability are two of the institution's principal commitments, and these qualities go hand in hand with the Bank's emphasis on personalized service and a "we're glad to see you and we want to help" approach to doing business.

There are nine BCI Bank branches in southwestern Ontario alone, including Mississauga. There are also three branches in the Montreal area and one in Vancouver. Mr. Gennaro Stammati, president and CEO of BCI Bank, emphasizes that across Canada, BCI Bank is dedicated to helping its customers meet their financial goals. "Our mission is straightforward—to build lasting relationships of trust and respect with our customers by understanding their needs, and through the committed professionalism of our employees, to contribute to the financial success of our customers and that of the Bank." Adds Mr. Stammati, "We strive for service excellence in everything we do, whether we are meeting the needs of individual depositors and borrowers, small or medium-sized businesses, or large corporations doing business within Canada or abroad."

BCI Bank's slogan is "We treat you like family." To that end, the Bank is continually looking for ways to make the services it provides more accessible and more competitive. In addition to being able to challenge the more "traditional" Canadian banks in the areas of commercial and personal accounts, residential mortgages and RSPs, clients may also take advantage of the convenience of ABM and debit cards with the "Expresso" card both in Canada and abroad. What's more, the Bank prides itself on its commitment to serving the community. According to Mr. Stammati, "We take an active role in communities throughout the world, and our Canadian branches are no exception. We are proud to support cultural events which enrich the lives of our Canadian banking family. In addition, we are very proud of our branch in Mississauga and of our employees who offer solutions that contribute to our customers' financial success, and that of the city."

Through an uncompromising standard of banking excellence at the corporate, business and individual levels, BCI Bank offers its clients the widest possible range of competitive products

BCI Bank

and services. As a financial institution that's able to offer the kind of efficient, individualized attention so highly sought after in today's banking world, it's no accident that BCI Bank is able to deliver on its promise to clients: "We treat you like family." Ⓜ

BCI Bank is a full-service bank ready to meet the needs of individuals, businesses and corporations alike with a "we're glad to see you and we want to help" approach.

$\mathcal{A}$sk just about any company what its biggest day-to-day business problem is and most will respond without hesitation: managing their employees.

"So just imagine what our situation must be like," says Bob Bryce, president and co-founder (with his wife Brenda) of TREBOR

TREBOR Personnel Inc.

Personnel Inc. (TPI) and TPI Staffing Inc.; "our whole business is managing people for others."

Bryce was president of the Canadian subsidiary of a German food services equipment company when, in November 1984, he decided to switch careers and start TREBOR Personnel Inc. Now, TREBOR is one of the biggest suppliers of temporary and contract industrial help in the Greater Toronto Area. It has offices from Belleville in the east to Kitchener-Waterloo in the west and annually supplies between 4,000 to 5,000 workers for firms from the pharmaceutical to the waste and recycling areas—and everything in between.

Pictured are Bob and Brenda Bryce, founders of Trebor Personnel Inc.

A separate division, TPI Driver Services, provides temporary, contract and permanent drivers, and with TPI's temporary-to-permanent worker program, clients no longer spend valuable time, effort and money on recruiting new workers. TPI will fit a worker to a particular need, thus allowing the client to monitor the person's competence before deciding whether or not to hire that person full time. If the fit isn't right, TPI will replace that worker and find a new one. If the person is hired, there is no additional cost associated with the placement.

"TREBOR truly supplies one-stop shopping for its clients," Bryce says. "We have a complete understanding of what companies go through with people. We, in effect, become their professional people managers, thus allowing them to do whatever it is they do best."

"We handle all the paper work associated with providing employees, whether it be for one day, one week or even one year. We pay the workers, look after all the administrative items such as Canada Pension Plan, vacation pay, Revenue Canada and Workers' Compensation."

TREBOR has a staff of fully trained placement coordinators at each office. It is their duty to supply each client with the right personnel:

quickly, efficiently and cost-effectively. TPI builds an extensive database of local workers for each office because it is easier to service the client locally and many of the workers use public transit.

The original office was based in Mississauga and remains the company's headquarters. TREBOR Personnel Inc. is ISO 9002 certified and its operations fully computerized.

When the Bryces started TPI 12 years ago, supplying industrial workers and drivers was a new concept. Now, however, the competition for business is fierce, and Bryce is looking to spread his wings both geographically and in TPI's breadth of services as TPI develops a greater focus on providing both part-time and contract employees in the general office environment.

"If a company has a need or a problem, we can help them solve it with one phone call," Bryce says. "TPI is here to provide good people with full-time hours. Our clients know they can depend on us—any time, all the time." Ⓜ

The Canadian Imperial Bank of Commerce's roots pre-date Canadian confederation, and, like the country, it has grown and prospered over the past 100-plus years.

CIBC is now the second largest financial services institution in Canada and has a significant presence throughout the world. It serves more than 6 million individual customers,

| CIBC, Port Credit, Ontario, since 1908

300,000 small businesses and 10,000 commercial clients. CIBC delivers services through more than 1,400 banking centres and a national network of more than 3,000 ABMs.

Through CIBC Wood Gundy, it offers investment and corporate banking operations worldwide to more than 5,000 corporate, government and institutional clients.

CIBC is the result of the amalgamation of 14 distinct banks, the first of which opened as the Halifax Banking Company in 1825. Over the ensuing years, amalgamations and acquisitions resulted in what was called the Canadian Bank of Commerce, which was based mainly in Ontario, as was its rival, The Imperial Bank of Canada.

But as Canada grew and the population spread from coast to coast, both institutions expanded. The final amalgamation that resulted in the Canadian Imperial Bank of Commerce took place in 1961.

Since then the bank has introduced a new, more modern logo and corporate strategy that better reflects its tradition of stability and integrity and meets the changing needs of its customers.

In Mississauga, the bank has been serving citizens since 1908 when a predecessor, the Sterling Bank of Canada, opened its first branch in Port Credit at the Lakeshore and Stavebank Road. It later became the Standard Bank of Canada and, finally, the CIBC in 1981.

As Mississauga has grown, so too has the CIBC. There are more than 25 local branches, as well as a commercial banking centre, a private banking centre and an Asian banking centre. It is the City's banker and has a long blue-chip list of local customers, including the Mississauga Board of Trade.

The businessmen who established the original bank more than 100 years ago said at the time: "Our policy is to benefit our respective localities by employing our own and the floating capital under our control, in the support of the trade and industry of the place."

CIBC management has never lost sight of that initial objective and is constantly introducing new products and services to help it retain its leadership position in the ever-evolving environment of both retail and commercial banking.

The introduction of telephone and personal computer banking, the debit card and the Mondex cash card are just a few of the areas where CIBC is recognized as an innovator.

Clients can now deal with a single account manager for personal or commercial banking, and customers have the option of using either telephone or personal computers for most transactions, to buy and sell stocks through CIBC's discount brokerage—or to receive quotes on car and home insurance and mortgages.

CIBC

CIBC's goal is to be Canada's pre-eminent financial services company—for its customers, its employees, its shareholders and the communities in which it is situated. In Mississauga, CIBC strives to do everything to support its goal of winning—and retaining—customer loyalty. Ⓜ

| CIBC, Mississauga City Centre

"**S**urety" means a security against loss or damage, and in its antiquated use it referred to something which is beyond doubt.

At Canadian Surety, one of the country's leading property and casualty insurers, protecting clients against loss is, of course, the nature of the business. The company is mindful

The Canadian Surety Company

of the second definition too, ensuring prompt and fair claims handling for customers, and superior service to brokers, both of which are, without doubt, recognized as being in the top level of the industry.

Canadian Surety was incorporated in 1911, and since 1982 has operated its Southern Ontario regional office out of Mississauga. (Sister company Canada West, founded in 1946, is based in Alberta, where it is a leading personal lines insurer.)

Southern Ontario Regional office is located at 5995 Avebury Road, a strategic location for brokers and customer access.

The office is strategically located to serve the company's regional customers and brokers, and was a cost-efficient alternative to the former office in Toronto. This segment of the Ontario market is integral to the company's success, representing about 25 per cent of the Canadian business.

The company markets a wide range of personal and commercial lines exclusively through a network of about 400 independent brokers across Canada, a quarter of them in Southern Ontario. These are the professionals who are closest to the clients and understand their needs best.

A sensitivity to customers' concerns isn't the only reason for Canadian Surety's ability to grow steadily to the point where it ranks, in an extremely competitive business, among the top 25 insurance groups in the country.

The Canadian Surety management team, *standing left to right:* **Carol MacDougal, Claims; Iain Galbraith, Senior Vice-President, Broker Relations; Victoria Taylor, Personal Lines; Cathy Glasser, Human Resources;** *seated, left to right:* **Barbara Addie, President and CEO; Joe Potter, Business Development; Lloyd Hobbs, Commercial Lines; Jane-Anne Barnes, Regional Manager.**

The company is also an innovative insurer, developing creative commercial packages for small and mid-sized business, risk management services for major and international accounts, and added-value extensions like its Home Assistance Program that is one of the keys to the company's continued success.

Canadian Surety and Canada West were the first insurers in North America to offer a program such as Home Assistance, which is automatically included in personal property polices. The coverage includes housekeeping after property damage, babysitting for sick children, homemaking and a visiting nurse after hospitalization, along with a legal information line.

If customers can't reach their broker in case of emergency, Canadian Surety also offers a 24-hour assistance line, all part of the desire to improve and measure service standards. The goal is quite simply to out-perform the industry.

Both Canadian Surety and Canada West are wholly owned subsidiaries of global giant A.G.F. (the Assurances Generale de France Group), whose head office is in Paris. That company has direct or indirect representation in 75 countries, boasts $22 billion in premium income worldwide, is the number two company in France and one of the 10 largest insurers in Europe, insuring such major international organizations as the U.N., N.A.T.O. and the French Aerospace program. **Ⓜ**

*K*PMG is Canada's largest professional services organization. The firm has 4,800 personnel in more than 60 locations across the country, including Mississauga. Canadian-owned and managed, KPMG delivers assurance, consulting, financial advisory and tax services to individuals and businesses, the public sector and not-for-profit organizations.

Partners, left to right: **John Krukowski, Dan Vance, Georgina Tollstam, Bob Rose and Managing Partner, Bill Dillabough**

KPMG is well-positioned to meet clients' international business needs. With a global network of more than 800 offices in 140 countries, KPMG provides access to information and insight into business practices around the world. KPMG has more than 6,000 partners and a worldwide staff of more than 73,000.

The firm's name reflects the four founding partners and their respective practices—Piet Klynveld (Holland), William Peat (England), James Marwick (United States) and Reinhard Goerdeler (Germany). Over the years, the firm, both internationally and in Canada, has

Client service team meeting, left to right: **Orest Szot, Gordi Ann Brisbin and Jim Cassidy**

established a broad geographic coverage and depth of professional resources which has placed it in the unique position to deal with local, cross-border and international matters.

The Mississauga office of KPMG has more than 140 employees and is one of the largest full-service practices in the greater Toronto area. The present client base has a strong focus on the manufacturing, retail and distribution sectors, and services provided to municipalities and not-for-profit organizations. In addition, KPMG's Japanese client business is based in Mississauga. The local office also has significant tax, consulting and financial advisory services practices, providing a wide range of services to the firm's clients.

The office of KPMG Mississauga opened in 1974, and presently occupies space in two of the four office towers on Robert Speck Parkway across from the Mississauga City Centre.

KPMG is proud to have been part of the significant development that has occurred in the Mississauga business community during the past 20 years. Staff members actively volunteer in the community, serving on civic groups, the Economic Development Council, committees involving the Credit Valley Hospital and Mississauga Hospital, the Arts Council, Living Arts Centre, Sports Council, Board of Trade and dozens of other worthy projects.

Such community involvement enables KPMG to make a significant contribution to the community in which it operates, and also where numerous of its staff reside and the majority of its clients operate. As Bill Dillabough, the local office managing partner, and managing partner of KPMG's manufacturing, retail and distribution practice in the Greater Toronto Area, puts it: "In Mississauga, I feel like I

have a voice not only as a businessman, but as a citizen. I continue to be excited about making my living in such a vibrant, prosperous and dynamic city."

KPMG is committed to providing leading-edge, highly creative advice and solutions to businesses of all types and sizes. The firm has

KPMG

the depth and scope of practice to meet the needs of any client in any assignment, and looks forward to the opportunity of continuing to serve clients in Mississauga in the years ahead.

Mississauga, for its part, is fortunate to have a firm such as KPMG. **Ⓜ**

Global strategic business and financial expertise

CHAPTER 15

Real Estate & Construction

Ⓜ

Hammerson Canada Inc. 256-257
Orlando Corporation 258-259
PCL Constructors Canada Inc. 260-261

Photo by Michael Scholz

*H*ammerson Canada isn't just located in Mississauga's City Centre; it is largely responsible for much of it.

As a property and development company, Hammerson owns almost 160 acres in this core area of the city. Its portfolio includes the Square One Shopping Centre.

Hammerson Canada Inc.

Overlooking the City Centre, Hammerson Chairman Bruce Heyland sees not only what exists today but what is yet to come.

"We have developed only 10 per cent of what is currently allowed under the official plan," he says. "There is a huge amount of capacity."

A British-based firm, Hammerson invests in and develops properties in the U.K., the rest of Europe and North America. It focuses on two major sectors: retail properties, particularly major shopping centres, and office buildings in major cities.

The company is listed on the London and Toronto stock exchanges, and its 4,500 shareholders include most of the U.K.'s leading investment institutions. Its portfolio is valued at more than $3.6 billion.

Hammerson was one of the first property companies to diversify internationally, and it branched out to Canada in 1968. In this

Hammerson's retail/entertainment facility usage includes Sega City at Playdium, Sport Chek and Famous Players cinemas and restaurants on Rathburn Road in Mississauga.

country, Hammerson has acquired or developed several premiere properties outside Mississauga. They include:

- 2 Bloor Street West and Cumberland Terrace in Toronto's prestigious Bloor-Yorkville district, a 530,000-square-foot office tower and shopping concourse.
- 70 University Avenue, a 235,000-square-foot highrise office building in Toronto's financial district.
- 11 King Street West, a 160,000-square-foot office building in downtown Toronto, also in Toronto's financial district.
- Westmount Shopping Centre in London, a 540,000-square-foot regional mall that leads the West London market area of Southwestern Ontario.
- Stone Road Mall in Guelph, a 492,000-square-foot shopping centre, the only regional mall in this fast-growing city.

The company has a three-pronged strategy for growth—acquire existing developed properties, and add value through continual upgrading; be highly selective in any ground-up developments or expansions; and focus on offering superior service through its property management teams.

Nowhere has the merit of this approach been more evident than in Mississauga. When Hammerson acquired Square One and the four office buildings in 1984, the appeal wasn't just the existing value of the properties but their potential.

"Back then you had a city that was the fastest growing in Canada, and about half of the city's land area had yet to be developed,"

Square One hosts a science and technology exhibit in its centre court.

says Heyland. "There was a huge amount of growth to come, an opportunity to build a City Centre."

Hammerson also realized that Square One was "outboard" of its population, a retailing industry term that meant that nobody was living yet in much of the area from which the shopping centre would naturally draw.

"If Square One was already doing well," he says, "down the road we foresaw a tremendous volume of business."

Since 1984, the city and the properties have both undergone a remarkable transformation. Mississauga's population continues to grow, and the city has become one of the most desirable parts of the Greater Toronto Area in which to live and work.

At Square One, the changes were dramatic. Under Hammerson's management, the shopping centre, which opened in 1973, has undergone two major expansions and upgrades.

It added a centre court, completely renovated the floor, ceiling and lighting, brought in another major anchor store, and increased the overall number of stores to 330

and almost 1.4 million square feet of retail space. This makes Square One the largest shopping centre in Eastern Canada in terms of retail store offerings.

Square One is one of the top-performing malls in the country, and draws almost 20 million visitors a year. But anyone who thinks of it as just another shopping centre doesn't understand its place in the fabric of Mississauga.

"I think of it as a huge community centre," says Heyland, "which is unusual in our business. But it has a hybrid of uses."

In addition to its top retailers, Square One houses a seniors centre, a teen centre, and even a church. Four highways—403, 401, 410, and 10—are at the centre's doorstep, and most of the bus routes in the city end up at Square One.

"It's not only a mall," Heyland says. "It's one of the community's resources."

To help cultivate this centre core, Hammerson deeded back to the city a parcel of land that was subsequently used to build the Living Arts Centre.

"We're a major supporter of the Living Arts Centre," he says. "All cities need a cultural heart, and it creates another reason for people to come to the City Centre."

Yet another is the Playdium, which opened in 1996, adjacent to Square One. Built on one of Hammerson's land parcels in the City Centre, this interactive sports theme park draws people of all ages to the area.

With so much of Hammerson's City Centre land still to be developed, Heyland envisions an even more vibrant core. The company has worked with the Mississauga Civic Centre on its Master Plan, examining the zoning and the mix of uses that will best benefit the city.

"It's important that we agree on what goes on what land," says Heyland. "It's their City Centre too. We're looking for synergistic uses that bring people here. Up to now, Square One has been a suburban mall sitting in a sea of parking. We want to create a downtown feel, with a people-oriented, accessible City Centre that becomes the place to go because there's always something to do."

He says parent company Hammerson plc is "bullish" about the Mississauga investment, seeing it as "a core property in the Group."

"They feel strongly about its uniqueness. It's very unusual to find one company that owns something as extensive as this outright. There are so many options as to what to do with the land. We consider ourselves fortunate." Ⓜ

A British-based firm, Hammerson invests in and develops properties in the U.K., the rest of Europe and North America. Pictured above is Hammerson's 2 Bloor Street West location in Toronto.

Square One Shopping Centre, under Hammerson management, is one of the top-performing malls in the country and draws almost 20 million visitors a year.

*T*he two most prominent landmarks as you drive along Airport Road from the Etobicoke border into Mississauga are Pearson International Airport on the left and Orlando Corporation's head office across the street. On the surface, they don't have much in common, but they share a common heritage in that both predate the city of Mississauga.

Orlando Corporation

Orlando, established more than 65 years ago, is a privately owned Canadian real estate investment company specializing in the design, construction and management of all types of industrial, office and retail properties and the development of major business parks. Orey Fidani, Orlando's founder, comes by his construction background naturally, working in his teens for his father as a bricklayer. Orey started off on his own establishing Orlando and continues as chairman and chief executive officer.

The head office of Orlando Corporation in Mississauga

Orlando's property portfolio is second only to the airport in the amount of municipal tax contributions to the city of Mississauga and the largest private municipal taxpayer in the city. As one of the largest companies of its kind in Canada, Orlando offers clients an integrated package of real estate development services, including product evaluation, site selection, architectural and engineering design, construction, financing, leasing and property management.

The company is currently recognized for developing the 1,250-acre Heartland Business Community centred at Highway 401 and Hurontario Street. Distinctive buildings designed and constructed by Orlando accommodate some of North America's leading corporations, such as AST Research, Inc., Bauer, Inc., Bridgestone/Firestone Canada, Inc., Canon Canada, Dun & Bradstreet, Federal Express Canada, GE Capital Technology, Government of Canada, Mattel Canada, Microsoft Canada, Inc., Oracle Corporation, Pepsi Cola, Red Cross, Suburu Canada, Sunbeam Corporation and Xerox Canada.

Orlando doesn't restrict its work to Mississauga, developing six business parks throughout the Greater Toronto Area, from Heartland Business Community on the west to Middlefield Business Park at Highway 48 on the east. Thus, the company is able to offer clients an excellent choice of sites for sale or lease on Orlando land. Forty years after introducing the total package design/build concept, Orlando remains the standard by which all others are measured.

Orlando is also a major retail developer and owner. It has built and manages more than 3 million square feet of retail space throughout Ontario, including Heartland Town Centre, Bayview Village and Bridlewood Mall in Scarborough.

Shopper-friendly surroundings, discreet security, attentive property management and

Orlando designs and constructs distinctive buildings for North America's leading corporations.

competitive occupancy costs are just a few of the reasons for Orlando's success in attracting leading local retailers as well as many of North America's most successful national tenants.

The company's expert staff is committed to excellence and has designed and developed more than 55 million square feet of industrial, office and retail properties. Orlando's portfolio of owned and managed properties now exceeds 25 million square feet.

Clients who choose Orlando's "lifestyle leasing formula" are assured of accommodation that is as unique as their business profile. They can also depend on Orlando to take full responsibility for all phases of the construction process, including site selection, regulatory approvals, architectural and engineering design, space planning, interior layout, building technologies and building operating efficiencies.

Because each of these services is offered in-house, Orlando is able to offer clients firm delivery dates, stipulated price contracts and fixed lease rates—the ultimate in accountability!

Orlando's construction division is well known as an industry innovator. At the heart

One of Orlando's multi-tenant industrial sites, Woodland Business Court is a 522,000-square-foot building in the Heartland Business Community.

Included in Orlando's multi-tenant office portfolio is Britannia Place, a nine-storey, 161,000-square-foot office building.

of the team is a dedicated group of construction experts, many of whom have been with Orlando for more than 20 years. On-site, the parallel progression scheduling of labour and materials, known as "fast-tracking," creates an environment where projects are consistently completed ahead of schedule, at a quoted fixed price and with award-winning attention to detail and safety.

Pave-Al Limited, an Orlando subsidiary, is extremely skilled in infrastructure development and serves the company, as well as the Province of Ontario, local municipalities and other developers. Pave-Al provides timely and cost-effective solutions for a diverse range of projects—including the construction and refurbishing of bridge and underpass structures, municipal underground services, highways, municipal roads, parking and trucking areas. Asphalt materials for these and other asphalt projects are supplied by Orlando's Mississauga manufacturing plant.

The property management division provides a comprehensive package of services,

each designed to safeguard the value of the company's assets and contribute to the comfort and well-being of its tenants. Properties are inspected regularly to ensure that each meets the company's environmental and maintenance standards.

Orlando's "life cycle" leasing program has been designed to accommodate tenants through each stage of their business growth. This unique program offers tenants a broad range of leasing options, plus an unparalleled degree of flexibility when choosing the size, type and location of their accommodations. And it's obvious customers appreciate it, because Orlando has one of the highest tenant retention rates and lowest overall vacancy rates in the industry.

Orlando has almost 2 million square feet of office space in its portfolio, all of which features a wealth of urban amenities with the preferred convenience and cost efficiencies of an established suburban environment. Low- and high-rise buildings offer quality office space ranging from a few hundred square feet to more than 100,000 square feet. Each property offers clients supervised building security systems and sophisticated heating, ventilating and

Left to right: **Carlo Fidani, vice president; Orey Fidani, chairman and CEO and Douglas Kilner, president**

air-conditioning systems that promote tenant safety and comfort.

Clients wishing to expand or relocate within Orlando's office portfolio receive priority attention under the company's innovative leasing options plan. No matter where you look in Mississauga, Orlando Corporation has made its mark; its buildings make a statement and reflect the city's image of excellence. Its "client first" philosophy is a key factor in preserving values within the community and setting new standards its competitors seldom achieve. **Ⓜ**

It would be hard to imagine Mississauga without the Living Arts Centre, Credit Valley Hospital, Trion Office Park or the Board of Education headquarters. Taking these city landmarks from imagination to reality was the job of one company—PCL Constructors Canada Inc. As construction manager on these

PCL Constructors Canada Inc.

and countless other buildings, PCL has literally changed the face of Mississauga and many other communities.

Incorporated in Ontario in 1983 and headquartered in Mississauga since 1992, PCL is an operating company within the PCL family of construction firms, a Canadian company that has been around since 1906. The company is known mainly for the major projects it builds—BCE Place and Scotia Plaza in downtown Toronto, the Air Canada Centre (home of the NBA's Toronto Raptors), the National Trade Centre at Toronto's Exhibition Place, and the Corel Centre (home of the NHL's Ottawa Senators). Along with these high-profile jobs, PCL also handles numerous construction projects valued at under $2 million, ranging from

Built by PCL, the HJA Brown Education Centre features an amphitheatre-style boardroom.

civil to residential, institutional and commercial in nature.

How has PCL secured a major share of the Ontario construction market? "A combination of competitive tendering and providing superior value is the short answer," says Paul Schmalz, vice-president and district manager. But that only hints at PCL's success in the demanding construction industry.

Start with PCL's people. A significant percentage of staff are shareholders in the company (formerly known as Poole Construction Limited until an employee group bought it from the Poole family in 1986). That helps generate a commitment to the company that's hard to match.

PCL has a similar commitment to its people, preferring to develop its own and promote from within. It starts by recruiting students midway through their university and college programs, and encouraging them to seek careers in construction by providing challenging work terms. In recent years, most entry-level PCL staff have been former education co-op students.

With a reputation for offering solid career opportunities, PCL also receives about 1,300

The cultural hub of Mississauga is its Living Arts Centre which features multiple performance venues, art studios and exhibition display areas.

résumés a year. This ensures a wide range of capable candidates when positions arise. Once employed, staff benefit from the in-house PCL College of Construction, which addresses skill gaps in technical and managerial areas, and encourages a continuous interest in learning. As a result, PCL Canada employees log training hours well above the average for the construction industry.

"An enquiring mind embraces new ideas and seeks unique solutions to difficult and often complex problems," says PCL President Paul Douglas. "Our ability to think and work together gives us an incredible competitive advantage."

Another advantage comes from the value PCL places on working partnerships. That means collaborating with trade unions to ensure quality workmanship, and encouraging youth to seek vocations in the trades. PCL also hires graduates from, and promotes the effectiveness of, union apprenticeship training programs.

Fostering partnerships with subcontractors is just as important. As the amount of work performed by the subtrades has increased, PCL has nurtured and recognized the subtrades' role in the company's success. This helps ensure competitive pricing, which helps PCL get the work in the first place. Each year PCL holds a subtrade appreciation event as just a small token of gratitude for their work.

The word "partnering" isn't just a platitude at PCL, but a formal business process. It's widely used in the U.S., though PCL is one of the pioneers at it in Canada.

"The process hinges on the concept of a cooperative team approach," says Brad Nelson, regional vice-president. "We use it to ensure quality projects on time and within budgets."

Essentially, all members of the team—PCL, the client, the architect, design consultants and

subcontractors—jointly develop the project goals, action plans, and the methods to solve problems and evaluate success. The result is a partnering "charter" and an environment in which respect and teamwork prevent disputes, foster cooperation and cost savings, and facilitate the successful completion of the project.

"To us, partnering marks a return to the way people used to do business," Nelson says. "While the contract establishes the legal relationships, the partnering process sets out the working relationships among all the project team members."

In fact, Roger Floyd of RPA Consultants and project director for the owner on the National Trade Centre states: "I do not believe that the successful completion of the project would have been possible without partnering."

The concept of partnerships extends to PCL's relationship with the community. To help make Mississauga a better place in which to live and work, PCL has designated United Way as its corporate charity and actively sponsors local sporting teams.

Within the construction community, PCL takes its role as a leader seriously. Its managers hold senior positions in various industry associations, and promote the industry and its advantages whenever possible.

What separates PCL from other companies is not only its people and partnerships but its performance. In its new work, billings, and profit, PCL boasts impressive numbers.

Trion Office Park is located in the heart of Mississauga and features a two-storey granite and marble lobby.

Beyond the figures are the beliefs that underline performance.

There's the belief in professional accreditation, which means encouraging PCL project managers, superintendents and estimators to become Gold Seal Certified by the Canadian Construction Association. There's the belief in safety, which goes hand in hand with performance, and which is evidenced by PCL having one of the best records in the industry.

There's the belief in value engineering, a service PCL voluntarily provides to clients to help them get the most for their construction dollar. PCL will scrutinize the construction documents and verify that design systems are appropriate, cost-effective and safe. If possible, PCL suggests alternate methods and materials to make the construction process even more efficient, while preserving the quality of the project.

Lastly, there's the belief in total quality management and continuous improvement initiatives, which fall under the company's unique motivational program, known as QUEST. It creates an attitude that produces excellence in quality and productivity, by involving those most knowledgeable about the work in deciding how it can be better done.

It's no wonder PCL has been named one of the top 100 companies to work for in Canada

Originally built in 1986, The Credit Valley Hospital is an acute care facility.

by the *Financial Post*, and one of the country's 50 best-managed private companies by the *Post* and Arthur Andersen. In addition, PCL was awarded the prestigious Outstanding Business Achievement Award for 1996 by the Ontario Chamber of Commerce for its innovation and excellence in business.

PCL hopes that its clients will add their own honour: one of the best construction companies to work with—for its people, partnerships and performance. **Ⓜ**

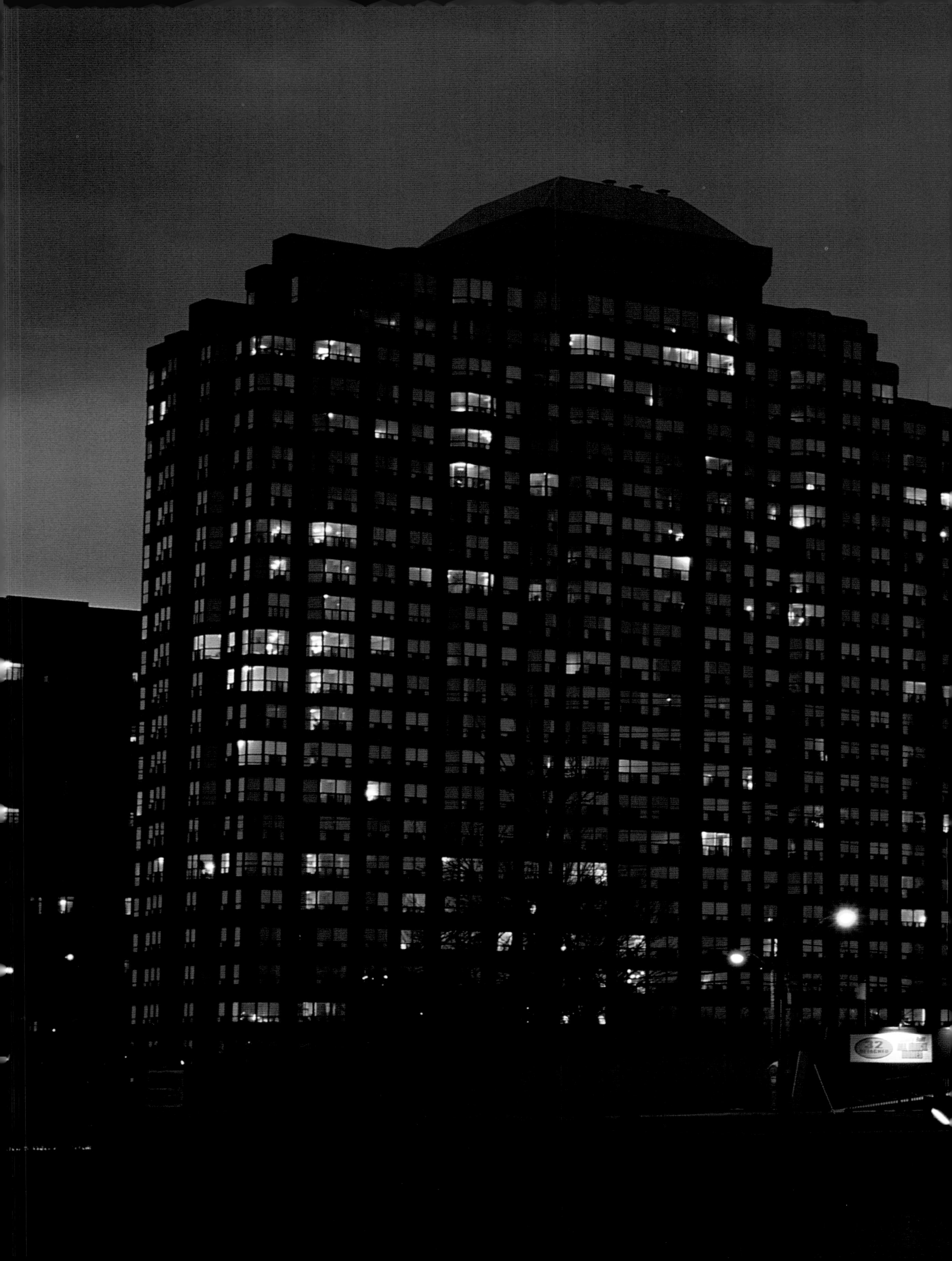

Photo by Jeff Chevrier

CHAPTER 16

Health Care, Education & Quality of Life

Ⓜ

Photo by Jeff Chevrier

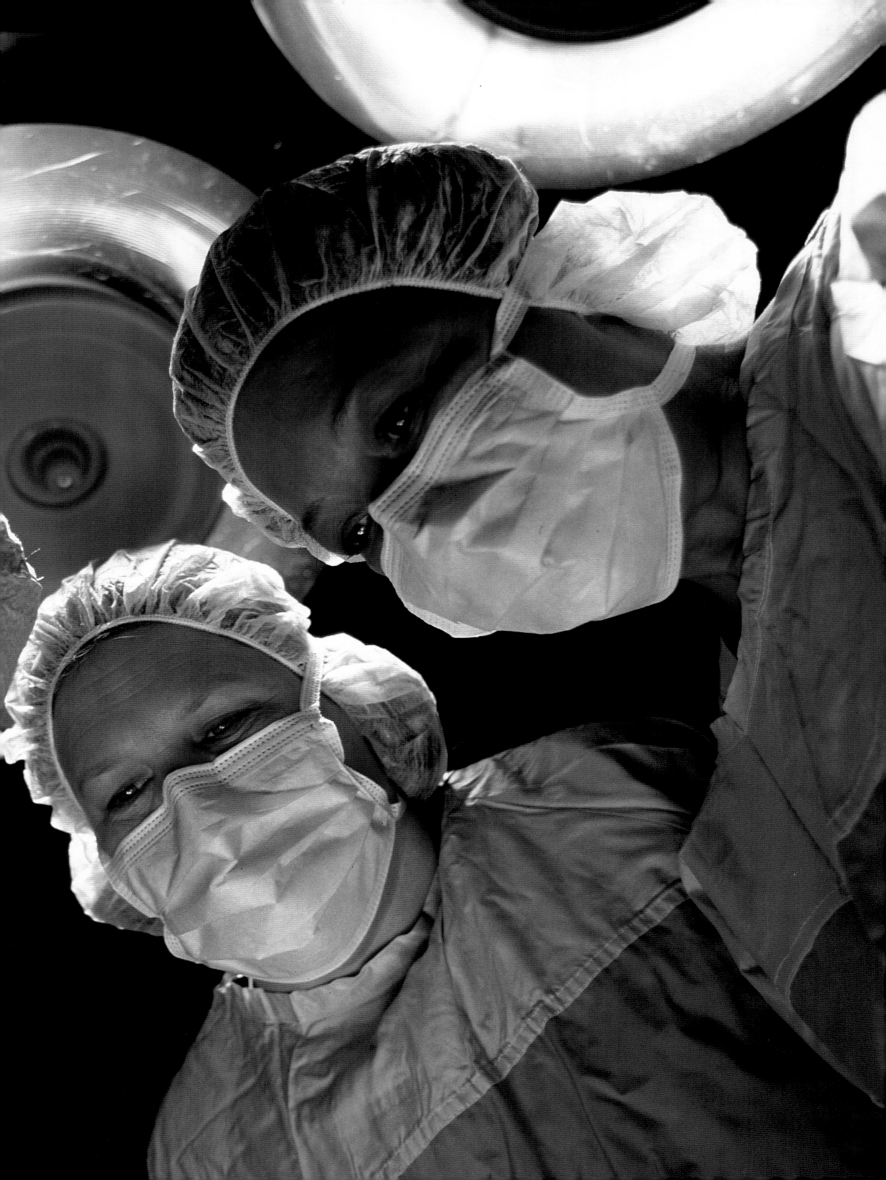

$\mathcal{A}$stra Pharma Inc. of Mississauga is a true partner in the delivery of health care in Canada. As an ethical, innovative, research-based pharmaceutical manufacturer, the company's management policies and decisions reflect its mission to be a key contributor to Canadians' quality of life and to help solve

Astra Canada

issues that detract from the high quality of the Canadian health care system.

Astra's view of the ideal health care system is one in which Canadians are encouraged to take care of their own health, and to prevent disease and illness. If drug therapy is necessary, consumers should then have access to the right type of treatment and drug therapies, fair prices and well-informed medical health professionals. Astra's commitment to being a partner in the system extends beyond the production and sale of drugs to impacting quality of life through ethical sales and marketing initiatives that focus on educating physicians and consumers and reducing costs, achieving therapeutic excellence in priority medical areas, and being a leading supporter of the community.

Astra is headquartered on Middlegate Road in Mississauga and houses a high-tech manufacturing facility, quality control laboratory, a video conference and development centre and an administrative complex.

Astra participates in and supports the development of clinical practice and prescribing guidelines that help physicians provide their patients with optimal treatment. Clinical practice guidelines and consensus guidelines direct prescribers on how to choose the right drug therapies, and the right regimens which should be considered first to treat a condition, as well as secondary choices and options for special prescribing.

Education is essential to the successful adoption of these guidelines. Astra is investing hundreds of millions of dollars to deliver much-needed continuing medical education and symposia promoting these guidelines. These education programs are becoming increasingly focused on the outcomes of drug treatments as well as alternatives.

In addition to educating the medical community, Astra is also working hard to educate Canadians through targeted health programs focused on prevention and self-care. The company has established an independent division called Health Alliance™ a consortium of companies with expertise in health and wellness programs. The goal of Health Alliance™ and its health management program Sharing a Healthier Future™ is to help individuals acquire new knowledge, attitudes

Astra's products undergo strict quality assurance testing. Raw materials and finished products are tested regularly in Astra's Mississauga laboratory to ensure they meet stringent quality standards.

and behaviours that will promote their ability to better care for themselves.

The Sharing a Healthier Future™ program provides consumers with regular newsletters and magazines containing the latest in disease prevention, healthful living and self-help treatments. Sharing a Healthier Future™ members receive:

- an SHF health card;
- a Healthwise™ handbook, a self-care manual with information on more than 180 health topics to provide general information and self-help guidance regarding common ailments;
- Bodyworkings™, a quarterly newsletter devoted to health and lifestyle information;
- Healthchoices™, a quarterly magazine that provides seasonally focused information about health, exercise and lifestyle in an informative and easily readable format and includes coupons for discounts on numerous health and health-related goods and services;
- access to the Sharing a Healthier Future™ Information Network, an electronic health information library with more than 200 pre-recorded messages on a variety of health topics in multiple languages, as well as customized hospital information that can be faxed or mailed on demand; and
- Bodyworkings™, an annual catalogue of health-related items.

Health Alliance™ through programs such as Sharing a Healthier Future™, works in partnerships with government, Canadian health care organizations and private-sector

employers to optimize utilization of public and private health benefits. Unique Canadian solutions, developed with a variety of Canadian health organizations, educate and inform the health care consumer on how to become a more responsible and empowered user of the health care system.

Health Alliance™ teamed with The Credit Valley Hospital in Mississauga to launch the Sharing a Healthier Future™ program to consumers in the area. This program was the first community health program of its kind in Canada.

Astra has developed other partnerships within the industry to tackle the issue of reducing health care costs. In 1994, the company co-founded with two other pharmaceutical companies a consolidated distribution network, the Canadian Pharmaceutical Distribution Network (CPDN), which allows hospital pharmacies to save up to 30 per cent

Trained operators carefully inspect these glass vial solutions before they can be labelled.

when they order their prescription drugs through the system. The network, which includes both brand name and generic companies, offers hospital pharmacies one method of ordering, invoicing and shipping products for no separate service fee. The CPDN is the only consolidated distribution network of its kind in the country.

The fundamental link in the health care chain is the research and development of innovative pharmaceuticals that meet identified medical needs. Astra is always seeking to develop new and better medications to help people find relief from disease and illness. Approximately one in five of Astra's employees worldwide is engaged in the research and development of pharmaceuticals to treat pain and diseases, such as asthma, Crohn's disease, hypertension and gastrointestinal disorders, which, when untreated, can impact patients' quality of life. In the past decade alone, Astra launched a number of new and innovative products including Losec®, a breakthrough

product for the treatment of gastrointestinal diseases, Entocort® for treating Crohn's disease, Naropin®, the first new local anesthetic in more than 20 years and Turbuhaler®, an innovative asthma device which administers a precise amount of asthma drug into patients' lungs improving the delivery and effectiveness of the medication.

Over the past decade, Astra has invested more than $152 million in R&D in Canada. Sixty-nine per cent of that amount has been invested since 1993, ranking Astra among the top 50 of the largest R&D spenders in Canada, regardless of sector.

While Astra's parent company, Astra AB of Sweden, conducts most of its basic research from five centres in Sweden and the U.K., it is increasingly looking to Canada and other countries in which to establish research centres. Montreal was the first location outside Europe to be chosen for the establishment of a basic research facility. Astra Research Centre Montreal (ARCM), inaugurated in May, 1997 is an impressive 10,000 square-metre facility located on 47,000 square-metres of land in Saint-Laurent.

ARCM is conducting pre-clinical research focusing on the development of new analgesic medications that do not induce addiction and a range of other side effects. Compounds are currently being investigated to treat severe and chronic pain.

The centre will represent an investment of $300 million by the year 2005, and employment is expected to grow to 150 by that time. The excellent calibre of Canadian universities and researchers and the fact the Canadian government supports innovative industries went into Astra's decision to locate in Canada, after a two-year review.

Astra strongly supports the medical research community in Canada as part of its ongoing R&D initiatives. The company initiates clinical trials both internationally and nationally in which leading medical researchers are chosen

To create the liquid, injectable medications, Astra scientists mix purifed water and chemical compounds inside stainless steel tanks under controlled manufacturing conditions.

to participate. These studies are commonly used in worldwide efforts to obtain drug approval and subsequently, market entry. This clinical research and development activity contributes to the development and eventual export of Canadian technological and scientific knowledge.

Astra often continues its product development research beyond that required by regulatory authorities once the product is on the market. For instance, in the past decade, Astra has launched two five-year international studies to investigate the treatment of two very prevalent diseases. The START Study is investigating the effects of early treatment on the development of asthma, and the HOT Study is investigating the optimal treatment for hypertension.

Astra Pharma was established in Canada in 1954 and seven years later moved to Middlegate Road in Mississauga, where it continues to be an important contributor to the community. Astra's 176,000 square-foot facility houses a high-tech manufacturing, laboratory and an administrative complex and is

home to two-thirds of Astra's 800 Canada-based employees.

For its employees, Astra's culture maintains a tradition of respect for all employees and flexibility to accommodate changing personal needs. The company established an Harrassment in the Workplace policy which stresses the importance of mutual respect in the workplace and is supported and reinforced through ongoing training. Astra also instituted a flex hours program whereby employees can choose the hours of work which suite their lifestyle as long as certain core hours are covered.

Astra offers employees access to a wide range of health information and has enrolled all employees in the Health Alliance™ Sharing a Healthier Future™ program. In-house programs on family health and wellness are also offered through the company's occupational health nurse. Astra also has an on-site fitness facility available to employees.

Over the past 10 years, Astra has spent $126 million in capital

expenses for expansions and general administrative improvements to its facilities in Mississauga. One example is the addition of a $40 million high-tech manufacturing facility which develops and produces injectable hospital products. Other products are shipped here to undergo quality control inspections and repackaging for compliance with Canadian standards and regulations for pharmaceutical packaging prior to distribution This investment has enabled Astra to integrate manufacturing, packaging, quality control, warehousing and administration, reduce costs, improve efficiencies and facilitate the export of key Astra products to markets in Latin America and Asia Pacific. Astra is the only Canadian manufacturer of a comparable size to merge these capabilities.

Astra Pharma's parent company, Astra AB of Sweden, founded in 1913, is the largest pharmaceutical manufacturer in the Scandinavian region. It employs more than 20,000 people, 67 per cent of whom are located outside Sweden. Astra has a presence in more than 40 countries and is listed on the Stockholm, London and New York Stock Exchanges.

Astra strives to develop, manufacture and market products which benefit health care and people's quality of life, while at the same time protecting the environment. Astra's management believes the continued success of the company, its employees and their communities is closely linked to sound long-term environmental health.

Astra's policy is to reduce to a minimum the potential adverse ecological impact of all company activities, while responsibly managing all

Regular inspection of Astra's water purification system ensures the water used in the production of Astra's liquid medications is purified.

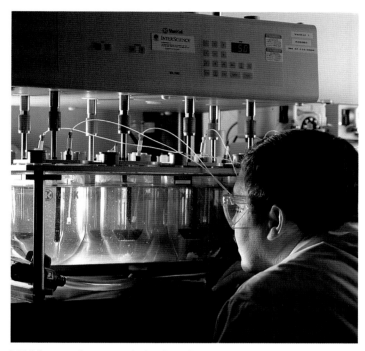

Tablet products, made by Astra's parent company in Sweden, receive a final test to determine how quickly the medication dissolves and how much of it is released, using dissolution equipment which simulates the human digestive system under controlled conditions.

United Way, making it the leading corporate supporter in its sector in the region. Employees contributed half from their own salaries.

Astra also reaches out to people in countries around the world in need of medicines and health supplies. In partnership with MAP (Medical Assistance Program) International of Canada, a non-profit, federally incorporated health organization, Astra donates products to help doctors and health care professionals working abroad.

In addition, Astra representatives work with patient associations such as the Heart & Stroke Foundation of Canada, The Lung Association and others to hold educational seminars for consumers at hospitals and pharmacies.

Astra's rapid growth has been fueled by its philosophy, commitment and dedication to excellence and innovation and its integrity. The city and its residents are fortunate and privileged to have such a company call Mississauga home. Ⓜ

aspects of waste generation, storage, transport and disposal. The company's goal is to meet or exceed all applicable government regulations, to work cooperatively with government, associations and other relevant groups to develop socially responsible standards, to incorporate environmental considerations into product development and service design and to support research and development efforts which provide for an enhanced environment.

Astra's efforts to protect the environment have been recognized by the Pharmaceutical Manufacturers Association of Canada, the National Packaging Association of Canada and the Regional Municipality of Peel's Waste Management Division.

Astra contributes significantly to Canadians' quality of life through its corporate philanthropy. The company has a generous corporate donations budget which increases annually. In 1996, the figure exceeded $400,000 and was allocated to deserving charities across the country based on requests from the charities and recommendations from local representatives. In that same year, Astra became a Caring Company under the Canadian Centre for Philanthropy's IMAGINE program, and committed to donate at least one per cent of its pre-tax profits to charitable organizations.

The United Way of Peel Region has become a major beneficiary of Astra's benevolence since 1991. In 1996, Astra contributed a record amount, more than $96,000, to the

An operator inspects Astra's largest breakthrough product Losec®, an acid-inhibitor used in the treatment of disorders of the gastrointestinal tract, to ensure the product is being packaged correctly.

*F*ritz Hoffmann's goal in 1896, when he started his commercial drug manufacturing business, was to provide high-quality, proprietary medicines that would revolutionize health care by making reliable medications more widely accessible and affordable.

Hoffmann-La Roche Limited

More than 100 years later, that focus has not changed. Swiss-based Hoffmann-La Roche—perhaps better known as "Roche"—is one of the world's leading health care companies, and sells its products in more than 70 countries. In Canada, the tradition Hoffmann started has been carried on for more than 65 years.

Roche Canada is a Canadian company, based in Mississauga, with the strength of a global organization, giving Canadians the benefit of Roche's international focus on the full medical spectrum of prevention, diagnosis and therapy. The company has grown through both

In 1980 Hoffmann-La Roche moved its Canadian headquarters from Etobicoke, Ontario, to the Meadowpine site in Mississauga. *Photo by André Van Vught.*

scientific discovery and strategic acquisitions, such as Syntex Pharmaceuticals in 1994 and Genentech BioPharm in 1996.

The company recently completed an expansion and consolidation of its corporate headquarters in Mississauga, and is now set to achieve its goal of ranking among the top three pharmaceutical companies in Canada by the year 2000. Roche has developed a strategic plan—Vision 2000—that will see it double its revenues by 1999.

During the expansion, a $10-million fibre-optic network and information structure was installed, giving all employees access to the Internet and the Intranet. As well, Roche's sales representatives are now armed with state-of-the-art laptop computers, enabling them to access sophisticated customer databases.

Few companies spend more on research and development than Roche. The 26 per cent of pharmaceutical sales invested is well above the industry average. The impact of this commitment

Roche Canada President, Vic Ackermann, left, **and Mississauga Mayor, Hazel McCallion,** right, **at an event in March 1997, celebrate the completion of the expansion made to the Roche Canada operations in Mississauga, Ontario.**

can be seen in breakthroughs for conditions as varied as Parkinson's disease, hypertension, angina and obesity. The anti-obesity drug, for example, is designed to block a portion of dietary fat from being absorbed by the body. Drugs such as these will alter the course of treatment for the patients of tomorrow.

Roche operates a branch in Montreal, manufacturing operations in Cambridge, Ontario

and High River, Alberta, and has representatives located across Canada. The staff of more than 500 throughout the country is involved in clinical research, professional and public education, manufacturing and quality control, as well as marketing, sales and distribution of Roche products across the company's three principal divisions: Pharmaceuticals, Vitamins and Diagnostics.

Although Roche Canada is not one of the largest Roche subsidiaries as measured by revenues, it does, nevertheless, play an important role in the company's global structure, and is one of just eight on Roche's international management committee.

Roche Canada's financial strength has enabled it to invest more than $1.6 billion annually in worldwide drug discovery research. Canada accounts for 20-30 per cent of Roche's global investment in clinical research outside the United States.

By concentrating on research and development of drugs for disease management and quality-of-life enhancement, Roche is able to market some of the industries' most promising discoveries.

In 1997 alone, Roche more than doubled the size of its clinical research team, and tripled the number of people working indirectly with Roche on clinical research. Virtually every medical institution in Canada derives benefit from these activities.

In addition, the research Roche conducts in this country gives Canadians early access to new treatments in key areas such as diabetes, heart disease, cancer, HIV/AIDS, infectious diseases and psychiatric disorders. It also gives Canadian clinicians a chance to contribute personally to the science of medicine, in a way that would not be possible in laboratory-intensive pure research.

Roche Canada is rethinking the very structure of its business. One strategy is to maximize the value of each compound by managing and extending its life cycle, from drug development, through the eventual loss-of-patent, to its potential conversion to OTC status. AltiMed, the branded-generic joint venture company with Glaxo Wellcome and Pharmacia & Upjohn, enables Roche Canada to benefit from its original drug development investments, even after patent protection expires, thus helping to finance the high costs of research and development for future breakthroughs.

Another example of Roche's efforts to expand its over-the-counter (OTC) business is the Roche prescription drug, Naprosyn®, for the treatment of arthritis, which is now marketed in the United States as an OTC product under the name Aleve®.

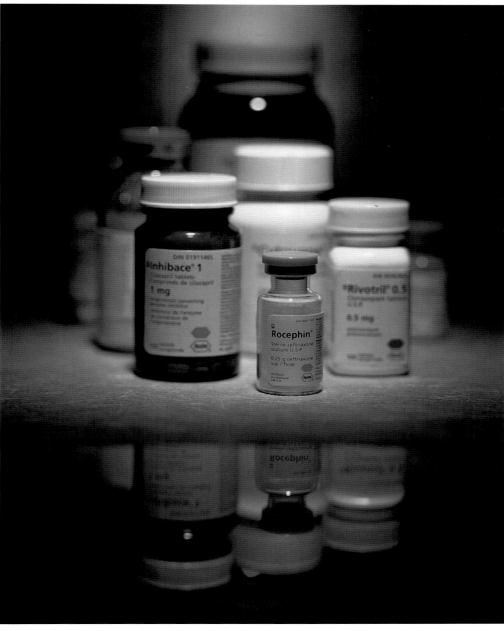

Pharmaceuticals

Pharmaceuticals is Roche Canada's largest division, representing approximately 62 per cent of revenues. The portfolio ranges from prescription drugs to generics, and from over-the-counter drugs to biotechnological products.

In Canada, Roche is a leading company in hospital sales. Its representatives have expertise in emergency medicine, infectious diseases, cardiovascular disease, anesthesia, endocrinology and respirology.

In the area of specialty medicine, Roche manages products for immune system disorders, such as HIV/AIDS, cancer and transplants—where patient groups tend to be small and treatment costs high. Roche works with policy-makers to set therapy guidelines, and with providers to ensure that these drugs are available to those who can benefit. Roche also works in the field, using highly trained specialist representatives and medical managers to

Hoffmann-La Roche conducts research around the world to provide early access to new treatments in key areas such as diabetes, heart disease, cancer, AIDS, infectious diseases and psychiatric disorders.

inform and support front-line caregivers or patient groups.

Roche's pharmaceutical portfolio is extensive. Central nervous system products make up 25 per cent of Roche's pharmaceutical line-up, pain and inflammation products 19 per cent, anti-infective products 18 per cent, cardiovascular products 16 per cent, dermatological and allergy products 15 per cent and metabolic and hormonal products 5 per cent.

The strong foundation on which Roche stands was established with the introduction of such well-known products as Librium®, Valium® and Bactrim®. Many of Roche's products are industry sales leaders in their particular category. Of the newer products, CellCept® is widely used because it significantly reduces the chance of organ rejection in transplant patients, compared to existing therapies. As kidney transplants have become more cost-effective, for example, the recipient is assured of a better quality of life than a lifetime of dialysis: CellCept® makes a positive contribution to both the patient and the health care system.

Roche's strength in HIV/AIDS research has produced such products as Invirase®, the first protease inhibitor available in Canada. In conjunction with such Roche drugs as

Roche has several drugs under development, many of which are expected to represent major breakthroughs. These include a unique treatment for obesity and weight maintenance; an add-on therapy that will significantly improve quality of life for Parkinson's patients; and the first in a new chemical class of drugs for hypertension and angina.

Hivid®, a nucleoside analogue, Invirase can prevent the virus from replicating, which has been shown to extend the healthy life of HIV-infected patients.

Roche Canada works with partners such as government and/or private insurers to deliver the optimal balance of leading-edge therapy and cost containment. In the area of widely used prescription drugs, Roche applies the principles of pharmacoeconomics to determine, then prove, that a specific drug is both economically and therapeutically superior to its alternatives.

The drug development division, working with clinicians, nurses, pharmacists and doctors, develops the clinical trials that give Canadians the opportunity to benefit from a drug before it becomes available on the market.

Vitamins

Roche Canada provides bulk products for human and animal nutrition and health. These include vitamins and fine chemicals such as pigments, or carotenoids, with a chemical make-up identical to those found in nature. Its customers are North America's consumer products manufacturers in the food, pharmaceutical and cosmetics industries, as well as nutrition specialists for livestock, companion and zoo animals.

Canadians use Roche products every day. The milk in breakfast cereal and the cereal itself are likely fortified by Roche vitamins—as was the diet of the milk cow. Roche citric acid may have helped produce the cheese in your omelette. Sunblock, your multivitamin pill and the DM in cough syrup, all likely contain ingredients from Roche.

Many leading brands of vitamin preparations and cosmetic products contain Roche vitamins—as do foods such as fortified breads, soft drinks and fruit juices. Roche pigments are also used to increase the appeal of certain foods.

Roche provides customers with regulatory advice and technical expertise. Its Vitamin Information Program (VIP) gives consumers and their health care advisers objective data about the role of vitamins in health.

Helping to keep Canada's agricultural industry competitive and healthy represents the biggest part of Roche's business in this division. The company's growing palette of medicinal feed additives helps ensure the health and productive efficiency of Canadian livestock. Roche supplies products in bulk or in custom formulated pre-mixes from its blending plants in Ontario and Alberta.

Diagnostics

The Diagnostic Division is responsible for research and development, manufacturing and marketing of diagnostic equipment. Roche addresses the wide spectrum of laboratory testing, from the small to the very large, institutional centres or private laboratories. This division also offers service engineering and technical support for customers.

Roche Diagnostics has been instrumental in placing numerous Cobas Mira Systems within Canada. Recently, the company launched its Cobas Integra, capable of testing up to 72 chemistries. The Cobas Core offers the flexibility to handle the testing of many chemistries within a small footprint—a considerable advantage when space and budget are an issue.

Roche also has a considerable market lead with its patented gene probes or polymerase

Roche Canada's strength in HIV/AIDS research is demonstrated by products such as Invirase®, representing a new class of HIV/AIDS drugs and the first protease inhibitor available anywhere in the world.

chain reaction (PCR) technology. PCR diagnostics enable medical teams to detect viruses or bacteria, even trace amounts, without the need to grow a culture. The technology amplifies, by millions of times, the presence of the suspect genetic material or DNA in a sample. This breakthrough has astounding implications for patients suffering from infectious diseases, HIV or cancer, where early detection and treatment matter most. It helps to solve problems across the complete spectrum of prevention, diagnosis and treatment.

People and Community

The future of Roche Canada is propelled by a team of knowledgeable, capable people committed to ensuring that the best health care solutions reach the Canadian market. To help its employees perform in such a high-pressure environment, Roche supports them with an open culture, one that stresses collaborative teamwork. Roche also has an ongoing commitment to training, so that together the company can continue to create informed customer solutions and

value-added approaches.

Roche carries its mission of providing solutions to improve the health and well-being of Canadians into the community through its employees, by promoting a culture that helps bring ideas into being.

Roche employees have a real concern for others. They know that Roche has a dedication to the highest level of integrity and are proud that Roche products can make a difference in people's lives.

That dedication extends to the way Roche contributes to humanitarian causes around the world. The Sight and Life Task Force is just one example at the corporate level. Through it, Roche donates and distributes Vitamin A to children in developing nations, to help combat deficiency-related blindness and other potentially life-threatening disorders.

In Canada, Roche contributes to a wide variety of charitable and non-profit organizations, such as the United Way of Peel Region, and has raised almost $200,000 over three years, earning it the United Way award for "Innovative" fund-raising.

Roche Canada is a member of Imagine, the Canadian Centre for Philanthropy program in which members pledge to donate at least one per cent of pre-tax profits to charity each year.

Roche is also involved in business-related issues such as a mentoring program in which experienced HIV/AIDS-treating physicians share their expertise with those physicians less familiar with treating the disease.

With its expansion and consolidation at its corporate headquarters complete, Roche Canada is well-positioned—through its core values of respect, creating a supportive environment and contributing to the well-being of all Canadians—to achieve its goal of becoming one of the three largest pharmaceutical firms in the country by 1999. Ⓜ

In May 1997, the Hoffmann-La Roche/MRC Donald B. Brown Research Chair in Obesity—the first obesity chair to be established in Canada—was awarded to Dr. Claude Bouchard, a researcher from Université Laval in Quebec. Dr. Bouchard will receive $1 million over five years to support his research efforts into the causes and treatment of obesity. Left to right: Vic Ackermann, Roche Canada president; Claude Roy, director of programs, MRC; Mrs. Don Brown, Dr. Claude Bouchard, Obesity Research Chair Recipient; Francois Tavenas, Rector, Laval University.

$\mathcal{E}$ven in the world of pharmaceuticals, where mega-mergers are commonplace, this was an electrifying alliance. When Glaxo plc acquired Wellcome plc in 1995, forming Glaxo Wellcome, it created the biggest pharmaceutical company on the planet.

Glaxo Wellcome

The company operates in 83 countries, has over 54,000 employees, has annual sales of $16 billion (Canadian), and spends about $2.5 billion a year on the research and development of new medicines. With a Canadian base of operations in Mississauga, Glaxo Wellcome Inc. employs more than 1,200 people in this country in R&D, manufacturing, sales and marketing. In addition, the company invests $60 million annually on R&D in Canada and donates nearly $5 million to health, educational, cultural and community causes across Canada.

Though functioning on a mammoth scale, Glaxo Wellcome never loses sight of the individual user of its medications, whose optimum health is the company's overriding mission.

"Our goal is to improve every aspect of disease therapy and enhance each patient's life," says Paul Lucas, President and CEO of Canada's Glaxo Wellcome Inc. "Our single commitment is to improve health care through discovering, developing and producing high-quality innovative medicines, services and programs."

It is a commitment that Glaxo Wellcome's predecessor companies have followed in Canada since the turn of the century. Glaxo Canada Inc. was founded in 1902 as Allen & Hanburys Co. Ltd. in Niagara Falls. Four years later, Burroughs Wellcome and Co. branched into Montreal, having been founded in London by two American pharmacists in 1880.

Both companies have a rich tradition of breakthrough discoveries. One of Glaxo's earliest accomplishments was the first mass production of penicillin. A research focus on respiratory disorders led to Ventolin® (salbutamol), which became the gold standard for treating acute asthma attacks.

Glaxo Wellcome's manufacturing operations are well known for their technological innovation, excellent customer service and a commitment to quality which has placed Glaxo Wellcome among the top manufacturing performers in North America.

With a Canadian base of operations in Mississauga, Glaxo Wellcome Inc. employs more than 1,200 people in this country in research and development, manufacturing, sales and marketing.

Burroughs Wellcome scientists were among the first to study nucleic acids (the chemical building blocks of DNA) in the search for compounds to block the cellular reproduction of disease-causing organisms. That led, for one, to the discovery of the first effective anticancer treatments. Two Wellcome doctors were awarded the highest honour in their field, with the 1988 Nobel Prize in Physiology or Medicine going to Gertrude Elion and George Hitchings for discoveries in drug treatment methodologies.

Today, Glaxo Wellcome is known for such landmark medications as Zantac® (ranitadine hydrochloride), the most prescribed medication in the world. Introduced in 1981, it has revolutionized the treatment of peptic ulcer and gastric acid-related diseases, often eliminating the need for surgery.

To combat the pain of acute migraine headaches Glaxo Wellcome developed Imitrex® (sumatriptan), the first major advance in treating this condition in years. Four out of five patients given Imitrex® by injection during a migraine begin to experience significant pain relief in 15 minutes, and users of Imitrex tablets begin to experience relief within a half-hour in 75 per cent of cases.

For the treatment of HIV/AIDS, the company is renowned for introducing Retrovir®

(zidovudine), also known as AZT, in 1987. In 1995, Glaxo Wellcome began marketing 3TC® (lamivudine), an even more effective treatment. The combination of these drugs is seen as the cornerstone for future treatments to prolong and improve the life of HIV/AIDS patients.

And for cancer patients the company produces Zofran® (ondansetron), used to treat the nausea and vomiting associated with therapy. By eliminating or reducing these debilitating side effects, many patients are better able to continue their therapy for longer periods.

While Glaxo Wellcome's R&D and manufacturing activities revolve around brand-name drugs, the company realizes that health care consumers are seeking economical alternatives. To give patients access to low-cost medications that are therapeutically equivalent to their branded counterparts, Glaxo Wellcome is part of AltiMed Pharmaceutical Inc., also in Mississauga. Created with the Hoffman-La Roche and Pharmacia & Upjohn drug firms, this alliance manufactures generic versions of medications from all three companies.

Under license AltiMed will also market generic versions of drugs from other pharmaceutical companies. Glaxo Wellcome distributes the AltiMed business across Canada, and has responsibility for quality control.

Along with its partners throughout the health care system, Glaxo Wellcome's shared goal is to ensure that patients receive the best and most appropriate treatment and services at every stage of their illness.

Those are just a few examples—the list goes on and on—of the ways in which Glaxo Wellcome is making a profound difference in the lives of patients in Canada and worldwide. Activities are organized around the following nine therapeutic areas:

- Respiratory: Diseases such as asthma and allergies are usually chronic and can interfere with the patient's everyday activities. As the world leader in respiratory medicine, Glaxo Wellcome aims to continue to produce a superior range of drugs in a choice of devices.

- Central nervous system disorders: In addition to the successful migraine medication, another key part of this therapeutic area includes treatment for epilepsy.

- Viral infections: Most common infections— colds, flu, measles, chickenpox, hepatitis— are caused by viruses. The challenge is to develop medicines that destroy viruses without destroying host cells. Leading therapies are proving effective against HIV and infections caused by herpes.

- Bacterial infections: Antibacterial agents are effective in preventing and treating a wide range of infections. However, continuous product development is vital as bacteria develop resistance to existing agents.
- Oncology: Glaxo Wellcome products not only treat the disease itself (lung cancer, breast cancer, colorectal cancer and leukemia), but also combat the effects of chemotherapy and radiotherapy.
- Gastrointestinal: Along with treatments for peptic ulcers, areas of interest include irritable bowel disease, where current therapies are ineffective.

| Paul Lucas, President and CEO of Canada's Glaxo Wellcome Inc.

- Anaesthesia: The company is pioneering exciting new medicines for use during surgery, notably neuromuscular blockers that relax the muscles, and a new class of analgesia-based anaesthesia to relieve pain and reduce stress responses.
- Cardiovascular: Glaxo Wellcome's portfolio of products include treatments for congestive heart failure and high blood pressure, a major risk factor for stroke and coronary artery disease.
- Dermatologicals: While not usually life-threatening, dermatological conditions can be debilitating, uncomfortable, and impact the patient's quality of life. Glaxo Wellcome's

products treat fungal infections and inflammatory diseases.

Beyond these main therapeutic categories, Glaxo Wellcome also carries out research in diabetes, obesity and urology.

"By integrating the strengths of Glaxo and Wellcome, we gained much greater therapeutic breadth and depth," says Lucas. "We're now even more responsive to the unique demands of the domestic market, and can compete more effectively in the global pharmaceutical arena."

As in other markets, the Canadian operation benefits from, as Lucas puts it, "being a strategic partner in the world's largest research-based pharmaceutical company."

He says the company aims to not only grow profits, but also to be number one in customer satisfaction in the Canadian pharmaceutical industry, and be the leader in improving disease outcomes in the health care system.

One sign of this leading role is the state-of-the-art manufacturing and product development facility that opened in Mississauga in 1997, adjacent to the company's Canadian headquarters.

"Along with raising our manufacturing capabilities," says Lucas, "the facility boosted the Mississauga economy, as we used local designers and labour."

This $180-million facility has helped expand Glaxo Wellcome's already significant exports to the U.S. and develop a regional supply centre for the North American market. Its advanced design has attracted acclaim from around the world, especially for the automated storage and retrieval system that forms the building's centre spine.

To support and ensure that the company's Pharmaceutical Sciences area remains on the frontiers of discovery, this group is also using the facility. The R&D division has spurred several international mandates, including the provision of clinical supplies to other Glaxo Wellcome companies, and has contributed enormously to the development of innovative drug delivery systems and new dosage forms.

Canada is among nine Glaxo Wellcome pharmaceutical R&D centres worldwide. Developing a new medicine is an intensive undertaking. On average, it costs over $450 million and takes in excess of 10 years to get a

new medication through development and regulatory approval. Any compound discovered has only a one in 10,000 chance of ever getting to market.

In Canada, Glaxo Wellcome's R&D investments have grown dramatically, and now total about $50 million annually. As a percentage of sales, that's more than the industry commitment to the Canadian government.

This country also boasts one of the largest groups of clinical research scientists of any Glaxo Wellcome operation—a unit that's also bigger, by far, than that of any competitor in Canada. "That speaks to the skilled and talented group of people we have here," Lucas declares.

On average, the company conducts 50 clinical trials per year at 500 hospitals and universities across Canada. This extensive clinical research gives health authorities the data required to approve experimental medicines or new uses of approved medicines.

"Canada is pivotal to Glaxo Wellcome's worldwide clinical drug development program," says Lucas. "Our Data Sciences Group plays a key role in analyzing clinical research information for the development of international registration applications."

In addition, the company has a licensing and research agreement with BioChem Pharma Inc. to focus on AIDS and anti-cancer therapy. Glaxo Wellcome holds a significant equity interest and has invested heavily in research contracts with BioChem, a strategic alliance that resulted in the development of 3TC®.

Research into AIDS, as well as herpes and hepatitis B, is the central concern at the Glaxo Heritage Research Institute, located at the University of Alberta in Edmonton. Glaxo Wellcome's largest commitment to extramural research, the Institute was established in 1992 with $800,000 in start-up funding, and continues to be supported with over $750,000 annually in operating grants.

Also in Edmonton, the company provided start-up funding in 1991 for the Glaxo Canada Research Laboratory, part of the Alberta Asthma Centre. In all, Glaxo Wellcome's external research portfolio includes about $10 million in annual funding for individual researchers at academic institutions across Canada. Among the basic research being conducted is the study of tuberculosis, asthma, cancer, neurological disease and ulcers.

The company also contributes over $5 million a year for continuing medical education for physicians and pharmacists throughout the country. In addition to regional investments, Glaxo Wellcome commits more than $50,000

Situated adjacent to the main office is Glaxo Wellcome's $120-million Technical Centre.

per year to support national medical and pharmaceutical organizations.

Medical relations are enhanced further through Glaxo Wellcome's funding of several fellowships (in collaboration with specialty societies) for research in respirology, gastroenterology, infectious disease and neurology, as well as training in allergies and otolaryngology (diseases of the ear, nose and throat).

Funding doesn't stop at medical and pharmacy efforts, but extends to overall community support.

"Being a good corporate citizen is an essential part of our operations, and we're proud to support charitable organizations at the local, regional, national and international levels," says Lucas. "Creating a healthy society isn't just a matter of introducing new medicines, but backing groups that do all sorts of good in the community."

The company also realizes that as part of the health care system its responsibility goes beyond the development of medicines. "We strive to understand and be sensitive to the impact of all aspects of a disease and therapies on a patient's life," says Lucas.

This "disease management" involves measuring the range of repercussions of a disease—from the cost of therapy to employee absenteeism to stress on the family. Part of Glaxo Wellcome's activities involve conducting sessions for employers and community groups to promote company wellness programs, encourage healthy lifestyles, and increase the understanding of specific diseases.

"With our partners in the health system, our shared goal is to ensure that patients receive the best and most appropriate care at every stage of their illness," Lucas says. "We advocate using the right treatment, for the right patient, at the right time, and in the right way—all treatments, not just ours."

It is Glaxo Wellcome's original discoveries, however, that form the cornerstone of the company's success. As Lucas says, the company's responsibility is to continually improve existing programs and therapies, and find novel ways of treating and curing disease.

"Whether on our own or through our research partnerships," he says, "we have the capabilities and the will to be part of significant breakthroughs for Canadians and the world." Ⓜ

The forward thinking of The Credit Valley Hospital founders is paying significant dividends in this era of reduced government funding, higher operation costs and smaller staffs.

And under the visionary direction of Dean M. Sane, president since the hospital's inception, The Credit Valley Hospital continues to

The Credit Valley Hospital

Since 1989, Credit Valley has been involved in the evolution of electronic imaging. A Picture Archiving and Communications System (PACS) has allowed the Diagnostic Imaging Department to acquire X-ray, CT, nuclear medicine and ultrasound images electronically. These images are stored on optical disks and can be reviewed in the doctor's office at the push of a computer key.

Early in its operation, the hospital earned two, three-year accreditations followed by a newly created Accreditation with Distinction. This four-year award is granted only to hospitals

"The concept was developed originally as a result of pressures on hospitals to control their costs," says Jocelyn Garrett, associate vice-president of marketing and community relations. "Because decisions made by physicians have a significant impact upon hospital expenditures, it is imperative that they participate in decisions designed to control costs."

Garrett goes on to explain how the hospital's progressive marketing strategy has created significant revenue generation. "At Credit Valley we are leaders in retailing. Partnerships have been developed within the hospital, where the private sector operates such ventures as coffee and bagel shops. We are always looking for new, innovative ways to develop partnerships with the corporate sector."

The Credit Valley Hospital Foundation plays a major role in bridging the gap between the shortfall of Provincial funding and the money required to provide a high level of patient care. The Foundation appeals annually to the community for funds and is indebted to the many service clubs, corporations, small businesses and individuals in the community who work together to help meet an annual goal of nearly $2 million.

Special events, including golf tournaments and an Annual Valentine's Gala, contribute important dollars for these needs. In addition to its original successful capital campaign for the building itself and then for a CT Scanner, the Foundation has funded the acquisition of infant warmers in the Special Care Nursery, portable pumps for the administration of medication to Oncology patients, toys for the Paediatric Unit, an operating table for Orthopaedics and other needs for every department in the hospital.

Each year, many organizations in the community undertake their own special events in order to donate the proceeds to the Foundation. Through the involvement of hundreds of volunteers, the Foundation is successful in helping every phase of patient care.

| The Credit Valley Hospital

be a leader in health care while maintaining fiscal responsibility.

Located on 30 acres in west Mississauga, The Credit Valley Hospital has approximately 300 beds. The hospital is a leader in obstetrics (delivering approximately 4,000 babies each year), and is the regional centre for dialysis and genetics.

"Wired" for complete computer communications when it was built, the hospital has been well positioned to accommodate the explosion in data technology. It was the first hospital in North America to equip its nursing staff with hand-held computers to monitor patients' vital signs and to access the patient data.

Data relating to patient care can be retrieved through confidential access by caregivers from any of the 700 terminals located throughout the facility. Doctors' offices are linked to the hospital by computer, enabling them to check medical records, prescribe medication and communicate with the hospital staff.

where the quality of patient care exceeds national standards and is a tribute to the commitment, talent and skill of the entire staff.

Credit Valley has done a masterful job of maintaining fiscal responsibility. The original promissory note for the Capital Building Fund was paid in full within a year, and through the generosity of the corporate sector and the residents of Mississauga, Credit Valley has continued to be fiscally responsible.

The hospital initiated Programme Management in 1989, and in 1991 expanded from four to ten programmes. Programme Management is a progressive management approach which allocates the hospital's clinical and support services into programmes and delegates responsibility for the effective and efficient operation of each programme.

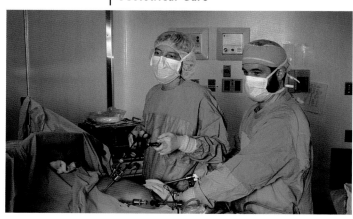

| Obstetrical Care

"Donor recognition is key to successful fund-raising," according to Norma Bandler, vice-president of resource development. "We are fortunate that there is a unique spirit in this community that compels citizens to give not only money, but also their time to ensure the ongoing high quality of health care. This commitment is unmatched anywhere."

Credit Valley, though, is more than a place for the sick. From the beginning, the hospital has concentrated on providing education and advice on wellness. The hospital organizes workshops for the general public on various topics such as child care, emergencies, CPR and proper diet.

In 1991, a Speakers' Bureau was started to promote wellness and the prevention of illness in the community. Through the programme, various staff members and professionals speak on a volunteer basis to groups. More than 50 such talks are given in any month. Credit Valley regularly holds focus group discussions whereby former patients evaluate the quality of care provided and offer suggestions for improvements. This feedback has led to many internal changes in the past. In addition to regular children's tours, a "travelling suitcase" programme assists teachers in promoting health care with children.

The Credit Valley Hospital has been selected as the site of the Peel Community Cancer Centre, which is scheduled to open by 1999. It will have three radiation machines and room for expansion.

As we approach the 21st century, health care facilities, under government scrutiny, will need to monitor their operations to ensure that they continue to provide world-class health care.

Adapting to challenging situations is not new to Credit Valley. Based on its track record, The Credit Valley Hospital will continue to be a leading health care provider and retain its reputation as "a hospital with a difference." **M**

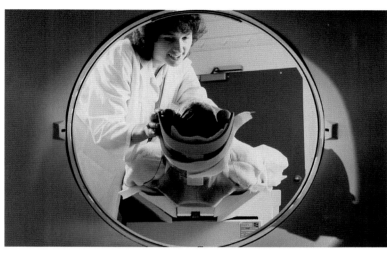

| **CT Scanner facilitates diagnosis**

| **Teddy Bear Clinic**

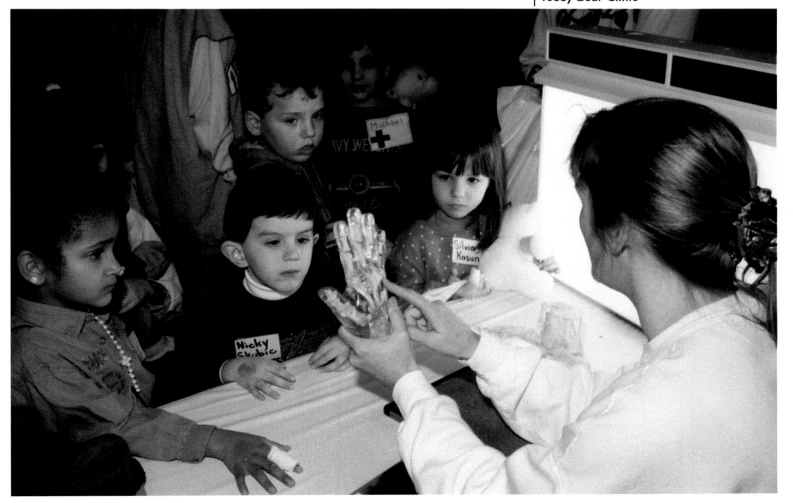

*F*ounded in 1967, world-famous Sheridan is not only one of Canada's largest colleges, but among its most entrepreneurial, respected, and influential.

The college delivers formal and continuing education to 65,000 full- and part-time students at campuses in Brampton and Oakville.

Sheridan College

Internationally, Sheridan is linked with post-secondary institutions in China, Singapore, Malaysia, Poland and the U.S., among other countries. Students are also attracted to

Sheridan's international leadership in animation is seen on movie and TV screens around the world and is continually recognized by Academy Award nominations.

Sheridan from abroad, with the college drawing applicants from Europe, Asia, the Middle East, Latin America and the U.S. Sheridan's reputation is founded on the ability to forge strong strategic alliances with government, education, business and industry—regionally, nationally and globally—and to be "first to the future."

This is fundamental to achieving Sheridan's educational vision. Back in the late 1970s, anticipating the evolving electronic information age, Sheridan committed itself to establishing world-class animation, computer graphics and multimedia curricula.

That foresight has resulted in Sheridan's leadership in each of these disciplines. Sheridan continues to earn acclaim for its work in fields that didn't exist 20 years ago—computer animation and computer graphics, multimedia, environmental technology, telecommunications, sports injury management, international business and entrepreneurship.

Sheridan's success as a teaching and learning institution comes from the accomplishments of its graduates; the college's prestige resides in their reputations.

Sheridan alumni are pushing the envelope of change in industry and technology, animation and design, theatre and crafts and more. Graduates—including Oscar and Grammy winners, renowned craftspeople and established business leaders—possess some of the most in-demand skills in the world.

The college's dynamic curriculum and faculty accomplishments position Sheridan as an integral part of the community, and a special and exciting place.

This has resulted in large part because of the

The Sports Injury Management Program is both unique and challenging and trains students to work with athletes, teams and sports facilities.

efforts of Sheridan's Program Advisory Committees. Comprising business and industry experts, the committees work with faculty to ensure that curriculum is always vibrant and relevant.

Evidence of this can be seen in the cooperative education component of Sheridan programs, which accommodates employer demands for graduates with hands-on skills. Sheridan students benefit from paid work terms in positions related to their fields of study.

Sheridan is recognized among the best for business, technology, community services, arts and design and as a centre for applied excellence and practical research.

This is demonstrated in facilities such as Theatre Sheridan for acting, dance and music; the sports injury clinic; computer graphic and computer animation labs; the CAD/CAM Institute (one of only 30 Autodesk multimedia training centres in the world); the Sheridan Environmental Technology Institute and the School of Crafts and Design, the largest in Canada devoted to textiles, furniture, ceramics and glass.

The college is world-renowned for animation and computer animation. The imaginative computer graphics and animated sequences of Sheridan graduates have created dinosaurs in *Jurassic Park*, and dazzled audiences in other Hollywood blockbusters such as *The Mask, Twister, Dragonheart, The Lion King, Aladdin, Beauty and the Beast*, and *Toy Story*.

Sheridan's animation program attracts students from over 20 countries, and graduates have senior responsibilities in leading animation, computer graphics and multimedia companies in Canada, Australia, Asia, England and

Germany—not to mention the U.S., where Sheridan alumni dominate the California animation and computer graphics scene.

While Sheridan-trained animators create an environment of imagination and fantasy, social and economic interest in the real environment and in sustainable development led to the creation of the Sheridan Environmental Technology Institute (SETI).

SETI is a great example of Sheridan's entrepreneurial spirit. Its mandate is to provide training, workshops and conferences, research and consulting on environmental issues to industry, government and the community.

A founding partner of the Halton Environmental Technology Group, SETI is working in Canada and abroad to help industry professionals learn from advanced environmental control systems, using resources developed at Sheridan. SETI also assists Canadian manufacturers and researchers in promoting

Telecommunications education provides students with the skills to network the world into an electronic village.

their technologies in Canada and other countries, including the U.S. and Poland.

Similar successes have been achieved in programs ranging from telecommunications and international business to the international award-winning CAD/CAM Institute.

From this applied, practical base, Sheridan has built relationships with industry locally and globally. Organizations as varied as Ford and Chrysler, Nelvana and Disney, the Toronto Blue Jays, Silicon Graphics, IBM and the Canadian Broadcasting Corporation have all partnered with Sheridan and benefitted from college programs and high-tech products.

Sheridan continues to strengthen its reputation for offering the corporate community the highest standard of customized training and product development. The college works with several hundred companies each year in needs analysis, planning and delivery.

The college has the capability and credibility to work with business in providing leading-edge curriculum and faculty expertise and distance and interactive learning. Continuing education and part-time studies courses have even been developed for Internet delivery on the World Wide Web.

Sheridan is also moving information and education into the corporate marketplace by developing CD-ROMs and other state-of-the-art technology.

Annually, hundreds of business executives, educators and government officials from around the world visit Sheridan to discuss joint venture opportunities, student and faculty exchanges and the transfer of Sheridan's curriculum.

The calibre and dedication of Sheridan's faculty, along with a market-driven and student-centred approach, have fostered a creative yet "grounded in reality" atmosphere.

It is an atmosphere that stimulates, motivates and supports the personal

The CAD/CAM Institute provides hands-on training in state-of-the-art facilities using the latest computer software and products.

interests and career paths of each Sheridan student, and the economic and human resource growth of each Sheridan partner.

Sheridan's status reflects more than 30 years of community support, academic development and instructional leadership and a philosophy of making the impossible possible. After all, this is the college whose graduates made dinosaurs come alive again. **Ⓜ**

The School of Crafts and Design is the largest in Canada and is recognized for its world-renowned faculty and graduates in textiles, furniture, ceramics and glass.

The University of Toronto at Mississauga (UTM) is unquestionably one of the city's most valuable assets. Over 80 per cent of the alumni either live or work within 40 kilometres of the campus, and are integral to the success of the local economic, research and business enterprises.

University of Toronto at Mississauga

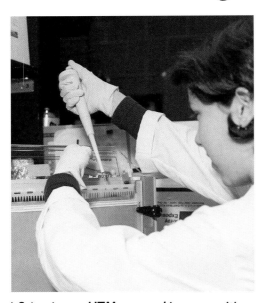

Scientists at UTM are working on exciting projects using advanced molecular-genetic tools, they are: designing and developing safer, more effective drugs; studying the effects of intracellular signaling; perfecting drug screening techniques using tumor cells and developing novel protocols to work in combination with chemo or radiation therapy for the treatment of cancers.

The school and the community have a symbiotic relationship—UTM educates the young people of the area, who in turn look to business for employment. This relationship helps fuel what is still one of the fastest growing regions in Canada.

UTM's 224-acre campus along the banks of the Credit River is larger in itself than five of Ontario's independent universities. Currently, 6,200 students attend full- and part-time classes, and the school is one of Mississauga's top 15 employers.

At the heart of UTM's academic program are the Sciences, Social Sciences and Humanities Divisions, which offer the foundation to produce well-rounded students and a well-educated pool of talent for the entire region.

For UTM to maintain its position as a top educational institution, it has developed several innovative programs in highly diverse fields—environmental studies, forensic science

(the only such program in Canada), molecular genetics, crime and deviance, computer-assisted language learning (French and Italian), women's gender studies and plant biotechnology.

Demonstrating a desire for academic partnerships, UTM has also developed joint degree/diploma programs with neighbouring Sheridan College in Art and Art History and Theatre and Drama Studies.

But much more distinguishes UTM. The school continually strives to build on its strengths—and expand links with the business and industrial sectors—by developing programs that are crucial to Canada's competitiveness in the new global economy.

A prime example is the Master of Management and Professional Accounting (MMPA) program. The program is educating the future leaders of the accounting professions, while giving graduate students a first-class understanding of the management skills that are essential for success in a changing economy.

UTM's strategy of developing graduate programs in technology management and biotechnology reflects not only the reality of today's economy, but also the status of Mississauga companies as leaders in these fields.

To take full advantage of biotechnology initiatives, UTM is forging industrial contacts that will result in new funding for research and development. Examples of research projects at UTM range from the design and development of safer and more effective drugs, to the creation

UTM's MMPA (Master of Management & Professional Accounting) students work on their team-building skills during their first week of classes each June. In one of the ice-breaking exercises, they must build the tallest possible self-standing structure out of straws and pins.

of environmentally friendly and species-specific pest controls. This new frontier of science holds major promise for Canada's social and economic growth.

In the area of technology management, UTM is ideally situated in a community that's home to an increasing number of technology-based corporate head offices. Already established as a centre of research and higher learning, UTM is going further by assisting in the transfer, management and understanding of technology's role in business and society. The future of advanced economies depends to a

Each year Erindale students graduate at commencement ceremonies held on the main U of T campus in Toronto. They can earn undergraduate degrees in Arts, Science, and Commerce or a graduate degree in Management & Professional Accounting.

great extent on the success of technologically based organizations.

Other fascinating examples of UTM's partnerships with the corporate and research communities include a financial risk management research endeavour called RiskLab, and the Hitachi Survey Research Centre.

Funded through Algorithmics Inc., the RiskLab project is dedicated to designing software solutions for risk management in the financial market. This is a vehicle for graduate students and post-doctoral fellows to perform theoretical and practical work in the mathematics of risk management. RiskLab forms a bridge between mathematics, physics, statistics and real-world finance.

The Hitachi Survey Research Centre provides much-needed demographic information for researchers and to the community. The centre is also being used by the community to

The University of Toronto at Mississauga opened its doors in September 1967 to 151 first-year students. This new "suburban" campus was given the name Erindale College and was established to meet the university needs of one of the fastest-growing communities in the country. Today, 6,200 students are engaged in full- and part-time studies.

produce statistical information for industry and commercial use.

UTM aggressively seeks to increase industry support and maximize relationships with the private and public sectors. One way of matching community and corporate needs with the school's expertise is through the Principal's Advisory Committee (PAC).

This team of industry and civic leaders—including CEOs, land developers and business professionals—is designed to bring the view of business to campus, and meets regularly to advise UTM's academic heads. The PAC is a fine complement to what is a research-oriented institution. A great advantage of being part of the top research university in the country is that students experience first-hand the interplay between research and scholarship. The faculty includes leading researchers in their fields, and even the research tools are inventive. Just look at Sniffy.

A computer-simulated rat developed at UTM, Sniffy is programmed to behave like a real rodent and exhibit 300 different rat-like behaviours. This virtual rat has been featured around the world in lectures and presentations, is an important means of replacing animals in

teaching, and is a key learning tool in psychology classes.

UTM is dedicated to discovery in the classroom, and to helping students discover how to excel in their studies. In fact, members of the faculty have won more of Ontario's top awards for teaching excellence than those of any other University of Toronto college.

Outside of the classroom, the Academic Skills Centre and the Quality Service to Students program offer personal counselling, teaching services and workshops—covering everything from essay-writing and note-taking, to listening skills and time management.

Academic support is provided too by the cornerstone of any university, the library. UTM's is among the best in Canada, holding more than 300,000 books, over 2,000 journal publications, voluminous CD-ROM indexes and many Internet links. Students can also access all of the other University of Toronto libraries—which have over 8 million titles—either from UTM or their home PC.

UTM is proud to be part of Mississauga, and through special events invites the community to visit the campus and share in the excitement of learning. Each year, thousands of people make use of UTM's theatre and public art gallery, its full-service conference operation and its athletic, leadership, science and art camps.

The community, local businesses and, most important, the students all benefit from a university that's dedicated to creating an environment in which knowledge, skills, creativity and imagination can flourish. Ⓜ

CHAPTER 17

Retail, Hospitality & Services

Ⓜ

Photo by Jeff Chevrier

Herron Chevrolet Oldsmobile

*O*ne hundred and fifty dollars a week may not seem like much of a wage today, but when the year is 1951, and you're making less than a third of that, it must have looked like a small fortune. That was the kind of money a buddy told Bob Herron he could make by running his own Shell station in Port Credit.

There was only one hitch—coming up with $3,000 working capital.

"I said 'No problem,'" Herron recalls of the meeting with Shell, "but I didn't know what I was talking about."

He managed to borrow half from friends and relatives, and based on that, convinced his bank to lend him the other half. That was how Herron ended up as the mechanic/operator of his own station. Ever since, the name Herron has been associated with motoring in Mississauga.

Today his car dealership, Herron Chevrolet Oldsmobile, is one of the best known and most successful in the region. Herron has won the President's Triple Crown—an award from General Motors that recognizes excellence in sales, service and customer satisfaction—an incredible 11 times.

Yet he remains humble about his accomplishments, takes nothing for granted, and doesn't view his Dundas Street East dealership as a Mississauga landmark.

"You don't consider yourself that important. You just always try to do as good or better the next time the customer comes in."

His career, he says, "just kind of happened." Born and raised in Mississauga, Herron served with the Royal Canadian Navy after which, upon his return home, his father gave him a simple piece of advice: "Get a trade."

Herron was always good with cars and had helped out at the corner gas station. So it was settled; he became a licensed mechanic, later taking a job at Bruce MacDougall Motors in Port Credit.

That's where Herron was working, for $48.50 a week, when the opportunity arose to lease the Shell station on Highway 5. Taking a fellow mechanic from MacDougall Motors with him, Herron opened for business.

"I just liked repairing things back then," he says simply.

It was a job he performed exceptionally well, and his station became known as the place to go for truck repairs. That attracted the attention of International Harvester. They suggested he become a dealer for them, selling trucks right off the Shell lot. Soon, Herron Motors was the largest International Harvester dealership in Canada.

When Shell's lease expired in 1956, Herron linked up with Gulf Oil, who built a dealership to his specifications. Eventually, Herron was able to stop doing repairs himself and concentrate on expanding the truck sales.

Business opportunities seem to have a way of seeking out Herron. In 1961, Chrysler approached him with a proposition to open a Dodge franchise about three miles away in Cooksville.

"I was so used to trucks, that at first I didn't want anything to do with cars," remembers Herron.

He soon changed his mind, and with an architect friend designed the Argyle Chrysler dealership (now Cooksville Chrysler Dodge). The building layout, designed to allow for simple expansion, was so successful that Chrysler uses it to this day. They even continue to send Herron a royalty cheque every time they build to the Argyle specifications.

Today, in Mississauga, the Herron name stands for superior car sales and service.

In 1966, Herron began his affilia-
tion with General Motors. Again, it
was a matter of one thing leading to
another, or as Herron puts it, "The
next thing you know… ."

The folks from General Motors
were interested in having Herron
Motors become a GM dealership.
Herron took on the challenge of
building up yet another car business,
selling Argyle and bringing aboard
key people from the Chrysler and
International Harvester staff. He
had the choice of the Pontiac or
Chevrolet lines, and picked Chevrolet,
as he felt it sold well during all kinds
of economies.

He has been a GM dealer ever since,
long enough to see son Bruce and
daughter Lynda join him in the business. Herron Chevrolet Oldsmobile has
about 90 employees, and actually com-
prises several businesses under one roof,
says Herron: leasing, new and used car
sales, the body shop, a mechanic service
and commercial truck sales.

Success isn't measured simply by
selling a car, but "by the satisfaction that
comes from doing everything well," he says.

The dealership adopted an innovative
approach in 1992, switching to a "no hassle"
policy. Herron recognized that most consumers were tired of haggling for the best
price—and being unsure if they ever received
it. When they sought a salesperson they were
looking for information, not a battle.

Of course, factors such as a down payment,
a trade-in, and the length of a car lease deter-
mines the eventual payments. But the price of
the vehicle is fixed. Herron calls it "value pricing." With all of the same terms, customer A
and customer B will pay the same price for the
same vehicle.

Along with their budget for purchasing a
vehicle, Herron says today's customers are on a
"time budget," and want to make the most out
of their visit to a dealership.

"We offer a more consultive way of selling,
giving customers all the information they
need to make their decision," says Herron.
"That's what makes a good shopping experience. We don't hire salespeople who want to
argue and negotiate."

He says this kind of approach benefits the
salespeople too. "If you're dickering back and
forth, back and forth, all day long, by the end
of the day you're pretty beat up."

The Herron name is known in Mississauga
not only for superior car sales and service, but

In the early 1960s the Herron Motors
International Harvester dealership was
located in the largely rural Dundas and
Dixie area of Mississauga.

also for supporting numerous community causes. Over the years, the dealership has donated
cars to Mississauga Hospital and Credit Valley
Hospital to be raffled for fund-raisers.

Herron also gives money to youth athlet-
ics, sponsoring local soccer, hockey and baseball leagues. And with the number of vehicles
he has sold over the years, you can bet that a
fair number of parents drive their children to
the games in cars they bought at Herron
Chevrolet Oldsmobile. 🖲

Under Bob Herron's direction, Herron
Motors grew to become the largest
International Harvester dealership in
Canada.

$\mathcal{W}$hen you're a business traveller heading out of town for an extended stay, you want your accommodations in order. But where do you stay while visiting England or Japan, the U.S., or, for that matter, Canada, or even Mississauga?

Try Global Travel Apartments (GTA). With

Global Travel Apartments

network offices worldwide, GTA provides corporate furnished apartments by the day, week or month. GTA's network covers 26 countries and 125 cities, from A (Aberdeen, Scotland) to Z (Zurich, Switzerland), including four sites in Mississauga.

GTA's corporate apartments are located in several high-rise towers throughout Mississauga and include a concierge, excellent security, full health club facility and parking.

"We provide the comfort, space, convenience and privacy that business travellers look for when relocating, on training or an assignment, at a more competitive rate than a hotel room," says Thomas Vincent, GTA president.

GTA is both a principal and broker. It owns furnished apartment properties, has leasehold interests in others and enters into management and marketing agreements.

The company has forged alliances with enterprises throughout the world, who ensure the quality of their furnished apartments. As part of this international network, GTA has over 200,000 apartments in its worldwide inventory.

In 1977, when Vincent founded GTA, he had only three units in one downtown Toronto apartment building. But his travel agency experience told him his concept was sound.

"Many business travellers were looking for furnished apartments, but when I researched what was available, I found the product wasn't customer-friendly. If I wouldn't stay there myself, why should I expect someone else to? I decided to come up with a better product and service."

GTA built an extensive apartment inventory, on its own or through partners, that met a higher level of service and comfort. Customers can now access a range of suitable accommodations in standard, executive and deluxe qualities and book their stay through the GTA central office. Downtown and suburban locations are available in most cities.

About 60 to 65 per cent of GTA's business derives from travellers coming to the Toronto area, the remainder from people seeking accommodation anywhere else around the globe. (About 10 per cent of GTA's customers are leisure travellers.)

Vincent says GTA's Mississauga sites are integral to their apartment network: Monarchy Suites and Enfield Suites near the Square One shopping centre and two other locations at Highway 10 and Burnhamthorpe and opposite the Toronto Golf and Country Club. GTA is looking to add other Mississauga sites.

"We watch where business is growing, and follow with our product," says Vincent. "Business has grown tremendously in the

Attractive and spacious corporate apartments offer more comfortable and convenient accommodation for the business traveller on an extended stay.

high-tech and consulting industries in Mississauga, so there's an enormous demand for our furnished apartments here."

GTA markets its inventory by approaching corporate HR managers, who are always looking for reliable accommodations for their incoming and outgoing business travellers on an extended stay. The company also has extensive marketing agreements with travel and real estate companies throughout North America who refer business to GTA.

Vincent is especially enthusiastic about its digital marketing on the Internet. An extensive

You can have meetings or entertain in the privacy and space of your own corporate apartment.

World Wide Web site lets people view GTA's accommodations in colour around the world and even book their stay immediately on-line.

"My vision is to remain the number one information source on furnished apartments worldwide," says Vincent. While GTA's counterparts abroad contribute to the overall apartment inventory, GTA heads up the worldwide Internet site.

With access to 200,000 homes away from home, business travellers know it doesn't matter where they're staying when they use GTA—they're staying in comfort. **Ⓜ**

Superb service, exceptional meeting rooms, exquisite cuisine and well-appointed guest rooms are some of the reasons visitors choose the Toronto Airport Hilton Hotel.

The hotel opened in 1971 and was purchased by Hilton International in 1972. The Toronto Airport Hilton plays an important role

Toronto Airport Hilton Hotel

| Pearson Boardroom

in Mississauga and Toronto commerce. It is conveniently located in Mississauga, on Airport Road, directly across from Pearson International Airport. Highways 401 and 427 intersect just east of the hotel. A complimentary shuttle service is available to and from the airport, and downtown Toronto is a 20-minute drive away.

The Toronto Airport Hilton introduced Meeting 2000 in 1997, a new approach to meeting services for use by companies and associations, and designed with customer input. It is part of a worldwide Hilton International chain initiative. Meeting 2000 conference facilities are now available at more than 60 hotels operated by Hilton International around the world.

A dedicated meeting services manager is on-site to help organize every aspect of a function. Two completely renovated meeting rooms offer the latest features and services most frequently requested by meeting planners, including comfortable chairs and state-of-the-art audio-visual facilities, including video conferencing. All Meeting 2000 rooms are located on the conference level and feature individual climate control, large windows, extra telephone outlets and data lines for computer hook-ups.

There is also a full-service Meeting 2000 Business Centre, operated by Hilton staff. Two private rooms are available for client use while typing or photocopying, and translation and courier services are available. Guests have access to fax,

modems, the Internet and personal computers loaded with the most popular software packages.

More than 100,000 people stay at the hotel for at least one night every year. There are 413 attractive guest rooms and suites, including 132 non-smoking rooms. A 152-suite tower is specially designed for the business traveller.

All guests enjoy a modern health club, saunas, squash courts and a heated outdoor swimming pool.

The hotel offers a wide range of banquet facilities and more than 200,000 guests visit annually for meetings, meals, special functions, trade shows and conferences. Banquet facilities for up to 960, including a 10,000-square-foot column-free ballroom, are available.

Award-winning chefs create imaginative menus to delight guests at both special functions and in the hotel's Harvest Restaurant. Fine cuisine, with a variety of choices for breakfast, lunch or dinner are featured daily. Friends meet to discuss the day's events at the Harvest Bar, and Misty's, one of Toronto's most popular night spots, caters to all music lovers.

Major shopping areas, including Square One, Woodbine Centre and Sherway Gardens, are close by. Toronto is home to more than

110 golf courses. Woodbine Racetrack, home to the 1996 Breeders Cup races, is five minutes away. Many tourist attractions are within easy driving distance, including CN Tower, SkyDome, Toronto Zoo, Canada's Wonderland, Royal Ontario Museum, Chinatown, Theatre District and Yorkville.

The Toronto Airport Hilton Hotel has been an integral part of Mississauga for more than 25 years and looks forward to continuing to be the business community's hotel of choice. **Ⓜ**

| Harvest Restaurant

| Toronto Airport Hilton Hotel Lobby

*I*n the heart of Mississauga's City Centre, Novotel is the place to be for both business and leisure travellers. With easy access to all major highways, Novotel's location is minutes from Pearson International Airport and only 20 minutes from downtown Toronto.

Novotel Mississauga Hotel

Square One, Canada's second largest shopping mall, is conveniently located across the street. Sega City at Playdium, Canada's first total physical and interactive entertainment complex, is also within walking distance.

A two-year, $4-million renovation is well underway, making the hotel even more attractive to its main clientele—business travellers. The renovation of the guest rooms is complete and has added new business services, such as keyless entry, video checkout, data modem

hook-ups and voice mail. The lobby and meeting room renovations will be completed by fall 1997.

Surrounding businesses make frequent use of Novotel's 16 meeting rooms and 325 guest rooms, some of which are wheelchair accessible. The friendly and experienced staff organizes meetings for groups as small as a half-dozen or as large as 400 and will tailor each one to suit the client's needs. Themes and special promotions often tie in with visiting dignitaries or special economic events in Mississauga.

The typical Novotel guest stays more than one night, is a business traveller and has likely stayed at the hotel in the past. Although the hotel is not on the "airport strip," it does host many airline crews and government officials because of its proximity to major highways, excellent restaurants and thriving entertainment venues.

The Mississauga hotel is one of nine Novotels in North America and is part of a

Novotel Mississauga—Welcome home!

worldwide chain consisting of more than 320 hotels. This is a special year for Novotel as it celebrates its 30th anniversary. Accor, the parent company to Novotel, is a global leader in the hospitality industry with more than 2,300 hotels worldwide.

Many centrally located firms use the Novotel as a second home, using the meeting rooms for off-site functions, holding special lunches or dinners at the Café Nicole Bistro or booking guest rooms for employees or clients coming to the city for meetings. With so many excellent entertainment choices to choose from within easy walking distance, the Novotel is also a prime choice for families visiting Mississauga.

"We focus on client comfort," Jack Nash, director of marketing and sales, says. "That's where our people come in. It's the personal contact with clients that emphasizes their importance to us. That's our key to success. Mississauga—and especially the City Centre— has grown quickly, and we have continued to grow with it. While we have benefitted from that growth, we have also contributed to it. The Novotel is a mainstay within the Mississauga community, and we intend to continue to grow to meet the community's— and our guests'—needs." **Ⓜ**

Novotel guest room—a new look focused on comfort

Photo by Jeff Chevrier

Who could have imagined that the most inspiring part of a business trip would be the hotel? When Jack Dodge visited Dallas in 1986, his purpose was to research self-storage units. Instead, the President and CEO of the Dodge Group, a Brockville, Ontario, development company, came away with a whole new

Dodge Suites Hotel

business concept. After staying at an all-suite hotel, he decided to bring the idea to Canada.

Through previous joint ventures with Journey's End, Dodge was familiar with the Canadian hotel market and saw an opening for a well-priced suite property.

"He felt an all-suite hotel could be built at a reasonable cost, with large suites offered at a competitive price to business travellers," says daughter Diana Dodge, now Director of Operations for the Dodge Group's hotel division.

In 1988 the first Dodge Suites Hotel opened in Mississauga, on a four-acre site at

Dodge Suites' pastoral courtyard, complete with resident ducks, peacocks and pheasants, offers a tranquil setting for business travellers ready to unwind at the end of a long day.

the entrance to the Airport Corporate Business Park. Two years later, the Dodge Group built a second hotel in Vaughan, just north of Toronto. The company's vision includes being the main provider and leader of extended stay accommodations in Greater Toronto. Dodge owns land in other cities, which allows for future consideration of expanding the "extended stay hotel concept."

Today, 75 per cent of the hotel's guests are business travellers. The others are vacationers or relocating families. The hotel's location is a large positive, as it is just minutes from Pearson International Airport and the major highways. The Corporate Centre Business Park provides a ready-made market, housing such corporations as Spar, Hewlett-Packard and Ericsson Communications Canada.

The 185 suites are filled regularly with stays ranging from a few days to six months or longer. Diana Dodge offers a simple reason for the hotel's popularity: "We provide the amenities that transform a hotel room into a home away from home."

Each suite has a living area and bedroom separated by a sliding door, a microwave, a coffee-maker, a kitchenette or full kitchen, and a Jacuzzi™-style bathtub. Guests have access to a laundry, complimentary breakfast, fitness facility and a 24-hour shop in the lobby that sells snacks and light meal entrees.

Each suite has a living area and bedroom separated by a sliding door, a microwave, a coffee-maker, a kitchenette or full kitchen, and a Jacuzzi™-style bathtub. Guests have access to a laundry, complimentary breakfast, fitness facility and a 24-hour shop in the lobby that sells snacks and light meal entrees.

Monday through Thursday evenings, guests also enjoy a hospitality hour, with complimentary food and theme events, such as "Wine Tasting" and "Hawaiian Luau." The three-storey hotel also boasts a pastoral courtyard, complete with resident ducks, peacocks and pheasants.

Such creature comforts, literally in the case of the courtyard birds—offer a tranquil setting.

"Business travellers work hard all day, and when they get in at night they want to put their feet up and relax," says Diana Dodge. "For people relocating, the Dodge Suites becomes a temporary home while they're looking for one. We want to create a comfortable atmosphere, with friendly faces and useful guest services and amenities."

Dodge has worked her way up in the business, starting as a hotel housekeeper and laundress in Ottawa.

"I was the worst housekeeper," she recalls with a chuckle. "I wanted to get into the hotel business, and I imagined that if I learned from the ground up, eventually I would succeed."

As for her current job? "A little more stress," she jokes, "but easier on the back." Ⓜ

$\mathcal{M}$ississauga is the City of Business. This suburb of the Greater Toronto Area (GTA) is home to many growing and successful companies, one of which is Meadowvale Security Guard Services, Inc. Meadowvale Security was founded 16 years ago in the city of Mississauga by two entrepreneurs, John Hughes and Chris Evans.

With the powerful combination of technology, training and management, Meadowvale Security provides its customers with the very best in service.

Under their direction, Meadowvale Security has grown to a reputable size of more than 12,000 hours per week of contract security that services the GTA. Meadowvale Security has become an innovative industry leader while providing superior quality services in the commercial, industrial and residential sectors.

Meadowvale Security's founders, John Hughes and Chris Evans have formed a new partnership with American Protective Services Inc. (APS) of Oakland, California.

Meadowvale Security has taken an even greater stride forward with its recent partnership with American Protective Services Inc. (APS) of Oakland, California, a privately owned company founded 52 years ago with a reputation for leadership in the industry.

Meadowvale Security and APS both embrace a commitment to excellence in quality service for the client. They are client focused and treat employees with respect and dignity. This shared commitment to quality led APS to acquire Meadowvale Security in early 1997.

Meadowvale Security continues to provide all the quality services that its clients have come to expect. With the application of new technology and superior management systems developed by APS, Meadowvale Security will develop complete security solutions for clients.

This technology includes computer software such as Integrated Voice Recognition (IVR), SiteTrack™ and CAPS™. IVR is an automated interactive check-in system that provides site management benefits. The computer receives check-in calls from the field staff, logs them and is able to randomly recall posts for verification. If the computer does not receive a check-in call from the field, IVR has been programmed to automatically call the communications centre or a patrol supervisor's personal pager. In this way, Meadowvale Security makes sure a site is always covered.

SiteTrack™ is a software system that tracks incidents which occur at individual sites and provides specific data for tailoring the best security solutions for each client.

Meadowvale Security Guard Services

CAPS™ is a computer-automated personnel-scheduling system. It integrates security officer qualifications, training, selection, scheduling, payroll and billing. All information is centralized onto one database, which ensures the assignment of the appropriate personnel for each post.

Technological advances are just part of Meadowvale Security's innovative approaches to achieve maximum efficiency and performance. New employees receive classroom instruction and are exposed to an extensive video-based training program that focuses on security knowledge and skills.

With the powerful combination of technology, training and management, Meadowvale Security provides its customers with the very best in service. **Ⓜ**

Photo by Jeff Chevrier

Bibliography

Economic Development Office, City of Mississauga. *Mississauga: Share The Excitement*; municipal information series. Mississauga, 1996.

Heritage Mississauga. *A Heritage Tour*; brochure series. Mississauga, 1995.

Manning, Mary. *Street: The Man, The Family, The Village*. Streetsville, Ontario: Streetsville Historical Society, 1983.

Murphy, Jim. "Progressive Architecture"; article. City of Mississauga, reprint; Mississauga, Ontario: Reinhold Publishing Company, Inc., August, 1987.

Murzin, Richard. *The History of the Mississauga Hospital*. Mississauga: Mississauga Hospital Community Relations Department; Boston Mills Press, 1983.

Ontario Ministry of Finance, Strategic Economic Issues Branch. *Ontario County Population Projections to 2021*. Toronto, 1995.

Pope, J.H. *Illustrated Historical Atlas of the County of Peel*. Toronto: Walker and Mills, 1877.

Region of Peel Planning Department. *Planning Peel*. Brampton, Ontario: 1996.

Riendeau, Roger. *Mississauga: An Illustrated History*. Burlington, Ontario: Windsor Publications, 1985.

Smith, Donald. *Sacred Feathers: The Reverend Peter Jones (Kahkewaquonaby) and the Mississauga Indians*. Toronto: University of Toronto Press, 1987.

Tardif, Joan. *The History of the City of Mississauga*. Mississauga: City of Mississauga, 1980.

Weeks, Verna Mae. *My Village of Mississauga*. Chelsey, Ontario: Verna Mae Weeks, 1986.

Enterprises Index

Index

This book was set in Berkeley Book, Gill Sans, Isadora and Minister at
Community Communications, Montgomery, Alabama.